Southern Europe in the Covid-19 Pandemic: The First Phase

This book investigates the fast-learning experience of Covid-19's initial onset in a region long renowned for low state capacity, political polarisation, and weak health systems.

Covid-19, a global health emergency entailing a major existential threat, presented a crucial challenge for national governments and political systems. It elicited drastic policy measures, including unprecedented lockdowns. The question of how and why some states acted more effectively in facing this emergency situation has important implications for future crisis management. The outcomes varied greatly across countries, ranging from examples for emulation to dire portents of the consequences of losing control. Case studies of Italy, Greece, Spain, Portugal, and Turkey examine crisis preparedness, policy response, political dynamics, and societal reception. A comparative overview chapter offers potential explanations for the divergence in national performance.

This volume will be of great use to students and researchers across the fields of European studies, political leadership, public policy, governance, and public health. The chapters in this book were originally published as a special issue of *South European Society and Politics*.

Juan Rodríguez-Teruel is Associate Professor of Political Science and Public Administration at the University of Valencia, Spain. His research focuses on executives, ministers and political parties. He recently co-edited *Digital Parties. The Challenge of Online Organisation and Participation* (2021). He is a founding editor of the Spanish political website *'Agenda Pública'*.

José Real-Dato is Associate Professor at the University of Almería, Spain. His current research focuses on the use of expert knowledge in public policy making. He was a principal researcher of the project *Impact of Specialised Knowledge on the Design and Adoption of Public Policy in Spain* and is currently the director of the project *Policy Analytic Capacities in Regional Public Administration in Spain: Mapping, Assessing, and Explaining.*

Susannah Verney is Associate Professor of European Integration and European Politics at the National and Kapodistrian University of Athens, Greece. She served as Editor of *South European Society and Politics* (with Anna Bosco) in 1999–2023. Her most recent book (co-edited with Anna Bosco) is *The Politics of Polarisation: Conflictual Competition in Italy, Spain and Greece* (Routledge, 2022).

South European Society and Politics

Series editors: Susannah Verney, *National and Kapodistrian University of Athens, Greece and* **Anna Bosco,** *University of Florence, Italy*

The parallel regime transitions of the 1970s, when Southern Europe was the vanguard of the 'third wave' of democratisation, the impact of EU membership and Europeanisation and more recently, the region's central role in the eurozone crisis, have all made Southern Europe a distinctive area of interest for social science scholars. The *South European Society and Politics* book series promotes new empirical research into the domestic politics and society of South European states. The series, open to a broad range of social science approaches, offers comparative thematic volumes covering the region as a whole and on occasion, innovative single-country studies. Its geographical scope includes both 'old' and 'new' Southern Europe, defined as Italy, Greece, Portugal, Spain, Cyprus, Malta and Turkey.

The AKP Since Gezi Park
Moving to Regime Change in Turkey
Edited by Susannah Verney, Anna Bosco and Senem Aydin-Düzgit

The Exceptional Case of Post-Bailout Portugal
Edited by Elisabetta De Giorgi and José Santana-Pereira

The Politics of Polarisation
Conflictual Competition in Italy, Spain and Greece
Edited by Anna Bosco and Susannah Verney

A Generational Divide? Age-related Aspects of Political Transformation in Post-crisis Southern Europe
Edited by Emmanouil Tsatsanis, Marco Lisi and André Freire

Affective Polarisation in Spain
Electoral, Regional and Media Conflictuality
Edited by Mariano Torcal

Southern Europe in The Covid-19 Pandemic
The First Phase
Edited by Juan Rodríguez-Teruel, José Real-Dato and Susannah Verney

For more information about this series, please visit: www.routledge.com/South-European-Society-and-Politics/book-series/SESP

Southern Europe in The Covid-19 Pandemic

The First Phase

Edited by

Juan Rodríguez-Teruel, José Real-Dato and Susannah Verney

Routledge
Taylor & Francis Group
LONDON AND NEW YORK

First published 2025
by Routledge
4 Park Square, Milton Park, Abingdon, Oxon, OX14 4RN

and by Routledge
605 Third Avenue, New York, NY 10158

Routledge is an imprint of the Taylor & Francis Group, an informa business

British Library Cataloguing-in-Publication Data
A catalogue record for this book is available from the British Library

ISBN13: 978-1-032-85621-6 (hbk)
ISBN13: 978-1-032-85639-1 (pbk)
ISBN13: 978-1-003-51912-6 (ebk)

DOI: 10.4324/9781003519126

Typeset in Myriad Pro
by codeMantra

Publisher's Note
The publisher accepts responsibility for any inconsistencies that may have arisen during the conversion of this book from journal articles to book chapters, namely the inclusion of journal terminology.

Contents

Citation Information

The following chapters in this book were originally published in *South European Society and Politics*, volume 27, issue 4 (2022). When citing this material, please use the original page numbering for each article, as follows:

Chapter 1

Southern Europe Managing the First Phase of the Covid-19 Pandemic: The Crucial Effect of Timing
Susannah Verney, José Real-Dato and Juan Rodríguez-Teruel
South European Society and Politics, volume 27, issue 4 (2022), pp. 431–458

Chapter 2

Italy, the Sick Man of Europe: Policy Response, Experts and Public Opinion in the First Phase of Covid-19
Giulia Vicentini and Maria Tullia Galanti
South European Society and Politics, volume 27, issue 4 (2022), pp. 459–485

Chapter 3

The Limits of Power Concentration and Expert Knowledge in Emergency Management: Spain's Government Response during the First Phase of the Covid-19 Pandemic
Juan Rodríguez-Teruel, Eloísa del Pino and José Real-Dato
South European Society and Politics, volume 27, issue 4 (2022), pp. 487–519

Chapter 4

A Portuguese Miracle: The Politics of the First Phase of Covid-19 in Portugal
Patrícia Silva, Edna Costa and João Moniz
South European Society and Politics, volume 27, issue 4 (2022), pp. 521–549

Chapter 5

Regaining Trust: Evidence-Informed Policymaking during the First Phase of the Covid-19 Crisis in Greece
Stella Ladi, Angelos Angelou and Dimitra Panagiotatou
South European Society and Politics, volume 27, issue 4 (2022), pp. 551–576

Chapter 6

Surviving the Covid-19 Pandemic under Right-wing Populist Rule: Turkey in the First Phase
Özge Kemahlıoğlu and Oya Yeğen
South European Society and Politics, volume 27, issue 4 (2022), pp. 577–606

Notes on Contributors

Angelos Angelou is currently a visiting fellow at the European Institute of the London School of Economics, having received his PhD from the same institute in 2020. His research focuses on crisis management by international and national bureaucracies and the political economy of reforms. He is currently posted as a junior professional in the Delegation of the European Union to the Council of Europe.

Edna Costa is a postdoctoral researcher at the Governance, Competitiveness and Public Policies Research Centre (GOVCOPP) of the University of Aveiro, Portugal. She holds a PhD in Political Science and works on political representation and social policies, from a gender perspective. She has participated in several national and international projects and co-coordinated the project 'The Political Participation of Portuguese Youth' (Calouste Gulbenkian Foundation).

Maria Tullia Galanti is Associate Professor at the Department of Social and Political Sciences at the University of Milan, Italy. Her research interests include entrepreneurship, leadership, and advice in public policy, with a focus on education policies, urban planning, and local public services.

Özge Kemahlıoğlu is Associate Professor of Political Science at Sabancı University, Istanbul, Turkey. Her research focuses on party politics, sub-national governments, distributive politics, and incumbency advantage. Her articles on these topics have appeared *in Comparative Politics, Journal of Politics, Journal of Theoretical Politics, Latin American Politics and Society, South European Society and Politics*, and *Public Choice*. She is the author of *Agents or Bosses? Patronage and Intra-party Politics in Argentina and Turkey* (2012).

Stella Ladi is Associate Professor at the Queen Mary University of London, UK, and at Panteion University, Athens, Greece. She previously worked as Lecturer at the University of Sheffield and the University of Exeter, UK. Her research interests include the Eurozone crisis, public policy and public administration reforms, and the role of experts in public policy. She has published in journals such as *Journal of European Integration, JCMS, Policy and Society, Regulation & Governance, Public Administration, West European Politics*, and *Comparative European Politics.*

João Moniz is a PhD student at the University of Aveiro, Portugal. His doctoral thesis, entitled 'Mapping Politicization in the European Parliament: A Longitudinal Analysis', examines how political parties use the European Parliament to politicise the European Union and the integration process, by using quantitative text analysis methods to analyse the plenary speeches of Members of the European Parliament from 1980 to 2019.

Dimitra Panagiotatou is a postdoctoral researcher at Panteion University, Athens, Greece, and teaching fellow at the University of Piraeus, Greece. She received her PhD in 2020 from the Queen Mary University of London, UK. Her research interests include multi-level governance, EU Cohesion policy, Europeanisation, European socialisation, and policy learning. She holds an Advanced Research MSc in Cultures and Development Studies from KU Leuven, Belgium, and an MA in European Economics from Université Libre de Bruxelles, Belgium.

Eloísa del Pino is a senior researcher at the Institute of Public Goods and Policies (IPP) in the Spanish National Research Council (CSIC). She was Chief of Staff of the Minister of Healthcare, Consumer Affairs and Social Welfare (2018–2020) and has been a visiting researcher at the Universities of Oxford, Kent, and Ottawa. She has published extensively on public policies and the Covid pandemic.

José Real-Dato is Associate Professor at the University of Almería, Spain. His current research focuses on the use of expert knowledge in public policy making. He was a principal researcher of the project Impact of *Specialised Knowledge on the Design and Adoption of Public Policy in Spain* (Ministry of Science and Innovation/Spanish Research Agency) and is currently the director of the project *Policy Analytic Capacities in Regional Public Administration in Spain: Mapping, Assessing, and Explaining* (Andalusian Research and Development Plan). His work has been published *in South European Society and Politics*, *Party Politics*, *European Political Science*, and *Journal of Comparative Policy Analysis: Research and Practice*, among other journals.

Juan Rodríguez-Teruel is Associate Professor of Political Science and Public Administration at the University of Valencia, Spain. His research focus on executives, ministers, and political parties. His most recent publications have appeared in *Party Politics*, *Nationalities Papers*, *Ethnicities*, and *Politics and Governance.* He recently co-edited *Digital Parties. The Challenge of Online Organisation and Participation* (2021). He is a founding editor of the Spanish political website *'Agenda Pública'.*

Patrícia Silva is Assistant Professor of Political Science and a researcher at the Governance, Competitiveness and Public Policies Research Centre (GOVCOPP) at the University of Aveiro, Portugal. Her main research interests are political parties, the recruitment of appointed elites, delegation processes, and bureaucratic autonomy. Her work has been published in international journals, most recently in *Public Policy and Administration*; *Public Administration*; and *South European Society and Politics.*

Susannah Verney is Associate Professor at the National and Kapodistrian University of Athens, Greece, where she is the director of the 'Master's Degree in Southeast European Studies: Politics, History, Economics' and a Athens coordinator of the 'International Master in South European Studies (Eurosud)'. She is Editor (with Anna Bosco) of *South European Society and Politics* and the related Routledge book series. Her most recent book (co-edited with Anna Bosco) is *The Politics of Polarisation: Conflictual Competition in Italy, Spain and Greece* (2022).

Giulia Vicentini is currently Research Collaborator at the Department of Social, Political and Cognitive Sciences at the University of Siena, Italy. She has been a postdoctoral fellow at the University of Trento, Italy (2014–2016); Scuola Normale Superiore, Florence, Italy (2016–2018); and University of Bologna, Italy (2018–2020). Her research interests include party politics, candidate and leadership selection, higher education policies, and political elites.

Oya Yeğen is Visiting Assistant Professor of Political Science at Sabancı University, Istanbul, Turkey. Before joining Sabancı, she received her PhD in Political Science from Boston University, USA, and worked at Simmons College, USA. Her research interests include politics of constitution-making, judicial politics, and authoritarianism.

Southern Europe Managing the First Phase of the Covid-19 Pandemic: The Crucial Effect of Timing

Susannah Verney, José Real-Dato and Juan Rodríguez-Teruel

ABSTRACT
This article, which introduces a special issue, compares the record of five South European states – Italy, Spain, Portugal, Greece, and Turkey – in managing the initial phase of the Covid-19 pandemic. Southern Europe's reputation for low state capacity, political polarisation and weak health systems all posed potential obstacles to an effective governmental response. However, despite these shared characteristics, these countries' records in Covid management varied widely. The article investigates whether this variation can be explained by national differences in degree of preparedness, state capacities, political dynamics or societal factors. It concludes that while the degree of decentralisation played a role in the initial response, the most significant factor was the timing of the virus' arrival in each country, resulting in different opportunities for governments to design and implement effective responses

Crises are super-wicked problems (Levin et al. 2012), where complexity encounters uncertainty and ambiguity. This significantly conditions decisionmakers' ability to produce an accurate diagnosis of the problems and develop the necessary response. These difficulties are especially pronounced at the early stage of a crisis. At that point, decisionmakers are still struggling to make sense of the situation by assembling myriad pieces of information into a coherent narrative which will allow them to design an effective course of action (Boin et al. 2005). This was very much the case with Covid-19, whose outbreak found countries around the world ill-prepared to face a fast-moving global health crisis, the biggest for a century.

The months to 30 June 2020 by no means marked the worst period of the pandemic: later phases brought a higher death toll. But by then, more was known about the deadly virus and what needed to be done to combat it. In contrast, in the first months, societies and governments were in a state of shock, suddenly facing a major existential threat from a largely unknown enemy. Everyday life was turned upside down through the implementation of unprecedented lockdowns, apparently the only tool available to limit the virus' spread. The speed at which the crisis developed was astonishing: in a matter of weeks, the virus spread around the globe, necessitating a rapid response from governments. It is this 'fast learning experience' of the first phase of the Covid-19 pandemic which provides the subject of this volume.

The onset of Covid-19 constituted a crucial challenge for national political systems. The nature of the crisis required politicians to react with speed and decisiveness and to be led by scientific expertise in crafting their response. That they would do so could not be taken for granted. In the United States, for example, the politicisation of Covid led to the flouting of the scientific evidence for partisan purposes and with deadly effect. The question of which states around the world responded most effectively to the initial onset of Covid-19 is not just an interesting political puzzle, but could also have implications for the management of future public health crises of this magnitude and urgency.

Investigating this puzzle, the current volume examines five South European states: Italy, Spain, Greece, Portugal and Turkey. In considering national responses to Covid-19, Southern Europe offers an interesting test-region. There are a number of reasons for this choice. First, South European countries have traditionally had a reputation for low state capacity. This suggests they might find it especially challenging to define and implement an effective policy under crisis conditions. Second, during the 2010s, most of the South European states had been in the frontline of the European economic crisis. Several of the eurozone member-states had been the recipients of international bailouts and had applied harsh austerity policies which had inevitably impacted negatively on their national health systems. This meant they were likely to be particularly vulnerable to a crisis in the field of public health. Third, South European politics had recently been characterised by political polarisation, which had been noticeably prominent in some of the 2019 elections in the region (Bosco & Verney 2022; Chiaramonte et al. 2018; Esen & Gumuscu 2019). This created a climate in which it seemed likely that any crisis response would be complicated by becoming an issue of political contention.

These factors might suggest that Southern Europe would not perform well in terms of crafting a swift and effective response to the crisis. Despite the regional similarities, however, the outcomes in these five countries varied significantly. While some appeared as a dire portent of what could happen if the authorities lost control, others performed better than expected and at least one was held up as an example to be emulated. This striking differentiation within a region with common characteristics makes Southern Europe a particularly interesting subject for study of the pandemic response.

In presenting the five national case studies in this volume, our authors were asked to follow a common format. Each country article first presents the background to the crisis, especially the extent to which the particular state was prepared to meet a health crisis. The main focus is then on the policy response, including the extent to which government strategy was led by expert advice and how state structures, particularly decentralisation, may have affected the outcome. This is followed by an examination of the political response, looking first at the institutional dynamics within parliament and the stands taken by political parties, and then at the societal dynamics, particularly as manifested in public opinion. After drawing conclusions about the country's performance during the first phase of the pandemic, each case study also briefly reviews developments during the second phase and the extent to which the national record changed during this period.

This introductory article aims to provide a comparative overview of the South European response to the first phase of the Covid-19 pandemic. While summarising what happened in our countries and when, it principally aims to address the question why the outcomes were so different. The article begins by developing an analytical framework, based on the literature, with which to investigate the reasons for this striking picture of national divergence. Applying this framework to our South European states, the article then combines data from a variety of sources with insights drawn from the case studies in this volume in order to indicate what might have been expected when the pandemic hit these countries. Next it presents data on the actual public health outcomes in our five countries up to 30 June 2020, followed by a discussion of these outcomes in the light of our theoretical expectations. Finally, the article addresses the impact of timing on the government responses, before drawing its conclusions.

Seeking explanations for diverse Covid-19 outcomes

In this section we develop a basic interpretative framework in order to compare the Covid-19 crisis management and its results in our five South European countries. We identify two basic types of factors at play: political and non-political, each with sub-categories. The first category includes those factors ultimately stemming from political decisions. The way a community can cope with a crisis greatly depends on its ability to produce well-targeted collective structures and decisions that promote resilience to the impact of the crisis. Among these political factors, we distinguish the level of crisis preparedness, politico-institutional factors likely to influence the national crisis response, and conjunctural political dynamics. While crisis management is unquestionably shaped by the previous political factors, the effectiveness of crisis measures also depends on non-political factors, i.e. factors which are relatively independent of political decisions (although the latter may influence them). Here we distinguish demographic characteristics, social trust, and timing.

Crisis preparedness

This concerns the existing structures and procedures designed to cope with crisis scenarios, including specific contingency action plans, early warning systems, standard operating procedures, and sufficient organisational, human, and material resources. This factor is strongly emphasised in the crisis management literature (Baubion 2013; Tierney, Lindell & Perry 2001; World Bank & United Nations 2010). Being able to detect critical threats, planning scenarios adapted to different levels of risk, clearly defining and allocating authority and responsibilities among the agents involved, stockpiling and maintaining necessary equipment and supplies, and/or having adequately trained staff quickly available are all critical variables. They can make the difference to how a country responds to a crisis and to the impact it has on the community.

Thus, in seeking to understand how different governments managed the initial onset of the Covid-19 crisis, many analyses have outlined the importance of crisis preparedness and administrative capacity (particularly in terms of healthcare capacities) (Capano 2020; Capano et al. 2020; You 2020). Yet it has also been suggested that higher levels of preparedness might have produced overconfidence and delayed responses (Toshkov, Carroll & Yesilkagit 2022).

Politico-institutional factors affecting crisis response and management

Crises cannot be predicted, and pre-existing contingency plans are frequently unavailable, or insufficient to cope with the uncertainty and ambiguity new critical events bring. During the Covid-19 crisis, many states lacked specific preparation (in terms of structures, plans, and/or resources) for a pandemic of such huge magnitude. Meanwhile, those which had prepared to face other similar pandemic threats (i.e. other respiratory viruses such as the MERS-CoV) found their plans insufficient, due to the different characteristics of the SARS-CoV-2 virus and the Covid-19 disease which it produced (IOAC Independent Ovesightand Advisory Committee for the WHO Health Emergencies Programme 2020). In such a situation, the ability of politico-administrative systems to produce on-the-spot reactions adapted to the unforeseen scenario becomes crucial (Baubion 2013; Boin et al. 2005).

Analyses of governmental responses to the first wave of the Covid-19 pandemic have tended to focus on the role of these politico-institutional factors. Some works remark on the importance of policy capacities (Capano 2020; Toshkov, Carroll & Yesilkagit 2022) as well as on centralised and/or well-coordinated structures in contributing to produce swift reactions,[1] while opposite results have been observed in decentralised and less well-coordinated systems.[2] Yet other works have emphasised the importance of local capacities when central actors fail (Capano & Lippi 2021).

Political dynamics affecting crisis management

Crisis management is also conditioned by other factors related to more or less conjunctural political dynamics. For example, minority governments could be expected to have reduced room for manoeuvre in adopting swift preventive or mitigating measures or in extending them over time. However, this can be compensated by rally-round-the-flag dynamics of increased popular support for the government during a crisis, particularly during its first moments. Meanwhile, political polarisation incentivises government-opposition dynamics, blame-games, and partisan approaches to crisis management that may also influence government decision-making or reduce public acceptance of government measures.

The literature on the Covid-19 crisis has also paid attention to the political dynamics of crisis management. Perhaps surprisingly, Toshkov, Carroll and Yesilkagit (2022) have demonstrated that a government's level of parliamentary support did not affect the timing of the response. However, polarisation and populist politics have been found to have a significant (negative) influence on how governments reacted to the pandemic (Bowling, Fisk & Morris 2020; Charron, Lapuente & Rodríguez-Pose 2023).

Demographic characteristics

In a public health crisis, a country's particular demographic characteristics may play a role. In the case of Covid-19, it has been shown that levels of incidence and mortality rates are higher among older people (Pijls et al. 2021) and the more socially vulnerable (Karmakar, Lantz & Tipirneni 2021). The proportion of the elderly within the general population might therefore be a potentially significant factor influencing the volume of cases and deaths.

Social trust

Other studies have demonstrated the effects of social trust on governments' response and on citizens' compliance with measures (Devine et al. 2023; Zaki et al. 2022). Thus, public distrust of government and politicians has been identified as reducing citizens' compliance with official guidelines (Jennings et al. 2021). Meanwhile, in the case of Covid-19, it has been shown that in countries with higher levels of social trust and trust in government, the authorities tended to delay their actions or rely on soft (non-coercive) measures (Toshkov, Carroll & Yesilkagit 2022).

Timing

The previous factors concern situations pre-existing before a crisis hits. However, there is another factor related to what happens once it has started. Specifically, *when* - at what particular time-point – authorities react in the development of a crisis has generally been acknowledged as a crucial factor in the existing literature. But reactions depend on having enough information about the situation and its possible developments. In the Covid-19 crisis, uncertainty and ambiguity were much higher in those countries where the virus arrived earlier. Taking into account the characteristics of the disease and its exponential expansion (Manchein et al. 2020), this suggests that early arrival of the virus could become a disadvantage with potentially crucial consequences for how countries initially dealt with the pandemic as well as the damage it caused in terms of cases and casualties.

To date, few analyses of the factors affecting the governmental response during the initial phase of Covid-19 have systematically analysed the importance of timing. Two exceptions are the studies by Toshkov, Carroll and Yesilkagit (2022, p. 15) and Plümper and Neumayer (2022). In the first case, the authors show that those European countries where Covid-19 cases appeared first were slower in reacting in terms of imposing measures like lockdowns and/or closing schools. In the second study, the authors emphasise the comparative advantage of those countries where the virus arrived later in the first wave. Their findings suggest that timing may also be an important factor to investigate.

Having identified some potential explanations for different national responses to the initial outbreak of the Covid-19 crisis, we will now consider what outcomes they might lead us to expect in the case of our five South European countries.

Anticipating a public health crisis in Southern Europe: what might have been expected?

Crisis preparedness: how robust were the national health systems?

As mentioned above, crisis preparedness concerns the knowledge and capabilities to detect the crisis-causing threat and to take timely and appropriate actions to prevent it or to mitigate its social and economic impacts. In the case of Covid-19, this mainly had to do with the capacities of national health systems.

There were clear differences among our five countries in terms of how ready they were to meet a major public health challenge like Covid-19. To measure this, we use the 2019 Global Health Security (GHS) index, which encompasses aspects related to each country's capacity to prevent, detect, and respond to public health crises, as well as the capacity of the national health systems, compliance with international norms, and an evaluation of the risks affecting each country.

Table 1 shows that of our five South European countries, Spain performed best overall in the Global Health Security (GHS) index in 2019. Its overall score of 65.9 was significantly above the European mean of 55.4, resulting in a ranking of 15th worldwide (out of 195 countries). However,

Table 1. Health sector capacity of South European countries in 2019.

	SPAIN	PORTUGAL	ITALY	GREECE	TURKEY	EUROPE (Mean)
	PERFORMANCE ON THE GLOBAL HEALTH SECURITY INDEX (2019)					
GENERAL SCORE	65.9	60.3	56.2	53.8	52.4	55.4
RANKING	(15)	(20)	(31)	(37)	(40)	
PREVENTION	52.9	52.8	47.5	54.2	56.9	52.9
DETECTION	83.0	50.5	78.5	78.4	45.6	63.3
RESPONSE	61.9	67.7	47.5	44.0	49.0	48.6
HEALTH SYSTEM	59.6	55.0	36.8	37.6	45.7	43.6
NORMS	61.1	63.0	61.9	49.1	64.3	57.4
RISK	77.1	77.3	65.5	58.2	56.5	69.8
	EXPENDITURE ON HEALTH (2019)					
AS % of GDP	9.0	9.6	8.7	7.8	4.4	

Source: 2019 Global Health Security Index (Cameron, Nuzzo & Bell 2019); for health expenditure OECD/European Union (2020) p. 161.
Note: Country ranking on the GHS index is out of 195 countries.

looking in greater detail at the components that form the GHS index[3] offers a more complete picture. Thus, though Spain scored comparatively quite high on most indicators, it lagged behind Greece and Turkey (though not significantly) in prevention capacity, which includes sub-indicators referring to immunisation, antimicrobial resistance, zoonotic diseases, biosecurity and biosafety. However, as Rodríguez Teruel, Del Pino and Real-Dato (2022) demonstrate in our Spanish case study article, lack of preparedness to cope with a health crisis was not an issue before the pandemic, as the country already had experience in dealing with previous pandemic episodes.

Portugal came overall second after Spain on the 2019 GSI. With a score of 60.3, it was ranked in 20th place globally. Table 1 also shows that Portugal scored above the European mean on response capacity, health system, norm compliance and low risk. Indeed, in the categories of response and risk, it had the highest scores of all our South European countries. However, it had a weaker score on detection compared to Spain, Italy, or Greece. In our Portuguese case study, Silva, Costa and Moniz (2022) note that Portugal's healthcare system came under pressure during the period of its sovereign bailout (2011–2014). But subsequently the new government installed in 2015 had come to power on an anti-austerity platform and as Table 1 shows, in 2019, the country's healthcare expenditure represented a higher proportion of GDP (9.6 per cent) compared with our other countries (OECD/European Union 2020, p. 161).

Italy, while significantly behind the two Iberian countries on the GHS index in 2019, still had an overall score (56.2) marginally above the European mean and ranked in 31st place worldwide. However, in terms of the sub-indicators of the GHS, Table 1 shows that it had some important weaknesses compared with the other South European states, registering the lowest score of all five in the categories of prevention and healthcare system, and the second lowest in terms of response. In this respect, Vicentini and Galanti (2022) in our Italian case study also remark on the rigidity of the system and the negative impact of the austerity measures imposed during the 2010s to cope with the economic and financial crisis.

Finally, in general terms, Greece and Turkey were apparently the least prepared of the five countries and as Table 1 shows, they both fell below the European mean on the overall GSI index. Of our group of five South European states, Turkey had the worst overall score (52.4) on the 2019 GHS and also had by far the lowest healthcare expenditure as a share of GDP. However, a closer look at the sub-indicators gives a more nuanced picture. Table 1 shows that Turkey comparatively excelled in the categories of prevention and international norm compliance, where it had the highest scores of our five states. Meanwhile in healthcare system and response, it scored higher than both Italy and Greece. In our Turkish case study, Kemahlıoğlu and Yeğen (2022) also refer to the improvements in Turkey's healthcare system during the 2000s which extended its coverage, as well as the country's experience with emergencies, which might also be expected to have a positive impact during the management of the Covid-19 crisis.

Although in the overall evaluation, Greece came out above Turkey, on four sub-indicators it actually performed worse than the latter. Indeed, Greece was also the only one of our South European states to fall below the European mean on four sub-indicators. In comparison with our other South European states, Greece had the worst score in terms of response and norms compliance, and the second worst in the categories of prevention, health system and risk. In their article in this volume, Ladi, Angelou and Panagiotatou (2022) refer to the structural inefficiencies of the Greek healthcare system (unequal distribution of personnel and facilities, problems of access, and a National Plan for Public Health which had been designed but never implemented). The system had also been significantly affected by the austerity associated with the three sovereign bailouts implemented in 2010–18 and, as Table 1 shows, in 2019 Greece healthcare expenditure as a proportion of GDP was significantly lower than in Portugal, Spain and Italy.

Politico-institutional factors affecting crisis response and state management

As we have mentioned, the literature emphasises how factors like state structure, policy capacities and coordination may affect the governmental response during a crisis and its ability to intervene on societal problems. Table 2 shows data from the Sustainable Governance Indicators (SGI) project (2023) concerning the overall executive capacity of the five countries. These scores are produced through evaluations of country experts on different governance dimensions.

We observe that the ranking is almost identical to our previous factor, with Spain first, followed by Portugal and Italy. Once again, Turkey and Greece lag

Table 2. Politico-institutional factors affecting crisis response in Southern Europe (score and ranking)

	EXECUTIVE CAPACITY	GOVERNMENT EFFECTIVENESS	EXPERT ADVICE	REGIONAL AUTHORITY INDEX (2016)
SPAIN	6.6 (15)	6 (18)	7 (8)	29.8 (3)
PORTUGAL	6.0 (25)	7 (12)	5 (26)	8.1 (26)
ITALY	5.1 (31)	6 (18)	3 (39)	23.9 (25)
TURKEY	4.6 (36)	6 (18)	4 (31)	8.8 (25)
GREECE	4.3 (38)	5 (30)	6 (14)	8 (27)

Source: Sustainable Governance Indicators (2019), data available for download from https://www.sgi-network.org/2020/ (see link to Scores (Excel) and Codebook) and https://www.sgi-network.org/2022/Publications (scroll down to Downloads SGI 2019); for the regional authority index, see the website 'Arjan H. Schakel, Regional Authority Index' (https://www.arjanschakel.nl/index.php/regional-authority-index, accessed 07/10/2023).

Note: In parentheses the country's rank (out of 42 countries in executive capacity, government effectiveness and expert advice; out of 45 countries in the Regional Authority Index). 'Executive capacity' and 'Regional authority index' are composite indexes, hence the decimals. In contrast, 'government effectiveness' and 'expert advice' are individual indices, scored in integers from 1 to 10. For the methodology of the regional authority index, see Schakel et.al. 2018.

behind the others, this time with Greece coming last. With the exception of Spain (ranked 15th among the 42 countries surveyed), our other South European states are not characterised by high executive capacities. Particularly striking is the low performance of Greece, occupying 38th position out of 42.

Within the SGI's general executive capacity index, we underscore two indicators likely to be important for the management of the Covid-19 crisis – those referring to government effectiveness (the government's ability to achieve its goals) and the use of expert advice from outside the government on a regular basis (Schiller, Hellmann & Paulini 2019). In government effectiveness, our South European states fared modestly, with the exception of Portugal, which ranked 12th out of 42. Once again, Greece seemed to be the South European country whose government would potentially face the biggest obstacles in achieving its stated goals. Regarding the regular use of expert advice, only Spain occupied a prominent position among the surveyed countries (ranked 8th out of 42). In contrast, Turkey and, particularly, Italy, were regarded by experts as countries where external expert advice hardly has any role in policymaking.

Decentralisation is another factor which some analysts have cited when analysing the performance of South European countries during the first phase of Covid-19. For instance, Casula and Pazos-Vidal (2021) and Mattei and Del Pino (2021) emphasise the impact of the decentralised nature of the Italian and Spanish states on coordination between the national and subnational governments in the adoption and implementation of healthcare measures. Table 2 also shows information about this, using the Regional Authority Index (Schakel et al. 2018). Here we observe the great contrast between Spain and Italy (two highly decentralised countries) on the one hand and the highly centralised Turkey, Portugal, and Greece, on the other.

Summing up these two key categories of crisis preparedness and policy capacity, we would expect that Spain would probably be in the best position to face a crisis, followed by Portugal and Italy. In contrast, Turkey and Greece looked likely to have difficulties in coping. However, crisis management may also be affected by other factors to which we will now turn, namely to conjunctural political factors as well as non-political ones.

Political dynamics

Our five countries were in different situations in terms of government stability, as shown in Table 3. It could be logical to expect that, during a crisis, stronger governments, particularly those not dependent on parliamentary allies, would be in a better position to produce swift decisions. This suggests that Turkey, with its strong executive presidency, installed after the regime change referendum of 2017 and the following year's presidential elections, might be well placed. Of the four parliamentary democracies, only Greece had a single-party majority government. Portugal also had a single-party government, but without a parliamentary majority. Both governments had recent mandates, dating from July and November 2019 respectively. Italy's majority government, the second to be formed from the parliament elected in 2018 and installed in September 2019 after the collapse of its predecessor, was an ideologically heterogeneous four-party coalition, described by Vicentini and Galanti (2022) as an '"unnatural" alliance with former "enemies"'. However, arguably the country in the weakest position was Spain, where it had recently taken two elections – in April and November 2019 – to form a government. A minority administration, this was the first governing coalition in Spain's post-1977 democratic history and its swearing-in, in early January 2020, came just days before the discovery of Spain's first Covid case.

Polarised politics might also be expected to make governmental decision-making harder, due to the likelihood that pandemic measures could become a contested issue in the confrontation among already warring parties. For the four eurozone member-states in our South European sample, the previous

Table 3. Political context of the first phase of the pandemic in Southern Europe.

COUNTRY	PARTY POLARISATION	MAJORITY/MINORITY GOVERNMENT	GOVERNMENT COMPOSITION	DATE GOVERNMENT FORMED
SPAIN	5.5*	Minority	Coalition 2 parties	January 2020
TURKEY	4.6	Executive presidency with minority cabinet	Single-party	June 2018
GREECE	4.4*	Majority	Single-party	July 2019
ITALY	4.1	Majority	Coalition 4 parties	September 2019
PORTUGAL	3.8*	Minority	Single-party	October 2019

Source for party polarisation: https://www.parlgov.org/ (2020 dataset); the estimates for Spain, Portugal and Greece were updated after the 2019 elections, using the EU Political Barometer (also based on parlgov information). See: https://eupoliticalbarometer.uc3m.es/dashboard/ideology.

Note: Values indicate the level of perceived ideological polarisation (ranging from 0 to 10), using Russell's method of estimation (2008).

years, marked by the sovereign debt and other crises, had seen the rise of challenger parties on the radical right and in Greece and Spain of the radical left as well, thus extending the ideological spectrum represented by the parties in parliament. Notably, just months before the arrival of Covid-19, the 2019 elections in Spain and Portugal had resulted in the first national parliamentary breakthrough for a radical right party. But while in Portugal, Chega elected a single MP, in Spain Vox emerged as third party with 52 out of 350 seats and became a highly vocal participant in parliamentary debates. Table 3 shows that, in terms of ideological distance among the parties represented in parliament, after the 2019 elections Spain emerged with the highest score, followed by Turkey, Greece and Italy. Portugal, in contrast, had the lowest level of political polarisation among our five South European countries.

In addition, some of our South European countries were riven around fundamental issues. Spanish politics in early 2020 continued to be marked by discord around the country's territorial integrity and the deeply polarising legacy of the attempted Catalan independence referendum, held in October 2017, just over two years earlier. Turkish politics was marked by disagreement around competing understandings of democracy (Türkoğlu et al. 2022) and the nature of the political regime. The Turkish referendum of 2017 had left the country almost equally split between supporters of the move to an executive presidency and adherents of the existing parliamentary republic (Esen & Gümuscü 2020).

A further dimension concerned the nature of political competition. Several of our South European political systems were characterised by a confrontational political style. It has been remarked that in Italy, Greece and Spain, adversarial politics, already an established pattern in their national political systems, had intensified in recent years, with the result that 'at the beginning of 2020, polarisation was at a high or even record level in each country' (Bosco & Verney 2020, p. 23). All of these features could be expected to make political understandings and compromise harder in a crisis situation.

Demographic characteristics

Given the higher incidence and mortality rate of Covid-19 among elderly people, as mentioned above, demographic characteristics might be expected to impact significantly on outcomes. As Table 4 shows, in four of the five South European countries – Italy, Portugal, Greece and Spain – the proportion of the

Table 4. Percentage of the population aged 65+ in Southern Europe in 2019.

	ITALY	PORTUGAL	GREECE	SPAIN	TURKEY	EUROPE (mean)
POPULATION 65+ (%)	23.0	22.4	21.9	19.6	8.7	17.9

Source: World Bank (World Development Indicators) (https://data.worldbank.org/indicator/SP.POP.65UP.TO.ZS, accessed 09/01/2024).

Table 5. Interpersonal trust and trust in government in Southern Europe.

	SPAIN	ITALY	PORTUGAL	TURKEY	GREECE	EUROPE (mean)
INTERPERSONAL TRUST (%)	41.0	26.6	16.9	14	8.4	31.5
TRUST IN NATIONAL GOVERNMENTS (%)	21	25	46	66	26	39.3

Sources: For 'interpersonal trust': European Values Survey 2017 (EVS/WVS (2021). European Values Study and World Values Survey: Joint EVS/WVS 2017–2021 Dataset – Variable Report (Documentation/Tables). Version: July 2021 (v.2). GESIS Data Archive, Cologne and JD Systems Institute, Madrid). For 'trust in national government': Eurobarometer 92 (Autumn 2019).

Notes: 1) 'Interpersonal trust' refers to those answering 'Most people can be trusted' and the mean refers to European countries with a population above 500,000 people. 2) Trust in national government refers to those answering 'Tend to trust the national government' and the mean refers to the EU average.

population aged 65 years or above was higher than the European mean, suggesting this region as a whole might be worse hit than some of its neighbours. The elderly populations of these four countries were similar in size. The only outlier in our South European group was Turkey, with a share of elderly population less than half the European mean.

Social trust

As noted above, the literature has established an association between country performance in the initial phase of the Covid-19 pandemic and levels of citizens' trust (both interpersonal and in government), suggesting that this factor is related to higher levels of compliance with difficult measures. Table 5 shows that, in terms of interpersonal trust, Spain was once again the leader and with a significant difference from the others. The other four South European countries fell below the European mean – and all but Italy were significantly below. Once again, Greece came last, with the percentage of the population ready to declare that 'Most people can be trusted' amounting to less than one in ten individuals – just one fifth of the equivalent proportion in Spain. Turning to trust in government, Turkey had by far the highest score, although this figure marked a rise of 20 percentage points compared with the previous Eurobarometer survey six months earlier, suggesting some volatility on this index. Of the other four South European societies, the Portuguese trusted their government most while the Greeks, Italians and Spanish all declared low levels of trust, significantly below the European mean and without major variations between them.

Having introduced some nuances to our expectations, let us now turn to see to what extent they were fulfilled when the Covid-19 virus arrived in Southern Europe.

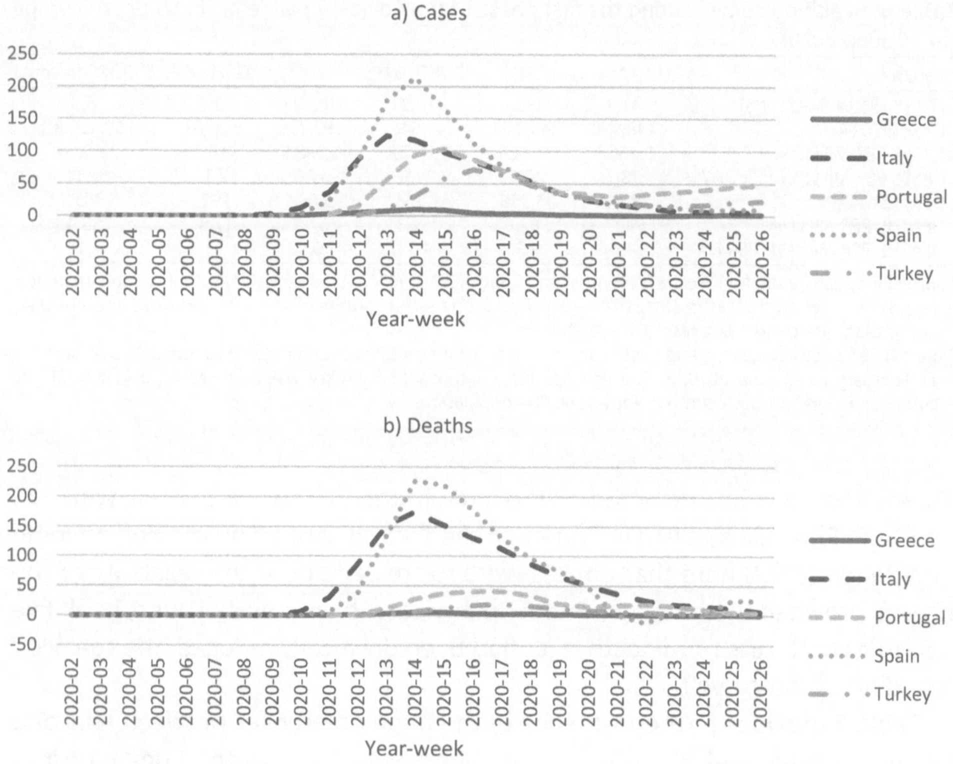

Figure 1. Evolution of the Covid-19 pandemic in Greece, Italy, Portugal, Spain and Turkey (cases and deaths per 100,000 population) until end of June 2020.
Source: Authors' elaboration of ECDC (European Centre for Disease Control) (2021) Data on 14-day notification rate of new Covid-19 cases and deaths (https://www.ecdc.europa.eu/en/publications-data/data-national-14-day-notification-rate-covid-19, accessed 11/08/2021).
Note: In Spain, for the last week of May (week 22), the indicator has a negative value (–12.3), reflecting an adjustment of the data (–875 deaths) in the previous week. In turn, the observed growth in weeks 25 and 26 is the consequence of a subsequent adjustment.

Southern Europe facing the first phase of Covid-19: what actually happened?

Figure 1 shows the weekly evolution of cases and deaths during the first wave of the pandemic in the five South European states. It illustrates how the numbers suddenly erupted in the early months of 2020 and underlines the diversity of national outcomes in terms of cases and deaths. It is clear at a glance that, completely contrary to our expectations, Spain and Italy were the worst hit among the five countries, while the impact of the first wave was much more moderate in the other three countries and especially in Greece.

According to the official records, at the acme of the tragedy, in the first week of April 2020, around 5,890 people in Spain and 5,108 in Italy lost their lives to the virus. In sharp contrast, at the worst point of the first phase in Greece (also the first week of April), 35 people died from Covid-19. In both Portugal and

Table 6. Health outcomes during the first phase of the Covid-19 pandemic in Southern Europe (to 30 June 2020).

Variable	SPAIN	ITALY	PORTUGAL	TURKEY	GREECE	EUROPE (mean)
POPULATION (MILLIONS)	47.3	59.6	10.3	83.2	10.7	16.9
CASES: TOTAL	248,970	240,310	41,646	192,239	3,376	58,525.8
CASES PER MILLION	5,266.4	4,031.4	4,070.7	2,388.5	316.3	2,450.4
CASES PER MILLION PER DAY	38.7	29.6	29.9	17.6	2.3	18.0
DEATHS: TOTAL	28,346	34,738	1,564	5,097	191	4,383.1
DEATHS PER MILLION	599.1	582.6	152.3	61.5	17.8	153.4
DEATHS PER MILLION PER DAY	4.4	4.3	1.1	0.5	0.1	1.1

Source: European Centre for Disease Prevention and Control (ECDC) (2021) Data on 14-day notification rate of new Covid-19 cases and deaths (https://www.ecdc.europa.eu/en/publications-data/data-national-14-day-notification-rate-covid-19, accessed 11/08/2021).

Notes: 1) Period covered: cases and deaths per million to 30 June 2020; cases and deaths per million per day from 15 February to 30 June 2020. 2) The first Spanish death on 13 February was reported on 3 March. 3) The European mean includes countries above 500,000 population.

Turkey, the peak was recorded a little later, in the third week of April, with 176 deaths in Portugal and 819 in Turkey. In the Turkish case, however, Kemahlıoğlu and Yeğen (2022) note that doubts were expressed about the reliability of the figures provided by the government. In any case, by the end of June, in all five countries both cases and death rates had been drastically reduced (the so-called 'bending of the curve').

Table 6 provides further evidence of the huge differences between Italy and Spain compared with the other three countries in terms of the human cost of Covid-19's initial phase. The highest total death toll was recorded in Italy, where almost 35,000 people died in the period to 30 June 2020, followed by 28,400 people in Spain. This was dramatically higher than Turkey's recorded total of 5,097 deaths, Portugal with 1,564 and especially Greece with what, by comparative standards, appears as a strikingly low 191 deaths.

Table 6 also shows data on cases and deaths in relation to the population in each country. Here it is clear that while Italy had the highest total number of deaths, in proportional terms Spain had the worst record, with the highest number of cases and deaths both per million and per million per day. Italy, however, did not lag far behind. Portugal, while experiencing a higher number of cases per million population than Italy, had a significantly lower rate of deaths – around one-quarter of the corresponding Italian figure. Turkey appeared to be in a different category from the other three countries, with ratios of deaths per million and per million per day less than half those of Portugal and less than one-eighth of the figures for Spain and Italy. Meanwhile, the proportional data further underline Greece's position as a significant outlier, with its death rates just a fraction of those of the Spanish and Italian figures.

Finally, how did our South European countries compare to the European mean? The region seemed to be characterised by extremes. During the period to 30 June 2020, deaths per million population approached a frightening four times the European mean in Spain and Italy. In contrast, Portugal was around the mean on this indicator, while Turkey was apparently significantly below that. At the other end of the spectrum from Spain and Italy, Greece's Covid-19 death rate was less than 12 per cent of the European mean. As can be seen from Table 6, Greece's low death rates were a direct reflection of its success in limiting the number of cases per million population (to about 13 per cent of the European mean).

Thus, during the first phase of Covid-19 in Southern Europe, Spain and Italy were the two countries which lost control of the pandemic to a frightening extent, while Portugal and Turkey were relatively effective in managing it. However, it was Greece which, in this early phase, emerged as the region's surprising success story, and a potential model to be copied. This was an astonishing turnaround for a country which, after the announcement of its sovereign debt crisis in late 2009, had been widely lambasted internationally as an example of administrative inefficiency and state incompetence (Tzogopoulos 2013).

Given that in the period examined, no differences were detected in the variant of the Covid-19 virus in the five countries,[4] how can these outcomes be explained? This is the subject of the next section.

Explaining national outcomes in the first phase of the pandemic in Southern Europe

Politico-institutional factors: state structure and coordination

During the first phase of the pandemic, in our five South European countries, the different national outcomes do not show a clear correlation with crisis preparedness, executive capacity, habitual use of expert advice, or government effectiveness. The worst outcomes occurred in the country rating highest in terms of crisis preparedness, executive capacity and expert advice (Spain), while the country with the worst score in government effectiveness and the second worst on crisis preparedness (Greece) had the best performance.

The country cases in the volume put flesh on these paradoxes. In the case of Spain, the prior assessments of the country's health security did not consider particular structural weaknesses that later became decisive, such as the low preparedness of nursing and elderly care homes, insufficient personal protection equipment, or a public health budget representing just one per cent of the total healthcare budget (Otero-Iglesias, Molina & Martínez 2020). However, it also seems that the apparent level of preparedness made national leaders and crisis managers overconfident about the capacity of the system to cope with the pandemic (Rodríguez Teruel, Del Pino & Real-Dato 2022). Something similar occurred in Italy, though in this case, as Vicentini and Galanti (2022) show, such overconfidence was less justified (see also Capano 2020). In the case of Greece, it seems likely that awareness of the country's weak public health and administrative capacity operated as an important motivation for the government to take decisive action.

We have mentioned above how the existing literature has emphasised the degree of (de)centralisation of the state structure and the ability to promote a coordinated response as factors explaining the different outcomes in some of our countries during the first wave (Casula & Pazos-Vidal 2021; Mattei & Del Pino 2021).

The articles in this volume concur with the view that decentralisation and coordination problems between national and subnational governments had a negative impact on the adoption and implementation of healthcare measures. Actually, the countries with the worst record, Spain and Italy, are also those which score highest on the regional authority index (see Table 2 above). In Italy, concurrent jurisdictions and coordination problems between national and regional authorities slowed down decision-making during the initial onset of the pandemic, while the decentralised structure of the healthcare system and ineffective national coordination led to asymmetries in implementation and policy outcomes across regions (Vicentini & Galanti 2022; see also Capano & Lippi 2021). In Spain, Rodríguez-Teruel, Del Pino and Real-Dato (2022), show how the competitive, bilateral style of intergovernmental relations (greatly influenced by more conjunctural political dynamics) resulted in weak coordination between the national and regional governments, which contributed to a reactive, and mostly soft, approach during the very first stage of the pandemic, just before the declaration of the state of alarm, when decision-making became centralised. That decentralisation probably played an important role in exacerbating initial problems in decision-making is consistent with previous findings (e.g. Toshkov, Carroll and Yesilkagit 2022). After the centralisation of powers implemented with the state of alarm decree, politicisation of intergovernmental relationships resurfaced during the easing stage, once the curve had been tamed.

In contrast, Ladi, Angelou and Panagiotatou (2022) argue that in Greece, concentration of responsibilities for the pandemic mitigation effort in a single authority (the General Secretariat of Civil Protection and Crisis Management) facilitated coordination and helped to build consensus with local authorities. Silva, Costa and Moniz (2022) and Kemahlıoğlu and Yeğen (2022) point to similar conclusions about the importance of centralisation in the swift responses of Portugal and Turkey. In the latter case, centralisation was reinforced by the recent switch to a presidential regime with authoritarian elements (see also Bakir 2020).

However, despite the apparent direct relationship between decentralisation and negative performance, it seems unlikely that this factor alone would be enough to explain the huge differences between the more decentralised Italy and Spain on the one hand and the other three more centralised countries on the other. Meanwhile, with regard to the latter group, it clearly does not offer an explanation for the big difference between Greece and the other two. It seems more likely that, rather than offering the main explanation, decentralisation acted to compound other, more critical, factors.

The role of experts

Outcomes during the first phase of Covid-19 also contradict expectations based on the countries' past records concerning the use of expert advice (Table 2). In all five South European countries, leaders resorted to experts to assist them in the management of the crisis, though their characteristics and use differed. For example, in Turkey, the government's claim it was following experts' advice contrasted with a lack of transparency about their role (Kemahlıoğlu & Yeğen 2022). In contrast, Greece's government decisions in the first phase were strongly based on the scientific input provided by an ad hoc advisory body formed by independent healthcare experts, which acted with a great deal of transparency (Ladi, Angelou & Panagiotatou 2022).

In the other countries, governments also created ad hoc bodies to advise them, though their influence varied. In Portugal, the initial influence of experts (intramural and external) on the government, apparent at the very beginning of the crisis, waned as economic concerns displaced healthcare considerations (Silva, Costa & Moniz 2022). The same occurred in Italy, where there was also a proliferation of expert bodies both within the national government as well as in the regions (Galanti & Saracino 2021), something also noted in Spain at the regional level. In the Spanish case, the national government heavily relied on intramural experts, while the ad hoc committees it created, formed of independent experts, had mostly a token function (Rodríguez Teruel, Del Pino & Real-Dato 2022). In both Italy and Spain, lack of transparency by the governments about how scientific evidence informed decisions, as well as disagreements both between experts and government on the one hand and within the expert community on the other, created confusion among public opinion and contributed to the politicisation of the crisis.

Political dynamics

The five countries also differed in their specific political dynamics when the pandemic hit. In this first phase, the three countries with single-party governments (Greece, Portugal, and Turkey) obtained better results compared with those ruled by coalitions. However, the case studies in this volume on Spain and Italy demonstrate that the nature of the government as a coalition did not affect the healthcare response during the first moments of the pandemic. Instead, frictions emerged between coalition partners at a later stage – in Spain in relation to the economic and social measures to cope with the consequences of the crisis (Rodríguez Teruel, Del Pino & Real-Dato 2022) and in Italy with respect to the length of the state of emergency and the rules during the easing phase (Vicentini & Galanti 2022).

It is also striking that the patterns of political polarisation in Southern Europe and the deep divisions within some of our countries did not condition the initial rally-round-the-flag dynamics that appeared in all of them at the beginning of the crisis. However, as time passed, these dynamics weakened. Only in Portugal and Greece did most opposition parties continue to support government policy throughout the period to the end of June 2020. In the Greek case, this responsible stance of the opposition was particularly striking in the context of the country's usual pattern of adversarial politics. In Portugal, with the lowest score on our party polarisation index in Table 3, this was less unexpected.[5] In addition, as noted by Silva, Costa and Moniz (2022) both the Portuguese prime minister and the President of the Republic involved opposition parties in decision-making and were successful in cultivating a shared national narrative.

In contrast, in Italy, Spain, and Turkey, criticisms about the government management of the crisis soon emerged. In Italy, the main opposition party, the Lega, as well as other parties (including one of the members of the governing coalition) urged the government to accelerate reopening as soon as late March (Vicentini & Galanti 2022). In Spain, parliamentary support for the six bi-weekly extensions of the state of alarm decreased from over 90 per cent of MPs in early April to slightly above 50 per cent in May. Opposition to the government was initially led by the radical right party Vox, but later extended successively to other parliamentary groups, including the official opposition, the Partido Popular (Popular Party). Moreover, in Spain, oppositional dynamics permeated intergovernmental relations, with some regions governed by opposition parties (like Madrid or Catalonia) adopting an explicitly confrontational approach towards the national government (Rodríguez Teruel, Del Pino & Real-Dato 2022). In Turkey, after the escalation of opposition criticisms, President Erdogan ended up accusing the official opposition of acting like a terrorist group (Kemahlıoğlu & Yeğen 2022).

It could be argued that growing contestation around the management of Covid-19 can be seen as an indication of the pandemic being normalised and incorporated into the dynamics of the existing political landscape. In any case, at this stage in the pandemic, the progressive politicisation of the crisis in these three countries did not seem to affect their ability to keep Covid-19 under control or to successfully bend the curve by June.

Demographic factors

If the proportion of the population aged 65+ had shaped the public health impact of the initial phase of Covid-19 in Southern Europe, we would expect four of our states to have roughly similar outcomes and worse records than their European neighbours. But as we have seen, there were major differences between Spain and Italy on the one hand, where deaths dramatically exceeded the European mean, and Portugal and Greece on the other. In other words, there does not appear to be an obvious correlation between the pandemic health outcomes and the demographic characteristics of our South European countries.

Social trust

As mentioned above, levels of citizens' trust (both in government and interpersonal) are expected to affect levels of compliance with governmental crisis measures. But again, this does not seem to be a relevant consideration for our South European states. Notably, Spain and (to a lesser extent) Italy presented higher levels of interpersonal trust than the other countries and, still, had a worse performance in the first wave. Furthermore, Greece registered the lowest level of interpersonal trust and similar levels of trust in government as Spain and Italy, yet was the best performing country. Perhaps even more to the point, all the case studies in this volume emphasise the high level of citizen compliance during the first phase of the pandemic, despite different levels of trust in the countries concerned (Table 5).

In sum, our initial expectations about the relative performance of our South European states in a public health crisis did not outlive the first onset of the Covid-19 pandemic. Given that of the factors we have examined, only decentralisation appears to offer a partial explanation of the differences, we now turn to our final factor: the effect of timing.

The importance of timing

Our basic hypothesis is that the major difference in crisis performance between Italy and Spain on the one hand and the other three countries on the other, can be explained in terms of where the virus appeared earlier (see Table 7). As Table 7 shows, Covid-19 arrived in Southern Europe in two stages. The first Covid-19 cases were detected in Italy and Spain at the end of January 2020. This was less than three weeks after the Chinese media officially reported the first death from Covid-19 and just one week after the imposition of the first lockdown in Wuhan. Meanwhile, the first deaths from Covid-19 in Italy and Spain occurred in February,[6] at a time when Greece, Portugal, and Turkey still had not recorded a single case (as can be seen in Figure 1 above). In contrast, the virus reached Greece at the end of February, and Portugal and Turkey in early March, with the first deaths in all three countries taking place in March.

This meant that governments and experts in Italy and Spain were acting in a much more uncertain environment than their counterparts in the other countries. In January and February, less was known about the virus and its consequences, and most of this was based on the initial Chinese experience in Wuhan. In Italy and Spain, this led to initial diagnostics (supported by national and international experts) which contributed to normalising the risk and delaying the taking of more stringent measures until it was too late. In the Spanish case, this initial misperception of the emergency was also supported by overconfidence in the level of preparation of the country's health system. Later, when the spreading of the virus seemed to escape control (in late February and

Table 7. Key dates in the evolution of the first phase of the Covid-19 pandemic in Southern Europe.

VARIABLE	ITALY	SPAIN	GREECE	PORTUGAL	TURKEY
First case	30/01	30/01	26/02	02/03	10/03
First death	22/02	13/02	12/03	17/03	17/03
Stay-at-home recommendation	–	09/03	27/02	18/03	21/03
Days from first case to stay-at-home recommendation	–	39	1	16	11
Nationwide stay-at-home order	10/03	14/03	22/03	–	–
Days from first case to nationwide stay-at-home order	40	44	25	–	–
Nationwide school closure	04/03	12/03	10/03	16/03	16/03
Days from first case to nationwide school closure	34	42	13	14	6

Sources: For dates of cases and deaths, see European Centre for Disease Prevention and Control (2021) Data on 14-day notification rate of new Covid-19 cases and deaths (https://www.ecdc.europa.eu/en/publications-data/data-national-14-day-notification-rate-covid-19, accessed 11/08/2021); for dates of policy measures, see the case studies in this volume. Data on non-pharmaceutical measures (stay-at-home recommendations and orders, and school closures) come from European Centre for Disease Prevention and Control (ECDC) (2021) Data on country response measures to Covid-19 (version 09/06/2021) (https://www.ecdc.europa.eu/en/publications-data/download-data-response-measures-covid-19, accessed 09/01/2024).

Notes: 1) The figures in the table refer to nationwide measures. In Italy, local lockdowns and school closures had already begun earlier. See Table 2 in Vicentini and Galanti (2022) in this volume for more information. 2) The first death in Spain occurred on 13 February but was not reported until 3 March. 3) The date for school closures concerns primary and/or secondary schools.

early March), uncertainty compounded by the coordination problems arising from the decentralised structures in both countries, contributed to delaying stronger containment measures.

In contrast, when the infection arrived in Greece, Portugal and Turkey, in addition to the cautionary Italian and Spanish experiences, dissemination of the virus was already under way in a series of other countries, including the United Kingdom and the United States. Thus, the authorities had more information about the urgent nature of the threat posed by Covid-19 and the need to take immediate and drastic measures to contain its spread.

To take the case of Greece: the first case was diagnosed in this country a full 27 days after Italy and Spain. The first Greek death on 12 March occurred the day after the World Health Organisation formally declared the Covid-19 outbreak to be a pandemic and several days after northern Italy had been placed under a compulsory lockdown. At this point, Greeks were already watching with horror the nightly news from their Italian neighbour and particularly the bulletins from the hospitals in Lombardy. They not only knew what was likely to happen but also what needed to be done to avoid it. Especially given the weak capacity of the national health system, the urgent need for proactive measures to limit the spread of the virus and the imperative for public compliance with them was apparent to both government and citizens. In retrospect, Greece's weakness in terms of crisis preparedness proved a strength as it meant the need for drastic action was undisputed.

The difference that the timing of the virus' arrival made to the government response in our South European countries is evident if we look at the number of days between the first case/death and the date main measures were taken, exemplified by nationwide stay-at-home recommendations or orders and school closures. In Italy, the initial approach was to implement local measures, with the first municipal lockdowns ordered three weeks after the first case, followed by regional stay-at-home orders two days later. However, it took more than a month from the first Italian case to the decision to close the schools nationwide, while in Spain it took 42 days. The stay-at-home recommendation in Spain was issued 39 days after the first case. In Italy there was no such recommendation: rather a compulsory national lockdown was ordered a full 40 days after the first case, while in Spain, the direct order decision took 44 days.

In contrast, Portugal, Turkey and Greece were much swifter in taking similar decisions. Thus, Greece recommended its citizens to stay at home just one day after the first case was declared, while this recommendation took 11 days in Turkey, and 16 in Portugal. Similarly, school closures took place in all three countries before their first deaths from Covid-19 occurred.

Particularly striking is the level of caution displayed in Greece, the only country where authorities were clearly proactive during this first phase of the pandemic. The actual date of the Greek stay-at-home recommendation (27 February) preceded the analogous Spanish decision by 11 days, despite the fact that in Spain the pandemic was significantly more advanced. Greek schools were also closed two days before Spain took similar action. Meanwhile, the stay-at-home order was issued less than two weeks after Italy and just over a week after Spain, despite the fact that Greece had comparatively very few cases at that time. In contrast to Greece's extreme caution – which brought exemplary results – Portugal chose not to order a compulsory lockdown at this point in the pandemic, while Turkey only imposed weekend lockdowns, which were lifted on weekdays.

The consequences are clear from Figure 1 above. For Italy and Spain, being first hit meant being worst hit, with cases and deaths rapidly soaring out of control. In contrast, the time lag in the arrival of the virus in Greece, Portugal and Turkey was accompanied by a significantly shallower curve in terms of both cases and deaths when compared to the South European Covid vanguard of Italy and Spain.

Conclusions

The goal of this paper was to investigate the performance of five South European countries in managing the first phase of the Covid-19 pandemic to 30 June 2020. While these countries shared some common characteristics, there was an extraordinary variation in their public health outcomes. The death rate per million population ranged from over 390 per cent of the European mean in Spain to less than 12 per cent in Greece.[7] Alongside Spain, Italy also suffered a dramatic spiral of cases and deaths as public authorities lost control. In addition to the Greek success story, both Portugal and Turkey also performed well in comparative European terms.

Also striking is the fact that these national outcomes generally confounded expectations, as crisis preparedness and policy capacity proved poor predictors of actual pandemic performance. Nor do political dynamics or societal factors appear to explain the differences at this stage in the pandemic. While centralised decision-making appears to have contributed to more effective crisis management, this article argues that in Southern Europe the key explanatory factor behind the variation was beyond states' control. Timing – the moment when the virus arrived in a country, and the amount that was known at that point about the disease and how to control it – proved crucial in conditioning the speed and decisiveness of the governmental response.

The virus was already circulating in Italy and Spain at a time when information about Covid-19 was still scarce and uncertain, and when available evidence (including that provided by experts) suggested that normal healthcare preparedness (proficient in the case of Spain, for instance) would be enough to cope with the threat. Therefore, these countries' reactions were mostly based on their actual capacities and institutions at that moment (Capano 2020). This is why the situation also exacerbated existing malfunctions and problems, such as the weakness of the elderly care system in Spain, or the problems of regionalisation affecting healthcare services in Italy. In this respect, the coordination problems observed in Italy and Spain as a result of their decentralised structures acted mostly as a factor compounding the underlying decision problems derived from the earlier arrival of the virus in these countries.

In contrast, the virus arrived later in Greece, Portugal, and Turkey, giving authorities in these countries more time and more information to adapt their policy reactions to their capacities. As a result, these governments were able to intervene at an earlier point in the diffusion of the virus than their Italian and Spanish counterparts, thus limiting the impact in their countries. Greece's success in controlling the pandemic, confounding expectations and making it a South European outlier during the initial phase, combined this time advantage with an especially cautious and pro-active approach, which can be attributed to a recognition that the country's weak health system and policy capacity would make it especially vulnerable if the virus was allowed to spread.

However, as noted by the authors of the case studies in this volume, the picture of comparative success and failure among our South European countries changed during subsequent phases of the pandemic. After the shock of the first few months, the initial focus on limiting the spread of the virus was counterbalanced by more complex calculations concerning the economic, social and educational consequences of the measures needed to achieve this, with different countries adopting different policy mixes. As can be seen in Figure 2, the record of all but one of our South European countries worsened, in some cases significantly, during the next phase of the pandemic.

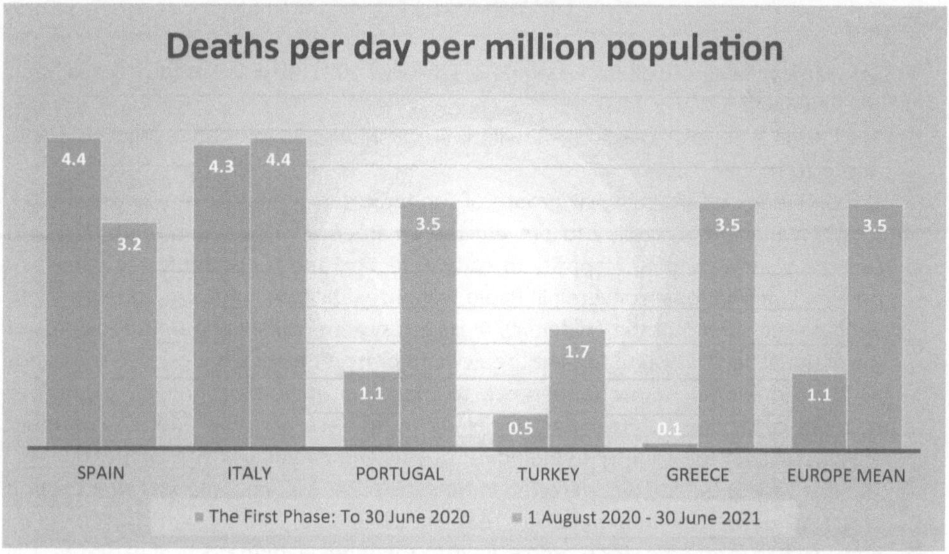

Figure 2. Covid-19 performance in Southern Europe: the first phase (to 30 June 2020) compared with the next six months (August-December 2020) (deaths per day per million population). *Source*: European Centre for Disease Prevention and Control (2021) Data on 14-day notification rate of new Covid-19 cases and deaths (https://www.ecdc.europa.eu/en/publications-data/data-national-14-day-notification-rate-covid-19, accessed 11/08/2021).

The initial comparative advantage offered to some countries by the later arrival of the virus was transient and could not be maintained. Inevitably, the next phases of the pandemic took a harsher toll on them. Portugal in early 2021 briefly became a world leader in terms of Covid-19 cases and deaths. As Figure 2 shows, between the first week of August 2020 and the last week of June 2021, the number of daily deaths as a proportion of the population in Portugal quadrupled compared to the first phase. Indeed, this country's performance during this second period approached that of Italy. The country which experienced the most spectacular increase compared to its earlier record, however, was Greece which, from a first phase outlier, now appeared to have 'normalised' in relation to the other South European countries and indeed the European mean. Meanwhile, although the figures officially reported by Turkey remained low, they had still tripled compared to the period before the end of June 2020. In contrast, Spain greatly improved its performance after the first phase, suggesting that once the passing effect of the virus' early arrival wore off, other factors are likely to have become more important in explaining comparative national performance.

Notes

1. See Hartley, Bales & Bali 2021; Hegele & Schnabel 2021; Toshkov, Carroll & Yesilkagit 2022; Kim, Oh & Wang 2020.
2. See Casula & Pazos-Vidal 2021; Bowling, Fisk & Morris 2020; Pattyn, Matthys & Van Hecke 2021; Pierre 2020.
3. The GHS index is formed by six groups of sub-indicators (Cameron, Nuzzo & Bell 2019, p. 65): 1) Prevention (ability to prevent the emergence or release of pathogens); 2) Detection and reporting (capacity of early detection and reporting for epidemics of potential international concern); 3) Rapid response (ability to offer a rapid response to mitigate the spread of the epidemic); 4) Health system (sufficiency and robustness of the national health system to treat the sick and protect health workers); 5) Compliance with international norms (adherence to global norms, commitment to improve national capacity, and financing for plans to address gaps); 6) Risk environment (vulnerability of the country to biological threats and overall risk environment).
4. The first variant (Alpha) was detected in November 2020, several months after the end of the period we are examining. See Thakur et al. (2022).
5. Portugal had form here. For example, in 2011 the three leading political parties had all agreed on the terms of the country's sovereign bailout, in sharp contrast to the corresponding debates in Greece.
6. In Spain the first death was officially reported on 3 March, though the passing occurred on 13 February.
7. Based on the figures in Table 6.

Acknowledgments

The authors would like to thank Anna Bosco for useful comments on an earlier version of this article.

Disclosure statement

No potential conflict of interest was reported by the author(s).

Funding

This work received the support of the Spanish Ministry of Science and Innovation [CONESPOL Project PGC2018-098319-B-C21 and PGC2018-098319-B-C22].

ORCID

Susannah Verney http://orcid.org/0000-0002-8554-7579
José Real-Dato http://orcid.org/0000-0001-9734-0850
Juan Rodríguez-Teruel http://orcid.org/0000-0002-7112-986X

References

Bakir, C. (2020) 'The Turkish state's responses to existential Covid-19 crisis', *Policy and Society*, vol. 39, no. 3, pp. 424–441.

Baubion, C. (2013) 'OECD risk management: strategic crisis management', *OECD Working Papers on Public Governance*, no. 23. available online at: https://www.oecd-ilibrary.org/oecd-risk-management_5k41rbd1lzr7.pdf?__cf_chl_tk=SVwqy0jilrqDnYHcWELCrcV7kGG4Q5.ailirkgAkRy8-1701801681-0-gaNycGzNC9A

Boin, A., 't Hart, P., Stern, E. & Sundelius, B. (2005) *The Politics of Crisis Management: Public Leadership Under Pressure*, Cambridge University Press, Cambridge.

Bosco, A. & Verney, S. (2020) 'Polarisation in Southern Europe: elites, party conflicts and negative partisanship', *South European Society & Politics*, vol. 25, no. 3–4, pp. 257–284.

Bosco, A. & Verney, S. (eds.) (2022) *The Politics of Polarisation: Conflictual Competition in Italy, Spain and Greece*, Routledge, New York and London.

Bowling, C. J., Fisk, J. M. & Morris, J. C. (2020) 'Seeking patterns in chaos: transactional federalism in the Trump administration's response to the Covid-19 pandemic', *The American Review of Public Administration*, vol. 50, no. 6–7, pp. 512–518.

Cameron, E. E., Nuzzo, J. B. & Bell, J. A. (eds) (2019) 'GHS Index (global health security Index): building collective action and accountability', in *Nuclear Threat Initiative, the Johns Hopkins Center for Health Security and the Economist Intelligence Unit*, Washington DC, Baltimore (MD), and London. available online at: https://www.ghsindex.org/wp-content/uploads/2019/10/2019-Global-Health-Security-Index.pdf

Capano, G. (2020) 'Policy design and state capacity in the Covid-19 emergency in Italy: if you are not prepared for the (un)expected, you can be only what you already are', *Policy and Society*, vol. 39, no. 3, pp. 326–344.

Capano, G., Howlett, M., Jarvis, D. S. L., Ramesh, M. & Goyal, N. (2020) 'Mobilising policy (in) capacity to fight Covid-19: understanding variations in state responses', *Policy and Society*, vol. 39, no. 3, pp. 285–308.

Capano, G. & Lippi, A. (2021) 'Decentralisation, policy capacities, and varieties of first health response to the Covid-19 outbreak: evidence from three regions in Italy', *Journal of European Public Policy*, vol. 28, no. 8, pp. 1197–1218.

Casula, M. & Pazos-Vidal, S. (2021) 'Assessing the multi-level government response to the Covid-19 crisis: Italy and Spain compared', *International Journal of Public Administration*, vol. 44, no. 11–12, pp. 994–1005.

Charron, N., Lapuente, V. & Rodríguez-Pose, A. (2023) 'Uncooperative society, uncooperative politics or both? Trust, polarisation, populism and Covid-19 deaths across European regions', *European Journal of Political Research*, vol. 62, no. 3, pp. 781–805.

Chiaramonte, A., Emanuele, V., Maggini, N. & Paparo, A. (2018) 'Populist success in a hung parliament: the 2018 general election in Italy', *South European Society and Politics*, vol. 23, no. 4, pp. 479–501.

Devine, D., Valgarðsson, V., Smith, J., Jennings, W., Scotto di Vettimo, M., Bunting, H. & McKay, L. (2023) 'Political trust in the first year of the Covid-19 pandemic: a meta-analysis of 67 studies', *Journal of European Public Policy*, pp. 1–23. 10.1080/13501763.2023.2169741

Esen, B. & Gumuscu, S. (2019) 'Killing competitive authoritarianism softly: the 2019 local elections in Turkey', *South European Society and Politics*, vol. 24, no. 3, pp. 317–342.

Esen, B.& Gümüşçü, Ş. (2020) 'A small yes for presidentialism: the Turkish constitutional referendum of April 2017', *South European Society & Politics*, vol. 22, no. 3, pp. 303–326.

Galanti, M. T. & Saracino, B. (2021) 'Inside the Italian Covid-19 task forces', *Contemporary Italian Politics*, vol. 13, no. 2, pp. 275–291.

Hartley, K., Bales, S. & Bali, A. S. (2021) 'Covid-19 response in a unitary state: emerging lessons from Vietnam', *Policy Design and Practice*, vol. 4, no. 1, pp. 1–17.

Hegele, Y. & Schnabel, J. (2021) 'Federalism and the management of the Covid-19 crisis: centralisation, decentralisation and (non-)coordination', *West European Politics*, vol. 44, no. 5–6, pp. 1052–1076.

IOAC (Independent Ovesightand Advisory Committee for the WHO Health Emergencies Programme). (2020) 'Interim report on WHO's response to Covid-19 January–April 2020', World Health Organisation, Geneva. available online at: https://www.who.int/publications/m/item/interim-report-on-who-s-response-to-covid—january—april-2020

Jennings, W., Stoker, G., Valgarðsson, V., Devine, D. & Gaskell, J. (2021) 'How trust, mistrust and distrust shape the governance of the Covid-19 crisis', *Journal of European Public Policy*, vol. 28, no. 8, pp. 1174–1196.

Karmakar, M., Lantz, P. M. & Tipirneni, R. (2021) 'Association of social and demographic factors with Covid-19 incidence and death rates in the US', *JAMA Network Open*, vol. 4, no. 1, pp. 1–12.

Kemahlıoğlu, Ö. & Yeğen, O. (2022) 'Surviving the Covid-19 pandemic under right-wing populist rule: Turkey in the first phase', *South European Society and Politics*, vol. 27, no. 4, pp. 577–606.

Kim, Y., Oh, S. S. & Wang, C. (2020) 'From uncoordinated patchworks to a coordinated system: MERS-CoV to Covid-19 in Korea', *The American Review of Public Administration*, vol. 50, no. 6–7, pp. 736–742.

Ladi, S., Angelou, A. & Panagiotatou, D. (2022) 'Regaining trust: evidence-informed policy-making during the first phase of the Covid-19 crisis in Greece', *South European Society and Politics*, vol. 27, no. 4, pp. 551–576.

Levin, K., Cashore, B., Bernstein, S. & Auld, G. (2012) 'Overcoming the tragedy of super wicked problems: constraining our future selves to ameliorate global climate change', *Policy Sciences*, vol. 45, no. 2, pp. 123–152.

Manchein, C., Brugnago, E. L., Silva, R. M., Mendes, C. F. O. & Beims, M. W. (2020) 'Strong correlations between power-law growth of Covid-19 in four continents and the inefficiency of soft quarantine strategies', *Chaos: An Interdisciplinary Journal of Nonlinear Science*, vol. 30, no. 4. 10.1063/5.0009454

Mattei, P. & Del Pino, E. (2021) 'Coordination and health policy responses to the first wave of Covid-19 in Italy and Spain', *Journal of Comparative Policy Analysis: Research and Practice*, vol. 23, no. 2, pp. 274–281.

OECD/European Union. (2020) *Health at a Glance: Europe 2020. State of Health in the EU Cycle*, OECD, Paris.

Otero-Iglesias, M., Molina, I. & Martínez, J. P. (2020) '¿Ha sido un fracaso la gestión española del Covid-19? Errores, lecciones y recomendaciones', *Real Instituto Elcano, Documento de Trabajo*, vol. 14, no. 2020, available online at: www.realinstitutoelcano.org

Pattyn, V., Matthys, J. & Van Hecke, S. (2021) 'High-stakes crisis management in the Low Countries: comparing government responses to Covid-19', *International Review of Administrative Sciences*, vol. 87, no. 3, pp. 593–611.

Pierre, J. (2020) 'Nudges against pandemics: Sweden's Covid-19 containment strategy in perspective', *Policy and Society*, vol. 39, no. 3, pp. 478–493.

Pijls, B. G., Jolani, S., Atherley, A., Derckx, R. T., Dijkstra, J. I. R., Franssen, G. H. L., Hendriks, S., Richters, A., Venemans-Jellema, A., Zalpuri, S. & Zeegers, M. P. (2021) 'Demographic risk factors for Covid-19 infection, severity, ICU admission and death: a meta-analysis of 59 studies', *British Medical Journal Open*, vol. 11, no. 1, pp. 1–10.

Plümper, T. & Neumayer, E. (2022) 'Lockdown policies and the dynamics of the first wave of the SARS-CoV-2 pandemic in Europe', *Journal of European Public Policy*, vol. 29, no. 3, pp. 321–341.

Rodríguez Teruel, J., Del Pino, E. & Real-Dato, J. (2022) 'The limits of power concentration and expert knowledge in emergency management: Spain's government response during the first phase of the Covid-19 pandemic', *South European Society and Politics*, vol. 27, no. 4, pp. 487–519.

Schakel, A. H., Danailova, A., Gein, I. & Hegewald, S. (2018) 'Final Report on Updating the Regional Authority Index (RAI) for Forty-Five Countries (2010–2016)', European Commission and Maastricht University, Brussels. available online at: https://op.europa.eu/en/publication-detail/-/publication/5562196f-3d3a-11e8-b5fe-01aa75ed71a1

Schiller, C., Hellmann, T. & Paulini, P. (2019) *Codebook: Sustainable Governance Indicators 2019*, Bertelsmann Stiftung, Gütersloh.

Silva, P., Costa, E. & Moniz, J. (2022) 'A Portuguese miracle: the politics of the first phase of Covid-19 in Portugal', *South European Society and Politics*, vol. 27, no. 4, pp. 521–549.

Sustainable Governance Indicators. (2023) "About the SGI", Bertelsmann Stiftung, available online at: https://www.sgi-network.org/2022/About

Thakur, V., Bhola, S., Thakur, P., Patel, S. K. S., Kulshrestha, S., Ratho, R. K. & Kumar, P. (2022) 'Waves and variants of SARS-CoV-2: understanding the causes and effect of the Covid-19 catastrophe', *Infection*, vol. 50, no. 2, pp. 309–325.

Tierney, K. J., Lindell, M. K. & Perry, R. W. (eds.) (2001) *Facing the Unexpected: Disaster Preparedness and Response in the United States*, Joseph Henry Press, Washington, DC.

Toshkov, D., Carroll, B. & Yesilkagit, K. (2022) 'Government capacity, societal trust or party preferences: what accounts for the variety of national policy responses to the Covid-19 pandemic in Europe?' *Journal of European Public Policy*, vol. 29, no. 7, pp. 1009–1028.

Türkoğlu, D., Odabaş, M., Tunaoglu, D. & Yavaş, M. (2022) 'Political polarisation on social media: competing understandings of democracy in Turkey', *South European Society and Politics*, vol. 27, no. 2, pp. 223–251.

Tzogopoulos, G. (2013) *The Greek Crisis in the Media: Stereotyping in the International Press*, Ashgate, Farnham and Burlington, VT.

Vicentini, G. & Galanti, M. T. (2022) 'Italy, the Sick Man of Europe: policy response, experts and public opinion in the first phase of Covid-19', *South European Society and Politics*, vol. 27, no. 4, pp. 459–485.

World Bank & United Nations. (2010) 'Natural Hazards, Unnatural Disasters: The Economics of Effective Prevention', World Bank, Washington, DC, available online at: https://openknowledge.worldbank.org/handle/10986/2512

You, J. (2020) 'Lessons from South Korea's Covid-19 policy response', *The American Review of Public Administration*, vol. 50, no. 6–7, pp. 801–808.

Zaki, B. L., Nicoli, F., Wayenberg, E. & Verschuere, B. (2022) 'In trust we trust: the impact of trust in government on excess mortality during the Covid-19 pandemic', *Public Policy and Administration*, vol. 37, no. 2, pp. 226–252.

Italy, the Sick Man of Europe: Policy Response, Experts and Public Opinion in the First Phase of Covid-19

Giulia Vicentini and Maria Tullia Galanti

ABSTRACT

Italy was the first Western country to be dramatically overwhelmed by Covid-19, the first country outside of China to implement lockdown measures and, until mid-April 2020, the country in the world most affected in terms of number of victims. This article aims to sketch the evolution of the first phase of the Covid-19 crisis in Italy and demonstrates that the health crisis moved forward hand in hand with some typical shortcomings characterising the Italian political, administrative and institutional system. The incremental reaction by the unprecedented M5S-PD coalition government showed the huge difficulties in facing the most serious challenge since the end of WWII, with the institutional system already afflicted by its scarce capacity and the economy still recovering from the 2012 crisis.

In 2005 *The Economist* described Italy as 'the real sick man of Europe', referring to the country's structural and political difficulties in promoting reforms capable of relaunching economic growth. From then onwards, this became a recurring cliché in the international media. Similarly, the scientific literature associated this definition with the characteristics of the Italian political and socio-economic systems and their (negative) effects on its capacity to adapt and respond to pressures and external crises (Cotta & Verzichelli 2007; Pasquino 2020; Moschella & Verzichelli 2021).

In March 2020, Italy became the first Western country to be dramatically overwhelmed by Covid-19, the first country outside of China to implement lockdown measures and the most affected country in the world in terms of contagions and victims. Thus, the 'sick' status finally assumed a 'literal' meaning. The images of rows of trucks taking away hundreds of coffins from the city of Bergamo (Lombardy) as graveyards had no more space circulated around the world, as did the drama of over-crowded hospitals in northern Italy.

This unexpected crisis found fertile ground in a country still affected by pre-existing shortcomings, which may have impacted the speed and strength of the policy response. First, the economy was still recovering from the 2012 crisis, which among other things had involved years of serious cuts to the public health system (Neri & Mori 2017). Second, the country's administrative system is largely considered ineffective (Di Mascio & Natalini 2014), while the distribution of competences between the various levels of government ultimately engenders increased institutional conflict between the central and local levels (Baldi & Profeti 2020). Third, the political stage was characterised by extreme electoral volatility, party system de-institutionalisation (Emanuele & Chiaramonte 2020) and a growing level of personalisation (Garzia 2017) and polarisation, reflecting the weaknesses of political parties and the government (Newell 2020a).

The first aim of this paper is to single out some 'crisis explanatory factors' by investigating the relationship between the pre-existing Italian political and institutional context and the policy response to the Covid-19 emergency. Second, we seek to evaluate the management of the health crisis by the Italian government and to assess the main political effects of Covid-19 in the short to medium term. Temporally, our analysis is focused on the first phase of the Covid-19 crisis, specifically on a period of approximately six months between January and June 2020.

The paper is structured as follows: the first section is devoted to the country background, namely the level of crisis preparedness and the evolution of the pandemic in the country. The second section focuses on the policy response: first, we look at the government's reactions to contain the spread of infection and its dramatic social and economic aftermath; second, we analyse the (unprecedented) role of experts in driving the government's choices and the 'narrative' of the epidemic presented to the Italian public; third, we focus on the interactions and disputes between the national government and regional authorities in the management of the crisis. Then, the third section deals with the political response, i.e. with the political debate in terms of government-opposition conflict and negotiations within the governing coalition, and with public opinion dynamics relating to the reactions from the media and citizens to anti-Covid measures. Finally, in the conclusion we summarise the main findings and discuss how far the experience of the first phase in Italy has differed from the subsequent phases.

Country background

Crisis preparedness and state capacity: a perfect storm scenario?

The literature on crisis management highlights that in the case of an emergency, the preparedness of the system is helpful in striking a fast and effective response (Boin et al. 2005). Accordingly, a brief overview of the characteristics of the Italian health, administrative and political systems before the onset of the Covid-19 crisis is necessary to better interpret what came next.

First, the Italian national health system has been progressively decentralised since the 1970s (and after the end of the 1990s), with the distribution of powers and resources (political, managerial and fiscal) from the national to the regional level (Terlizzi 2019). Although the Ministry of Health maintains a role in financing the system and in setting general principles, the regions organise and deliver all the services and have progressively acquired autonomy in spending and (partially) taxation. This decentralisation has progressively led to different levels of performance among regions and, most notably, to different regional healthcare models in terms of the organisation of services based on hospitals versus territorial public health, as well as in terms of protocols and operational response (Mapelli 2012). Most importantly, the austerity policies adopted in response to the 2008 economic crisis entailed an overall block on the hiring of medical personnel (doctors and nurses in particular) whose financing still depends on the central government, and a tendency to a 'differentiated federalism', in which the more 'virtuous' regions enjoy greater spending autonomy than their more 'vicious' counterparts (Neri & Mori 2017). Furthermore, the Italian healthcare system did not have any recent experience with epidemics or pandemics: even though an 'influenza pandemic plan' had been approved years earlier (Ministero della Salute 2007), it has never been updated or implemented. Moreover, the governmental body dealing with risk management, the Department of Civil Protection, had considerable experience and expertise in the management of natural catastrophes, but never with a sanitary emergency (Capano 2020).

Second, austerity affected the (already) scarce Italian state capacity (World Bank 2020; Di Mascio & Natalini 2014). Cutbacks on personnel in public administration have undermined reforms aimed at dealing with the rigidities and inefficiencies derived from a legalistic administrative culture and this ultimately resulted in frequent implementation gaps in several policy domains.

Finally, the country was facing a situation of extreme political weakness following the failure of the first 'entirely populist' government in the history of the Italian republic (Bressanelli & Natali 2019), which had been supported by an unprecedented coalition between the main party in Parliament, the M5S (Movimento Cinque Stelle – Five Stars Movement) and the rightist party Lega (League). In summer 2019 the Lega leader Matteo Salvini decided to break the alliance and the Prime Minister (PM) Giuseppe Conte – a lawyer and academic completely extraneous to politics up to the year before – was forced to resign. In order to avoid early elections (and a prospective defeat against a newly united centre-right coalition) the M5S was finally able to embark on a second Conte government thanks to the 'unnatural' alliance with the former 'enemies' of the centre-left PD (Partito Democratico – Democratic Party) plus two smaller parties.

Yet, the PD and the M5S had divergent views on the main economic issues and the coalition was further weakened by the internal divisions and leadership crisis of the M5S. Furthermore, as the government counted on an unstable majority of only a dozen members of parliament (MPs) in the second chamber, it depended on the unconvinced support of the small centrist party IV (Italia

Viva – Italy Alive), founded by the former PM Matteo Renzi (Newell 2020a). Finally, many components of the executive did not have any previous governmental experience (Capano 2020), including the PM and the 41-year-old Minister of Health Roberto Speranza, who was the only government representative of the small left-wing party LEU (Liberi e Uguali – Free and Equals).

In such a context, the already limited political capacity of the Italian government in terms of decision making, policy formulation and implementation (Capano & Pritoni 2016) diminished further. Moreover, beyond political and social factors, many scholars (e.g. Perone 2021) have underlined that Italy also presented some problematic demographic, urban and environmental conditions (i.e. the oldest population in Europe, a high residential density and a high level of pollution, especially in the most industrialised areas in the north of the country). Consequently, it was easy to anticipate a 'perfect storm' scenario when the Covid-19 emergency exploded in Italy.

The evolution of the pandemic in Italy: the first phase

The first two cases of Covid-19 in Italy – two Chinese tourists – were confirmed and immediately hospitalised in Rome on 30 January 2020. In the following weeks, while the virus was spreading in other Asian countries and a few cases of contagion were confirmed in other European Union (EU) member states, both experts and Italian authorities reassured the public that the situation was under control. The dynamic changed on 21 February, when 38-year-old 'Patient No. 1' was finally tested and confirmed in Codogno, Lombardy. Notably, the decision to test the patient for Covid was taken against the protocol in force at the time, which did not allow patients who apparently had no contact with the Chinese cluster to be swabbed. Subsequently, extensive screenings and checks were performed on anybody who had possibly been in contact with or near the infected subject. Within two days, the registered number of infected people in Lombardy exceeded 200 and the government established isolation and lockdown protocols for the first 'red zones'. However, these were insufficient to contain the exponential spread of the virus, especially in some Regions of the country such as Lombardy, Veneto, Piedmont and Emilia-Romagna.

On 9 March – when the government announced the national lockdown – cases numbered about 10,000 and deaths touched 500, with more than half of the cases recorded in Lombardy. As shown by Figure 1, by the end of March the exponential increase in cases and deaths had rapidly made Italy the most affected country in the world, with more than 10,000 victims, while in China they had officially stopped at about 3,300.

On 31 March, after more than three weeks of lockdown, the government announced that the pandemic had reached its peak in the country. In the following days, the curves of both cases and deaths showed a slow but continuous decrease, somewhat relieving the pressure on national hospitals and

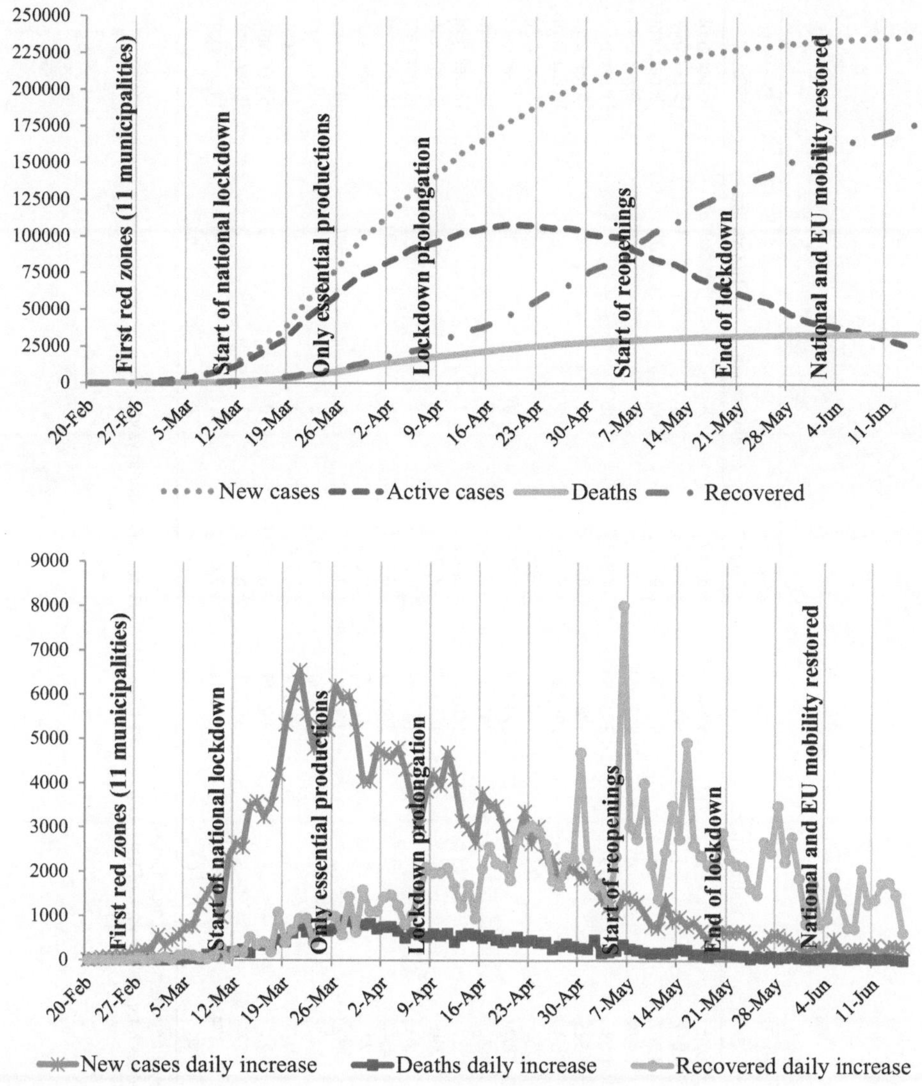

Figure 1. The evolution of the pandemic in Italy (20 February-15 June).
Source: authors' own elaboration from official ministerial data (http://www.protezionecivile.gov.it/)

intensive care units in particular.[1] Meanwhile, a number of public prosecutor's offices across the country (but mostly in Lombardy) started investigations into the inefficiencies and violations of protection measures against Covid-19 in various retirement homes, where the virus killed thousands of people (ISS 2020).

At the beginning of May, the number of deaths had passed the significant threshold of 30,000, with almost 220,000 people infected. Yet, the daily increase in active cases had become negative since mid-April, as the (daily) number of those who recovered exceeded new contagions. At the end of the period considered (15 June 2020), intensive care units had almost emptied, while active cases were below 26,000 and in continuous decline. The daily increase in cases

Table 1. Covid-19 distribution by region on 15 June 2020.

REGION	Total cases	Cases/ Pop*	Total deaths	Deaths/ Pop*	Total test	Test/ Pop*	Intensive care	Hospitalised	Deaths/ Cases
Lombardy	91,917	914	16,457	164	899,278	8,939	94	2,018	18 per cent
Piedmont	31,061	707	4,012	91	369,294	8,407	28	517	13 per cent
Emilia Romagna	28,084	630	4,207	94	410,984	9,216	13	188	15 per cent
Veneto	19,220	392	1,978	40	817,064	16,649	1	38	10 per cent
Tuscany	10,188	272	1,088	29	293,683	7,847	16	31	11 per cent
Liguria	9,887	632	1,525	97	127,913	8,172	2	87	15 per cent
Lazio	7,958	135	811	14	299,590	5,079	37	304	10 per cent
Trentino A.A.	7,060	664	756	71	180,651	16,997	1	13	11 per cent
Marche	6,762	440	997	65	121,620	7,907	0	18	15 per cent
Campania	4,837	83	430	7	241,380	4,134	2	58	9 per cent
Apulia	4,516	111	534	13	148,627	3,657	2	56	12 per cent
Sicily	3,458	68	280	6	180,327	3,566	4	30	8 per cent
Friuli V.G.	3,296	271	343	28	161.945	13,297	1	15	10 per cent
Abruzzo	3,279	248	456	34	91,700	6,935	3	71	14 per cent
Umbria	1,436	162	77	9	82,235	9,251	1	9	5 per cent
Sardegna	1,363	82	132	8	69,134	4,182	0	12	10 per cent
Valle d'Aosta	1,191	939	144	113	16,650	13,122	0	7	12 per cent
Calabria	1,162	59	97	5	82,392	4,193	1	17	8 per cent
Molise	439	141	23	7	19,125	6,160	0	0	5 per cent
Basilicata	401	70	27	5	35,233	6,177	1	0	7 per cent
Total Italy	237,515	392	34,374	57	4,648,825	7,666	207	3,489	14 per cent
Italy vs. others**	7	29	4	6	7	27	25	n.a.	3

Source: http://www.protezionecivile.gov.it/ and https://www.worldometers.info/coronavirus/.

Notes: *Cases/deaths/tests per 100,000 inhabitants **The number refers to the rank of Italy with respect to all the other countries in the world.

was zero or lower than ten in most regions but Lombardy, which clearly remained 'the sick man of Italy' for the entire first phase of Covid-19, as shown by Table 1.

The policy response

The government's management of the crisis: from risk normalisation to incrementalism

Just like most other Western countries, the dynamics of the reaction to the Covid-19 crisis in Italy began (in January 2020) with a substantial underestimation of events in China, resulting in what has been called 'the normalisation of the risk', i.e. a cognitive attitude minimising the perils of the pandemic on the presumption that such events could not happen in Italy (Capano 2020).

On 30 January the Minister of Health Speranza reported to the Italian Parliament about Covid-19, explaining that the General Assistant Director of the WHO (World Health Organization) recognised Italy as 'the most attentive and equipped' among Western countries (Ministero della Salute 2020, p. 5). On the same day, the first two cases in Italy were confirmed. In response, the Italian government suspended all direct flights to and from China, introduced thermal scanners and temperature checks on international passengers and declared a 'state of emergency' with a duration of six months.[2] The same act empowered a specific governmental branch, the Department of Civil Protection, which in turn appointed the brand-new CTS (Comitato Tecnico Scientifico – Scientific and Technical Committee) to deal with the health emergency (see following section). Nevertheless, at first these were mostly symbolic and bureaucratic actions (not implying any specific policy or allocation of funding) to show the public that the government was seriously considering the problem, in compliance with the WHO's acknowledgement that the Covid-19 outbreak was a public emergency of international concern. However, even though the new prevention protocols and the secret Health Ministry plans for the 'worst-case scenario' had been arranged in the previous days (Guerzoni 2020), the quick spread of the virus in northern Italy during the last days of February demonstrated that it had started circulating much earlier and that local and national authorities, hospitals and doctors had been taken by surprise.

Accordingly, what came next was a slow, incremental response to the fast-moving crisis, consisting of several small steps before a complete lockdown (Capano 2020). On 23 February, the PM issued a decree imposing the quarantine of more than 50,000 people from 11 municipalities (so-called red zones, namely geographical areas where the level of risk is highest), ten in Lombardy and one in Veneto. The Italian military and law enforcement agencies were instructed to secure and implement the lockdown, with penalties for violations ranging from a small fine to three months' imprisonment. Due to the initial scarcity of tests

Table 2. Policy response: list of national Italian government measures in relation to Covid-19 (31 January-15 June 2020).

Government acts	Main content
31/01/2020 Cdm deliberation	State of Health Emergency until 31 July 2020; stop direct flights from China
4/02/2020 Note of Pcm	Guidelines for health surveillance in airports, thermal scanners and temperature checks on international passengers
23/02/2020 Decree Law 6	First red zones (11 municipalities in northern Italy): isolation and lockdown, closing of non-essential services, no free movement
05/03/2020 Law 13	Conversion into law of Decree-Law 23/02/2020, with updates
25/03/2020 Dpcm	School closures and prohibition of public gatherings in six northern Regions
1/03/2020 Dpcm	Italian territory divided into three areas: red zone (11 municipalities); yellow zone (Lombardy, Veneto and Emilia-Romagna: cultural, social, sport events, religious services suspended; schools, theatres, clubs and cinemas closed; commercial activities reduced); rest of Italy (no particular limitations)
2/03/2020 Decree-Law	Economic support for the population of the 'red zone'
4/03/2020 Dpcm	Shutdown of all schools and universities nationwide for two weeks, sporting events behind closed doors until 3 April
8/03/2020 Dpcm	Lockdown of the whole of Lombardy + 14 other provinces in Veneto, Emilia-Romagna, Piedmont and Marche
9/03/2020 Dpcm	Lockdown for the entire country (go out only for reasons of necessity: work, medical and serious family reasons)
11/03/2020 Dpcm	Closing of all commercial and retail businesses except those providing essential services
17/03/2020 Decree-Law 18, *Cura Italia*	Allocation of 25 billion euros to strengthen the national health system against Covid-19 and support workers, families and industries during the lockdown
22/03/2020 Dpcm	All non-essential production and industries halted
25/03/2020 Decree-Law 19	Regional governments allowed to impose additional restrictive regulations in their own territory; higher fines for the violation of the restrictive measures; possibility of reducing or suspending public and private transport
1/04/2020 Dpcm	Lockdown extended until 13 April
8/04/2020 Decree-Law 22	New procedures to conclude the school year and the Matura in case schools are not able to restart their activities by 18 May
8/04/2020 Decree-Law 23, *Decreto liquidità*	New economic stimulus plan intended to unlock €400 billion of state-guaranteed loans to companies + interventions concerning health and labour and prorogation for administrative and processual deadlines
10/04/2020 Dpcm	Prolongation of the lockdown until 3 May, 'symbolic' reopening of bookstores and baby clothing shops; appointment of Colao's 'task force' in charge to provide advisory activity to the government with regard to the progressive re-opening of production sectors
24/04/2020 Law 27	Conversion into law of Decree-Law 17/03/2020*Cura Italia*, with modifications
26/04/2020 Dpcm	From 4 May people allowed to move within the regional borders to visit close kin; moving within or outside the Region is allowed for work or medical reasons, as well as for return to the place of residence; reopening of public parks; manufacturing, construction, estate agencies and wholesale trade allowed to restart their activities
30/04/2020 Decree-Law 28	National platform to trace infected people by *Immuni* app for mobile phones (downloaded on volutary basis)
10/05/2020 Decree-Law 29	Replacement of provisional prison with home detention agreement because of Covid-19 emergency
10/05/2020 Decree-Law 30	Start of sierological tests for specific sample of people; new provisions concerning privacy and use of personal heath data for Covid-19 monitoring and statistical studies
12/05/2020 Dpcm	Composition of the expert task force changed with integration of five women
16/05/2020 Decree-Law 33	Freedom of movement within regional borders and reopening of all activities from 18 May (leaving to regions the discretion to decide specific closures); inter-regional mobility and international mobility allowed from 3 June; cinemas, concerts and theatre events allowed from 15 June (provided that social distancing can be maintained)
17/05/2020 Dpcm	Implementing provisions for Decree-Law 33
18/05/2020 Dpcm	Modifications to Dpcm 17/05 with regard to Covid-19 management in penal institutions

(*Continued*)

Table 2. (Continued).

Government acts	Main content
19/05/2020 Decree-Law 19 *Decreto Rilancio* (former April-Decree)	55 billion euros to support enterprises, families and workers: funds for the heath system, Civil Protection, renewal of social safety nets + emergency income (*reddito d'emergenza*) for families most in need, funds to stabilise school teachers and 1.4 billion for universities, bonus for holidays in Italy, 6 months regularisation for migrant workers
22/05/2020 Law 35	Conversion into law of Decree-Law 19, 25/03/2020, with modifications
05/06/2020 Law 40	Conversion into law of Decree-Law 23, 8/04/2020, with modifications
06/06/2020 Law 41	Conversion into law of Decree-Law 22, 8/04/2020, with modifications
11/06/2020 Dpcm	Implementing provisions for Decree-Law 19: sporting events and competitions allowed behind closed doors; reopenings of cinemas, theatres, concert halls, community and fitness centres

Source: authors' own elaboration from https://www.governo.it/it/coronavirus-normativa.

Notes: (1) Dcpm = Decreto della Presidenca del Consiglio dei Ministri, namely administrative acts that do not require conversion into law by Parliament, differently from Decree-Laws; Cdm = Consiglio dei Ministri (Council of Ministers); Pcm = Presidenza del Consiglio dei Ministri (Prime Minister's Office). (2) The table only reports legislative acts and emergency acts issued by the Prime Minister (Dpcm). Actually the government as a whole (including the various Ministries and the government agencies) produced almost 300 acts between January and mid-June, with the Health Ministry and Civil Protection accounting for half of the cases (Capano 2020). Moreover, in June 2020 80 per cent (165) of the implementing acts concerning anti-Covid measures (especially economic measures such as *Cura Italia* and *Decreto Rilancio*) still had to be adopted (Openpolis 2020a, 2020b).

available, the CTS resolved that swabs could be performed only on symptomatic patients, contrary to the practice in other countries and the opinion of other national experts. In addition, a quarantine of two weeks was established for those who had been in close contact with an infected person and for people coming back from China and the new Italian red zones. Limitations on commercial activities and the closure of schools as well as cultural, sporting, religious and social activities (but not lockdown or mobility limitations) were also established for so-called yellow zones (those with a lower level of risk), including the rest of Lombardy, Veneto and Emilia-Romagna. At the beginning of March, the Italian government imposed a shutdown of all schools and higher education institutions nationwide for two weeks, also deciding that all sporting events in the country would be played behind closed doors (see Table 2).

Yet, the curve was rising so quickly that the risk that medical facilities would be overwhelmed became real and required a complete reframing of the emergency, so as to force the government to opt for a quicker and stronger reaction (Capano 2020). On 8 March the PM announced lockdowns throughout Lombardy plus 14 other provinces in Veneto, Emilia-Romagna, Piedmont and Marche. This was the most aggressive response taken in any country beyond China until that moment, involving more than 16 million people from one of the wealthiest areas of Europe. A few days later, the lockdown was extended across the entire country.

On 11 March, when the WHO officially declared Covid-19 a pandemic, Conte announced a further tightening of the lockdown, with the closing of all commercial and retail businesses except those providing essential services. On 17 March the government allocated 25 billion euros to strengthen the national health system against Covid-19 and to support workers, families and industries during the lockdown. Meanwhile, police controls and sanctions to prevent people from leaving their homes for unnecessary reasons were intensified. Nevertheless, interpretations concerning free movement limits were not univocal. Accordingly, on 20 March further regulations banned open-air sports and individual running, except in close proximity to one's residence, and all parks, playgrounds and public green spaces were closed. Two days later, following pressure from trade unions, medical professionals and regional and local administrators, the government also halted all non-essential production and industries, notwithstanding the opposition of Confidustria (General Confederation of Italian Industry), the main pressure group supporting entrepreneurs' interests.

Thus, a month passed from the discovery of the first clusters to the imposition of the complete lockdown (25 March), an incremental response that is both an indicator of the government's low political capacity and also a sign of a certain subjection to the country's major economic interests, which were clearly lined up against the prospect of a complete lockdown and consequent block on production for most Italian enterprises (Capano 2020). However, exceptions also remained, as several industries (including many of those in Lombardy) could waive this regulation by self-certificating their 'essentiality' to keep working.

Many measures (such as the purchase of appropriate protective equipment for health workers) faced implementation problems. The confusion caused by the continuous issuing of new, sometimes repetitive, and sometimes conflicting directives during the dramatic weeks of March 2020 was exemplified by the fact that the government's self-certification form, which each citizen had to bring with them whenever they went outside, was changed four times in under twenty days.

Nevertheless, the passing of time also allowed the government to redress the balance in its policies towards a more proactive and centralised approach. Facing the health emergency remained the primary concern even after the peak was overcome at the end of March, as the hospitals in northern Italy were still dramatically overwhelmed. Accordingly, the lockdown was extended, initially until 13 April and then to 3 May. The forthcoming economic emergency also started to be considered more attentively. On 6 April the government announced a new and unprecedented economic stimulus plan. However, this so-called April decree only saw the light in mid-May, still needing 92 additional ministerial regulations to be fully implemented, due to the complexity of Italian law-making, the long negotiations between government partners and difficulties in finding economic coverage. Similarly, many payments and unemployment benefits provided by the economic measures already adopted were subject to considerable delays because of political and bureaucratic restrictions. The collapse of the website of the National Social Security Institute (INPS) on 2 April, the first day it opened applications for individual subsidies, is telling in this regard.

At the same time, the Italian government started long and difficult negotiations with the EU institutions, calling for extraordinary recovery measures, and these efforts finally brought some results. The initial offer was a controversial agreement for a condition-free loan of 37 billion euros through the European Stability Mechanism, to support the health system. Of the governing parties, PD and IV were in favour of it, but the main government party M5S was against,[3] and finally the loan was not requested. Instead, the final EU agreement on the Recovery Fund was presented as a huge success, since Italy obtained more than 170 billion euros, half in the form of loans and half as non-repayable grants.

On 26 April, Conte announced the long-awaited new decree on reopening, intended to start uniformly across the entire national territory on 4 May. Expectations for the end of the lockdown were initially disappointed: people were allowed to move within regional borders just to visit close relatives; only manufacturing, construction, estate agencies and wholesale trade were allowed to restart their activities. However, following a substantial decrease in cases and deaths, the definitive end of the national lockdown was only postponed for two weeks. On 18 May freedom of movement within regional borders was finally restored and all commercial activities could reopen across the entire country. Inter-regional and international mobility was also restored from 3 June, although many foreign countries maintained restrictions on Italian travellers. Further reopening occurred in the following weeks, such as cinemas, theatres and sporting events behind closed doors. Nonetheless, contrary to many other European countries, the reopening did not include nurseries, schools and universities.

The role of experts: uncertain science and inconsistent communication

Although Italian public opinion is generally supportive of science (Bucchi & Saracino 2020), evidence-based policymaking has always been quite negligible (Dente 1995; Capano 2020, 329). In the so called First Republic (1948–1992) different experts and policy advisers were traditionally connected to the mass political parties as the *domini* of the Italian political system (Lippi 2012, pp. 102–103). After the breakdown of the old party system in 1992, the policy advice system became increasingly fragmented and politicised (Di Mascio & Natalini 2016). More recently, the dynamics regarding experts, politicians and public opinion over health issues have proven particularly controversial. Well before the actual crisis, doctors and virologists advocating compulsory vaccination were strongly resisted by a widespread 'no vax' movement and by several individual policymakers in the former M5S-Lega government, thereby pitting populist 'common sense' against the complex scientific arguments of experts (Casula & Toth 2018). Suddenly, the spread of Covid-19 brought scientific expertise into the spotlight and, most importantly, provided an opportunity for the appointment of different experts to various task forces and scientific committees in various policy domains (Galanti & Saracino 2021). Meanwhile, at the media level, the Italian scientific community of virologists, epidemiologists and infectivologists started to be constantly consulted on information broadcasts from February, often offering contradictory warnings about the seriousness of the new virus (Ruiu 2020, p. 1011).

At the institutional level, this multiplication of experts occurred rapidly but incrementally, with different timings and strategies across central and regional governments. At the central level, even before the spread of the contagion, the brand new CTS – mainly composed of ministerial personnel from different departments (e.g. Health, Defence, and Infrastructure) – was intended to provide strategic guidance and non-binding advice with regard to anti-Covid measures. At the local level, some regions started to create their own CTS, with very different strategies in terms of the number of external health experts appointed. For example, Lombardy nominated an impressive number of 150 experts and stakeholders, while Veneto appointed a more limited number of experts who anticipated a strategy for the mass testing of the entire population (including asymptomatic subjects) as early as February (Macciò 2020), thus setting a very different model for testing from that recommended by the experts at the national level.

At the national level, the appointment of advisors rapidly increased, but their impact on the different policy domains (except for health) remained incidental (Galanti & Saracino 2021). On 10 April, the PM appointed a new task force to plan operations after the lockdown: the Economic and Social Experts Committee (ESC), also called the 'Colao Commission' after the name of its chairman, a former Vodafone chief executive officer. On 18 April, the composition of the CTS was complemented by the integration of a higher number of experts in the medical sector and by the main stakeholders in the health system. In mid-May, further experts were added, mainly in response to accusations of gender bias in the government's appointments of experts. The same kind of gender-sensitive integration occurred in the ESC, which reached a final membership of 21, mostly academics, alongside a few managers and professionals. The ESC ultimately delivered its proposals for economic and social recovery in early June, but they received a lukewarm reaction from government parties and scarce attention from the media.

As for containment policies in health, neither governmental nor external experts publicly sought drastic containment measures until the beginning of March, perhaps contributing to the normalisation of the risk in the eyes of the public and national and regional authorities. Only when the national lockdown was finally implemented did the entire Italian scientific community align on the need to stay at home and maintain social distancing. Nevertheless, in preparation for the first re-openings (expected to start from May 2020), contradictory views and different diagnostics emerged, along with the mediatisation of expertise and increased numbers of experts and task forces at the various territorial levels.[4]

All things considered, the health advisers proved quite influential in driving the decisions of the central government in the acute phase of the crisis, but were less considered or even contradicted thereafter. At first, the national CTS and the ISS (Istituto Superiore di Sanità – National Institute of Health) followed the WHO guidelines. These were ambiguous about the importance of masks in preventing transmission, delayed the declaration of the pandemic until 11 March, and waited until mid-April to underline the importance of the so-called 3Ts (test, trace and treat), thus contributing to the tendency in Italy to normalise the risk and adopt an incremental approach (Capano 2020). However, thereafter the CTS became the most prudent adviser in the crisis, advocating a complete lockdown and fiercely opposing the non-gradual strategy for reopening demanded by important interest groups (Confindustria) and members of the governmental coalition (Renzi, see below).

At the same time, the debate among health experts inside and outside government remained lively during the entire first phase (and later), especially regarding the use of tests, which were actually administered by the regions at the local level. In fact, the contradictions emerging in the debate puzzled public opinion (Bucchi & Saracino 2020). Simultaneously, the opacity of the procedures and the initial inaccessibility of the documents of the various task forces weakened the transparency of the process, while negatively affecting accountability (Openpolis 2020).

Though all the governments facing the pandemic called upon experts before taking dramatic decisions, the chaotic and over-abundant use of experts observed in the Italian case might also be connected to the lack of experience of most of the ministers in the second Conte government. In this regard, it is significant that, with the notable exception of the CTS, none of the other task forces proved to be influential in the first phase of the crisis (Galanti & Saracino 2021). All in all, this over-abundant use of experts surely offered several opportunities for policymakers to either shift the blame onto experts in cases of unpopular decisions, or to claim credit in cases of successful initiatives.

The impact of the state structure: regionalism vs. centralisation

The Italian Constitution defines the country as a 'multi-level polity' (Longo & Mobilio 2016, p.2) with different intermediate bodies between the state and the local level – including municipalities, metropolitan cities, provinces, and the regions. Legislative power is shared between the central state and the regions, which have exclusive legislative jurisdiction over some policy issues and concurrent jurisdiction over others, such as health and labour. In practice, when a health issue is on the government agenda, some types of decisions must be negotiated among the state and the regions, while others can be taken autonomously by the local governments. Nonetheless, the legislative power of the 21 regions (five of which have special statutes) is subject to certain constitutional limitations, the most important of which is that regional acts may not conflict with national interests (Bolgherini 2014, p. 198). The State-Regions Conference and its articulations – such as the Conference of the Regions – are the institutional venues where most of these negotiations take place. This contributes to a weakly cooperative regionalism that negatively affected the management of the crisis and policy implementation (Baldi & Profeti 2020).

As far as crisis management is concerned, the declaration of the state of emergency empowered the central government and brought about the creation of the crisis unit of the Department of Civil Protection and several crisis units coordinated by regional presidents, with very different timings and compliance in terms of organisation (i.e. small and bureaucratic units versus large and representative units). Most importantly, the concurrent jurisdiction over health between the state and the regions made the decision-making process slower (owing to the need to negotiate the content of the decisions) and ultimately uncertain, given that each region could adopt more restrictive regulations than those approved by the national government. This produced an incredible number of (sometimes contradictory) norms at the national and local levels over crucial issues such as the use of masks, restrictions on movement and the administration of tests. Furthermore, it complicated the implementation of measures like the distribution of medical equipment and unemployment benefits.

Looking at results, the models of healthcare in the regions (Mapelli 2012) helped differentiate outcomes in terms of capacity to contain the spread of the contagion. Different observers have attributed the successful strategy of the Veneto region in stopping the spread of the virus during the first phase both to the early decision to mass test the population already in early February 2020 and to the organisation of the regional healthcare system around a focus on territorial medicine and community care. By contrast, the centralised organisation of healthcare services in Lombardy – a renowned model of excellence centred on the importance of hospitals and residential care units – turned out to be a terrible fuse for the explosion of the contagion, as patients with symptoms filled the hospital emergency rooms (Pisano, Sadun & Zanini 2020).

Second, during the first phase of the Covid crisis, the functioning of conventional institutional venues for coordination between the state and the regions, such as the State-Regions Conference, was uneven and ultimately ineffective (Baldi & Profeti 2020). In particular, frictions between the central government and the regions (especially between the PM and the Lega President of the Lombardy Region) emerged several times during official press conferences from the very start of the crisis, with mutual accusations about the responsibility for decisions that may have affected the spread of the contagion. A paradigmatic case was the failed establishment, at the beginning of March 2020, of red zone status in one of the most affected areas in the country, namely the cities of Alzano and Nembro in the province of Bergamo, Lombardy.

Weeks later, the media reported mutual recriminations between the national government and the Lombardy leadership about who had the responsibility to declare the red zone. The case was finally put under the spotlight of the courts in June 2020 after numerous accusations by relatives of Covid-19 victims (Sarzanini 2020).

In this regard, the crisis inevitably triggered some political clashes between the national government and those regions administered by the centre-right. For instance, there was a tug of war between the Minister for Regional Affairs, Francesco Boccia (PD) and the centre-right President of the Calabria Region, Jole Santelli, concerning a regional ordinance that allowed bar and restaurant activities to recommence earlier than the dates established by national decrees. Ultimately, the minister successfully asked for the intervention of the Regional Administrative Courts (TAR) to stop Santelli's ordinance, even if a few days later a new government decree allowed for the general reopening of all commercial activities in Italy.

At the same time, dialogue between the central government and the regions in the State-Regions Conference seemed listless while the internal debate at the Conference of the Regions was lively. In particular, the virtual meetings of the representatives of all the regions were frequent, often producing a cohesive position against the government's decisions regardless of each region's political allegiance, such as in the case of the recruitment of doctors, or in the definition of the rules for re-openings concerning industries and commercial activities. In this regard, another episode is particularly telling: on 16 May 2020, the PM anticipated the content of an impending regulation concerning the reopening of several activities, which had not been discussed with the regions themselves. After a night of tough negotiation with the regions, the regulations were amended, and the institutional crisis was resolved (Custodero 2020a). Not by chance, the President of the Republic invoked national unity and the need for 'fair institutional collaboration' between the state and the regions in several public discourses thereafter.

The political response

Institutional dynamics: same old polarisation?

The Italian political system is known for being highly polarised and fragmented (Sartori 1982; Cotta & Verzichelli 2008). The pivotal positioning of the M5S – which refused to be framed within the left-right spectrum and was indeed able to ally with the right wing Lega first and the centre-left PD thereafter – implied that the traditional ideological cleavage has more recently been accompanied by a sort of populist versus anti-populist cleavage able to drive sudden and unpredictable changes in coalition dynamics, which nevertheless has not reduced the level of confrontation between political actors (Newell 2020a). On the eve of the Covid-19 crisis, the relationship between government and opposition forces was accordingly extremely adversarial, but tensions were also present within the governing parties.

At the end of January, when Covid-19 was still considered a 'Chinese problem', it simply became one of dozens of contentious issues for Italian political forces. Lega leader Salvini rode the issue to support his general demand for border defence, stating that the contagion could arrive in Italy through migrant boats coming from Africa. After the two Chinese tourists tested positive, he sought to 'close any access by air, land and sea' (Custodero 2020b). On the other side of the political spectrum, many voices were raised against Salvini for political manipulation of the Covid-19 crisis and later for fuelling episodes of intolerance towards Asian tourists and Chinese residents. In fact, a number of initiatives were organised in order to convince the population not to fear the Chinese communities living in the country: the centre-left Mayor of Milan, Giuseppe Sala, organised a traditional breakfast with citizens in the local Chinatown (Dazzi 2020), while the President of the Republic visited a school in a multi-ethnic district in Rome attended by a large number of Chinese students (Lupia 2020).

Nevertheless, when the first clusters were discovered in Lombardy and Veneto, the opposition voted with the government for the establishment of the first red zones (see Table 3). Furthermore, different political leaders united in opposing the image of Italy as an 'infected country': on 27 February the PD party chair, Nicola Zingaretti, joined a crowded aperitif with sympathisers in the centre of Milan to support the campaign promoted by Mayor Sala – *'Milano non si ferma'* ('Milan Doesn't Stop'). The same day, Salvini invited the government to reopen all commercial and leisure businesses. A few days later, the other right-wing leader Giorgia Meloni (FdI, Fratelli d'Italia – Brothers of Italy) released a reassuring promotional video to invite foreign tourists not to give up

Table 3. Parliamentary votes on anti-Covid-19 measures (lower chamber).

Acts	In Favour	Against
23/02/2020 Decree Law 6 *Red zones*	462: All groups	2: Misto
05/03/2020 Law 13 *Red zones*	462: All groups	2: Misto
17/03/2020 Decree-Law 18, *Cura Italia*	229: LeU, M5S, PD, IV, Misto (6)	123: FdI, FI, Lega, Misto (7)
25/03/2020 Decree-Law 19, *reg. restrictions*	241: LeU, M5S, PD, IV, Misto (5)	166: FdI, FI, Lega, Misto (2)
24/04/2020 Law 27*Cura Italia*	229: LeU, M5S, PD, IV, Misto (6)	123: FdI, FI, Lega, Misto (7)
22/05/2020 Law 35 *conversion of DL 19*	241: LeU, M5S, PD, IV, Misto (5)	166: FdI, FI, Lega, Misto (2)
05/06/2020 Law 40 *Decreto liquidità*	269: LeU, M5S, PD, IV, Misto (?)	193: FdI, FI, Lega, Misto (?)
06/06/2020 Law 41 *schools and Matura*	245: LeU, M5S, PD (63), IV, Misto (4)	122: FdI, FI, Lega, PD (1)

Source: https://www.camera.it/.

Notes: (1) The number in parenthesis indicates the votes in favour or against for each parliamentary group. If there are no numbers in parenthesis, it means the group has voted unanimously. (2) Key to political parties: LeU (Liberi e Uguali - Free and Equals); M5S (Movimento Cinque Stelle - Five Star Movement); PD (Partito Democratico - Democratic Party); IV (Italia Viva - Italy Alive); FdI (Fratelli d'Italia - Brothers of Italy); FI (Forza Italia - Go Italy), Lega (League); Misto (group of non-aligned MPs). (3) Most of the acts issued during the crisis are not reported in this table because they were in the form of administrative acts (Dpcm).

their Italian vacations, while the M5S Foreign Minister, Luigi Di Maio, promoted a campaign to defend products 'Made in Italy'. Similarly, all political forces criticised limitations on Italian people travelling abroad.

This normalisation of the risk by political forces was forced to change in the following days. On 7 March, Zingaretti announced that he had tested positive for Covid-19, followed by the President of Piedmont, Alberto Cirio (Lega), the day after. When the country was put under lockdown, the opposition publicly supported the decision in the name of 'national unity' (Segatti 2020). Contrary to what he had said a few days earlier, Salvini declared: 'For weeks I've been saying that everything has to be closed, let's close before it's too late ... the entirety of Europe has to be closed and turned into a red zone in order to avoid trade wars' (Mari 2020).

In the following weeks, all political forces hurried to support the 'Stay at Home' campaign and the 'heroic' work of medical staff all around the country. Nevertheless, the opposition was not really involved in the decision-making process and new political clashes emerged over the economic measures to counter the crisis, as much as the centre-right unanimously voted against the March economic decrees. Meloni even accused the government of using 'methods of communication typical of a totalitarian regime' (Newell 2020b, p. 110) because of Conte's massive media presence, while the entire opposition denounced as defeatist the government approach of asking for EU support. In fact, the initially low level of solidarity seen at the European level provided fertile ground for eurosceptic leaders such as Salvini and Meloni and further increased Italian citizens' dissatisfaction with the EU (Circap & SWG 2020; Newell 2020b). The negotiations with EU institutions also created skirmishes among the government parties, with the M5S heavily lined up against the possible recourse to the ESM, contrary to PD and IV.

In April 2020, new political conflicts exploded in view of the re-opening. Salvini was among the first to ask for the end of the lockdown. First of all, he proposed reopening the churches for Easter, but this was rejected by both his centre-right allies and Vatican institutions (Mari 2020). Subsequently, he supported the requests of the Lega presidents of the northern regions and major economic interests to return to work, but obtained more support from the IV leader Renzi than from his allies in the centre-right camp, Silvio Berlusconi (leader of Forza Italia) and Meloni. Finally, after Conte's announcement of 26 April, Salvini threatened protests in the streets against the overly slow implementation of reopening, stimulating criticism from the rest of the centre-right as well. Two days later, Meloni's party organised a flash mob against the government in front of the Palazzo Chigi in Rome without involving their allies (Il Messaggero 2020). The following day, 70 Lega MPs symbolically occupied the two parliamentary chambers, declaring that they would remain locked in Parliament until the government guaranteed the reopening of all productive sectors. However, both Berlusconi and Meloni distanced themselves from the initiative (La Stampa 2020) and just two days later Salvini decided to stop the occupation. Nonetheless, apart from these different strategic and communicational approaches, the centre-right coalition remained cohesive in opposing the new government's acts within and outside the Parliament. The opposition's unity was officially sealed by a joint demonstration against the government on 2 June and its refusal to participate in the States General, a consultation with stakeholders organised by the PM in mid-June 2020 to discuss a post-Covid recovery plan (see Table 3).

On the government side too, there were different points of views concerning reopening. Renzi accused Conte of having an interest in prolonging the emergency situation in order to secure his political survival and maintain full authority. The IV also threatened to support the opposition's motion of no confidence against the M5S Minister of Justice, who was attacked by the opposition for enabling the house arrests of Mafia bosses because of the Covid-19 emergency in jails. Nevertheless, despite various caveats, the IV unanimously voted in favour of all the government's decrees concerning anti-Covid measures. In fact, rumours suggested that Renzi intended to prompt Conte's dismissal in favour of a national unity government, possibly led by the former President of the European Central Bank, Mario Draghi. This solution was supported by large industrial groups and mainstream newspapers (Ajello 2020), but Renzi did not find enough political backing to force a government crisis until February 2021.

That said, it is clear that the crisis did not encourage collaboration between political actors (apart from in the first weeks before and after the lockdown), but considering the pre-existing high level of conflict, we can probably maintain that it did not exacerbate polarisation either (Segatti 2020). Furthermore, the 'schizophrenic' communication of the various Italian political leaders during the first phase of the emergency may be explained by the constant quest for political visibility and the parties' incapacity to develop coherent long-term strategies (Emanuele & Chiaramonte 2020). Although personalisation of politics is not a new phenomenon in Italy (Garzia 2017), the Covid-19 crisis further encouraged this trend. In fact, during the first phase, political parties largely disappeared in terms of the visibility of their leaders, particularly compared to the constant media presence of the PM Conte who, not by chance, was not affiliated to any party. In this regard, De Luca (2020) recognised that Conte's 'half-populist leadership' was accompanied by a 'careful and thoughtful use of the media', as each new government act was introduced by a prime ministerial press conference and/or live coverage on social media, enabling him to communicate an image of reliability, political competence, empathy, reassurance and personal sharing, thereby helping him to increase his popularity (Vassallo 2020). This is exemplified further in the following section.

Societal dynamics: an unexpected 'rally around the flag'

In situations of collective danger for a country (e.g. wars, natural disasters) it is normal to expect public opinion to rediscover some forms of patriotism and possibly gather around the government (Baker & Oneal 2001; Healy & Malhotra 2009). Despite the clichés about Italian society being scarcely cohesive, intolerant of regulation and inclined to accuse public authorities when things go wrong, the pandemic progressively triggered a generalised acceptance of anti-Covid measures and this kind of 'rally around the flag' dynamic (Segatti 2020).

In February, opinion polls suggested that trust in the government and in PM Conte was below 40 per cent. Even so, this was the highest approval rating among the various political leaders of the moment and also greater than the average level of trust in the previous governments led by Renzi, Letta and Gentiloni (Circap & SWG 2020). Until the beginning of March – in line with the above-mentioned normalisation of the risk by politicians and experts – the Italian media and the majority of citizens underestimated the problem, while people emptying the supermarkets or stocking up on masks and hand sanitisers were ridiculed on social media and satirical shows. In the following weeks, public awareness of the magnitude of the emergency progressively increased, thanks also to the U-turn on the issue by the Italian scientific community and the media. In fact, the choice to extend the lockdown to the entire country was endorsed by almost 90 per cent of the population, while 80 per cent even agreed that stricter regulations should be applied if the situation did not improve (Istituto Ixè 2020; Termometro politico 2020).[5]

This situation translated into a patriotic and community reaction to the emergency: the images of people singing from their balconies, waving Italian flags and clapping their hands for the 'heroes' working in hospitals circulated around the world. Celebrities from all fields initiated a massive media campaign to encourage citizens to stay at home, while 'transgressors' became the intended victims and scapegoats of social media and TV shows. The motto '*andrà tutto bene*' ('Everything will be fine') was obsessively repeated on the media, while the 'Italian model' of reaction to Covid-19 was portrayed as an example to be followed abroad, where – in the view of Italian public opinion – governments were underestimating or even hiding the problem.[6] In fact, the choice of both the government and the national media was to be as transparent as possible in data communication and crisis 'storytelling', in order to raise citizens' awareness about the importance of respecting the lockdown and maintaining social distancing.[7] In this respect and in contrast to other countries, 'fake news' did not have such a strong impact during the first phase of the crisis. Furthermore, in this first phase, a large part of public opinion embraced the call by trade unions and medical professionals for a total lockdown, against the opposition of the industrial sector.

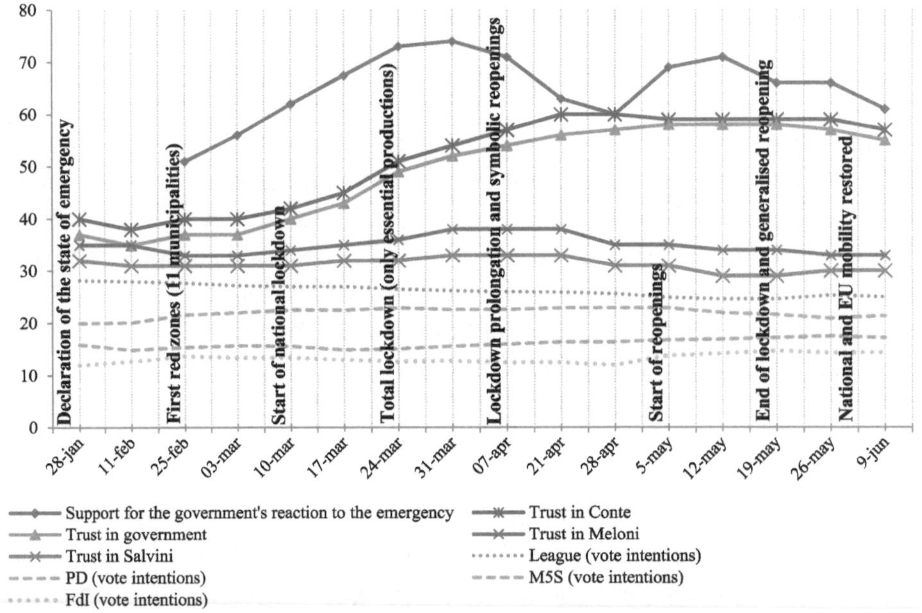

Figure 2. Trust in government and in political leaders during the first phase of the Covid-19 pandemic in Italy and voting intentions for the four main parties (%).

Source: authors' own elaboration from polls by Istituto Ixè S.r.l for Cartabianca (Rai3) http://www.sondaggipoliticoelettorali.it/

By the end of March 2020, support for the government and the PM had increased about 15 percentage points compared to the pre-crisis period and about 70 per cent of people declared that they appreciated the government's management of the emergency (Newell 2020b). Polls also reported a huge level of support (between 90 and 77 per cent) for containment measures such as preventing movement from one municipality to another, the obligation to stay at home, the closing of non-essential productive and commercial activities and the use of any means (apps, drones, army) to control transgressors and track individual movements (Emg 2020a). Similarly, more than 80 per cent of respondents supported the government's decision to extend the lockdown beyond 3 April (Emg 2020a) and the same percentage endorsed the subsequent prorogation until 3 May (Demopolis 2020a, 17/04). Interestingly, Segatti (2020) has noticed that the increase in the government's popularity started long before citizens had the chance to evaluate the efficiency of the anti-Covid measures undertaken, showing a latent disposition to obey the authorities and to renounce their own personal liberties in exchange for security, just as in cases of international crises.

In turn, negative feelings about the adversarial behaviour of the opposition during the emergency increased, reflected in the dwindling popularity of the centre-right leader Salvini (Atlante Politico 2020), also due to his contradictory messages and lower media exposure (Vassallo 2020). At the same time, neither the M5S nor the PD seemed to gain much advantage from the growing popularity of the government (see Figure 2). This further confirms the importance of personalisation mentioned in the previous section. In fact, regardless of party/coalitional affiliation, also those regional presidents who were recognised as reacting effectively to the first phase of emergency – Luca Zaia (Veneto, Lega), Vincenzo De Luca (Campania, centre-left) and Nello Musumeci (Sicily, centre-right) – faced a huge leap in the polls compared to the pre-crisis period, while the Lega President of the most affected region (Lombardy), Attilio Fontana, experienced a decline of 16 percentage points (Demopolis 2020b).

Of course, the PM's popularity varied considerably according to political self-placement (Segatti 2020) and party preferences, with voters of the governing M5S and PD extremely satisfied while supporters of the opposition parties, Lega and FdI, were much more sceptical. Proportionally however, centre-right voters' trust in Conte during the crisis increased more than that of the government parties' supporters (Circap & SWG 2020). Similarly, variations emerged by geographical area: unsurprisingly, respondents from less affected regions were more supportive compared to people from more badly hit northern areas. Most importantly, the government's popularity has been associated with economic insecurity: the more a person considered his/her economic situation had worsened since the onset of the Covid crisis, the less he/she was likely to support the government (Segatti 2020).

In any event, with the amelioration of the health emergency, Italians started to request fewer restrictions. However, after 4 May, some surveys observed a growth in the percentage of respondents wanting to see the restrictions increased (Vezzoni et al. 2020). Although 80 per cent supported the general reopening of 18 May, more than 60 per cent feared a new increase in cases and the risk of a new lockdown, while a similar percentage did not agree with the return to complete freedom of movement among the regions and entry from abroad from 3 June and were not satisfied with the measures adopted by the national and regional governments to trace and isolate cases (Demopolis 2020c; Emg 2020b).

In any case, the end of lockdown in mid-May 2020 also implied a re-appropriation of participation spaces and a progressive recommencement of public protests by opposition forces and various sectors of civil society affected by the crisis: school workers, taxi drivers, precarious healthcare personnel and workers in the entertainment and cultural industries, as well as Covid-19 'negationists' from radical right and marginal populist movements. In this regard, with the (first) health emergency (provisionally) overcome and the dramatic effects of the economic crisis just beginning to be felt, discontent towards the Conte government and the management of the crisis progressively increased.

Conclusions: 'sick man' or bad luck?

The article sketched the evolution of the first phase of the Covid-19 crisis in Italy in order to assess the possible relationship between the health crisis and national political, institutional and societal dynamics. Was Italy a 'sick man' even before March 2020 or did it just happen to be the first Western country to be badly hit by the pandemic?

The findings confirm that the legacy of the economic crisis (which also implied many cuts to the health system), the pre-existing weaknesses affecting the institutional and administrative system, and the political volatility (together with some social and demographic characteristics) anticipated a 'perfect storm' scenario at the onset of the crisis. Furthermore, our analysis has confirmed a low-capacity response by the Italian government, as much as the incremental progression towards a complete lockdown occurred approximately one month after the discovery of the first clusters. Problems were also linked to the unprecedented but relatively uninfluential use of experts, the inefficient coordination between the different territorial levels of government and the usual Italian political polarisation.

Actually, the scarce preparedness and the initial normalisation of the risk were common to most Western governments worldwide and also ascribable to the contradictory indications of scientific experts and the WHO. Moreover, the strictness of the Italian anti-Covid measures during the first phase of the pandemic – which encountered an unexpected level of compliance by the Italian people – was praised and imitated by many other countries. In fact, the (first) lockdown seemed to have reached the desired outcome by the onset of summer 2020. The health system appeared better prepared for an eventual second wave, with the number of intensive care beds having significantly increased during the first emergency phase and expected to double by the end of the year thanks to new government funding (Capano 2020). The Conte government could also boast the commitment to unprecedented financial support from the EU. Nonetheless, what came next demonstrated that the 'storm' had not ended and Italy was still 'sick'.

What's next?

At the end of the period considered in this study (mid-June 2020), the epidemiological situation in Italy was apparently under control. As in many other countries around the world, after a summer with light limitations, the situation quickly got worse with the restarting of all working activities and the reopening of schools in September. A new differentiated system by regions was implemented in autumn 2020, dividing the country into red, orange, yellow and white zones according to the level of risk and re-evaluated weekly. A curfew from 10 p.m. to 5 a.m. was applied to the entire country (from November 2020 until mid-May 2021). All Italian regions experimented with new periodical lockdowns, which mostly affected restaurants, bars and commercial activities, while people were allowed to move around the country for work reasons. Still, the number of new cases and deaths remained incredibly high and hospitals were overwhelmed again in most of the regions, this time much more homogeneously than in the first phase. As expected, the 'rally around the flag' effect did not hold in the medium-long run. Intolerance towards closures and personal and collective episodes of disobedience to the rules multiplied, often encouraged by opposition political forces.

Furthermore, the Italian management of the mass vaccination campaign during the first months of 2021 showed many deficiencies, beyond the obvious responsibilities of EU institutions for the delays in the supply by big pharma. Various setbacks occurred to the regional platforms intended to organise the appointments, while many regions set different criteria to identify priority groups with respect to the state's guidelines, creating confusion and institutional conflicts. Meanwhile, scepticism increased about the M5S-PD government's capacity to face the health and economic crisis and implement the Italian Recovery Plan to get EU funds. Thus, although the PM Conte had personally maintained a (declining but still) quite high level of popularity, he was not able to survive the government crisis initiated by IV in February 2021. In the words of the former centre-left PM, Massimo D'Alema, 'the most unpopular man (Renzi) throw out the most popular one (Conte)' (Cappellini 2020), and this further exacerbated political conflicts and citizens' annoyance. Yet, the subsequent rapid formation of the new Draghi government – supported by all political forces but FdI and a few individual MPs from M5S and LeU – demonstrated that political and social opposition to the previous government had become widespread.

However, although Draghi was welcomed as a 'saviour of the homeland' by public opinion, the long-awaited 'change of pace' was neither immediate nor striking. In fact, the ministerial reshuffle was only partial (i.e. the Minister of Health Speranza kept his place, as did other former Ministers), showing the will not to dismantle most of the anti-Covid measures adopted by the Conte government. Actually, in order to suit the new centre-right coalition partners, Draghi immediately replaced the Special Commissioner for the emergency, and some changes occurred in the composition of the CTS. Still, vaccinations proceeded quite slowly at least up to April 2021, measures for immediate economic recovery continued to encounter implementation problems, and reopening was delayed notwithstanding the Lega's pressures.

Luckily, from the end of April 2021 the epidemiological situation in the country began slowly improving and progressive reopening was implemented, just like one year before (when vaccines were not available). Still, Italy remains one of the countries most dramatically affected by Covid-19 in the world, with more than 125,000 deaths from the beginning of the pandemic to late May 2021. Up to now, not much has been done to face the structural problems that contributed to earn Italy the 'sick man of Europe' label long before the pandemic. Thus, only time will tell whether the change of government towards a more 'consensual model' based on the controversial rhetoric of 'the rule of the best' (where competence counts more than ideological positioning), the continuation of the vaccine campaign and most of all, the prospect of receiving an unprecedented amount of money from the EU in exchange for structural reforms, will finally cure Italian 'sickness'.

Notes

1. Between mid-May and the first days of April 2020 the number of people hospitalised in intensive care units because of Covid-19 doubled from 2,000 to 4,000. Considering that the total ICU places available in Italy (for any kind of critical patients, not only those suffering from Covid) was around 5,000, it meant most hospitals (especially in the northern regions) had no chance to accept other urgent cases.
2. This is a governmental act that allows the government to directly approve regulations to face emergencies such as natural catastrophes.
3. Both the 2013 and 2018 M5S election manifestos proposed the dismantling of the ESM and of the 'Troika', seen as the main agencies responsible for the austerity policies imposed on Southern eurozone countries.
4. Journalists estimated an overall number of 15 task forces and 450 'experts' appointed during this period by different Ministries (Perrone 2020).
5. The website http://www.sondaggipoliticoelettorali.it/, managed by the government's Department for Information and Publishing, collects the various polls published in national or local newspapers and/or presented on TV information programmes. All the poll data presented in this section were collected by the most important Italian survey institutes (Ixé, Emg, Demos, Demopolis, Tecné etc.) and refer to CATI and/or CAWI analysis with a representative sample of at least 1,000 people.
6. According to a survey (Emg 2020c), the absolute majority of Italians were convinced that the government was facing the emergency better than all other countries in the world, while only 11 per cent felt that its performance was inferior.
7. Every day at 6 p.m. from the end of February until the end of April, the Chief of Civil Protection – from time to time accompanied by an 'expert' from the CTS – held a TV press conference intended to present the daily data concerning the number of new cases, hospitalisations, deaths and recoveries.

Disclosure statement

No potential conflict of interest was reported by the author(s).

ORCID

Giulia Vicentini http://orcid.org/0000-0002-6378-8515
Maria Tullia Galanti http://orcid.org/0000-0002-1984-9085

References

Ajello, M. (2020) 'Conte, ipotesi governissimo Draghi dietro lo scontro tra premier e Renzi', *Il Messaggero*, 2 May.

Atlante politico (2020), Indagine Demos & Pi per la Repubblica, n.87 (April), available online at: http://www.demos.it/2020/pdf/5351ap87_20200503.pdf

Baker, W. D. & Oneal, J. R. (2001) 'Patriotism or opinion leadership? The nature and origins of the "rally 'round the flag" effect', *Journal of Conflict Resolution*, vol. 45, no. 5, pp. 661–687.

Baldi, B. & Profeti, S. (2020) 'Le fatiche della collaborazione. Il rapporto stato-regioni in Italia ai tempi del COVID –19', *Rivista Italiana di Politiche Pubbliche*, vol. 3, pp. 277–306.

Boin, A., 'T Hart, P., Stern, E. & Sundelius, B. (2005) *The Politics of Crisis Management: Public Leadership under Pressure*, Cambridge University Press, New York.

Bolgherini, S. (2014) 'Can austerity lead to recentralisation? Italian local government during the economic crisis', *South European Society and Politics*, vol. 19, no. 2, pp. 193–214.

Bressanelli, E. & Natali, D. (2019) 'Introduction', *Contemporary Italian Politics*, vol. 11, no. 3, pp. 208–219.

Bucchi, M. & Saracino, B. (2020) 'Scared, supportive and confident in science (but a little confused by expert communication) trends and changes in the perception of the pandemic: the new data from the science in society monitor', available online on: https://sagepus.blogspot.com/2020/04/italian-citizens-and-COVID-19-one-month.html?m=1

Capano, G. (2020) 'Policy design and state capacity in the COVID-19 emergency in Italy: if you are not prepared for the (un)expected, you can be only what you already are', *Policy and Society*, vol. 39, no. 3, pp. 326–344.

Capano, G. & Pritoni, A. (2016) 'Mirror, mirror on the wall, who is the most reformist one of all? Policy innovation and design coherence of the Renzi government', *Contemporary Italian Politics*, vol. 8, no. 3, pp. 289–302.

Cappellini, S. (2020) 'Governo, D'Alema: "Non si manda via l'uomo più popolare del Paese per volere del più impopolare', *La Repubblica*, 6 January.

Casula, M. & Toth, F. (2018) 'The yellow-green government and the thorny issue of childhood routine vaccination', *Italian Political Science*, vol. 13, no. 2, pp. 104–114.

Circap & SWG (2020) 'Gli effetti del COVID-19 sulla politica italiana', *Rivista il Mulino*.

Cotta, M. & Verzichelli, L. (2007) *Political Institutions in Italy*, Oxford University Press, Oxford.

Cotta, M. & Verzichelli, L. (2008) *Il sistema politico italiano*, Il Mulino, Bologna.

Custodero, A. (2020a) 'Coronavirus, Salvini: "Il governo ha perso tempo. Chiudere accessi via aria, terra e mare". Conte: "Non era possibile bloccare subito i voli"', *La Repubblica*, 31 January.

Custodero, A. (2020b) 'Fase 2, nella notte accordo Stato-Regioni su Dpcm. I governatori erano insorti: "Rischio caos normativo"', *La Repubblica*, 17 May.

Dazzi, Z. (2020) 'Il sindaco Sala a Chinatown contro la psicosi coronavirus: "Speriamo si riaprano presto i voli, qui per portare solidarietà"', *La Repubblica*, 8 February.

De Luca, M. (2020) *The Italian Style: Giuseppe Conte's 'Half Populist' Leadership during COVID-19*, EUROPP - European Politics and Policy blog, London School of Economics and Political Science.

Demopolis - Istituto di Ricerche (2020a) 'L'Italia in tempi di Covid-19', 15 April, available online at: http://www.sondaggipoliticoelettorali.it

Demopolis - Istituto di Ricerche. (2020b) 'Barometro Politico Demopolis: gli italiani e le istituzioni regionali dopol'emergenza Covid', 11 June, available online at: http://www.sondaggipoliticoelettorali.it

Demopolis - Istituto di Ricerche. (2020c) 'L'Italia, tra voglia di "ripartenza" e timori del virus', available online at: http://www.sondaggipoliticoelettorali.it, 19 May.

Dente, B. (1995) *In un diverso stato. Come rifare la pubblica amministrazione italiana*, Il Mulino, Bologna.

Di Mascio, F. & Natalini, A. (2014) 'Austerity and public administration: Italy between modernization and spending cuts', *American Behavioral Scientist*, vol. 58, no. 12, pp. 1634–1656.

Di Mascio, F. & Natalini, A. (2016) 'Ministerial advisers between political change and institutional legacy: the case of Italy', *Acta Politica*, vol. 5, no. 4, pp. 517–538.

Emanuele, V. & Chiaramonte, A. (2020) 'Going out of the ordinary. The de-institutionalization of the Italian party system in comparative perspective', *Contemporary Italian Politics*, vol. 12, no. 1, pp. 4–22.

Emg Acqua. (2020a) 'Osservatorio OMG', 26 March, available online at: http://www.sondaggipoliticoelettorali.it

Emg Acqua.(2020b), 'Osservatorio EMG', 19 May, available online at: http://www.sondaggipoliticoelettorali.it

Emg Acqua. (2020c) 'Osservatorio OMG', 9 April. available online at: http://www.sondaggipoliticoelettorali.it

Galanti, M. T. & Saracino, B. (2021) 'Inside the Italian Covid-19 task forces', *Contemporary Italian Politics*, pp. 1–17.

Garzia, D. (2017) 'Party transformation, leadership change and closeness to parties: the case of Italy, 2013', *Contemporary Italian Politics*, vol. 9, no. 1, pp. 30–43.

Guerzoni, M. (2020), 'Coronavirus, "Da gennaio c'è un piano segreto: troppo drammatico per dirlo', *Corriere della Sera*, 21 April.

Healy, A. & Malhotra, N. (2009) 'Myopic voters and natural disaster policy', *American Political Science Review*, vol. 103, no. 3, pp. 387–406.

Il Messaggero. (2020) 'Fase 2, Flash mob di Fratelli d'Italia a Palazzo Chigi, Meloni: "Non resteremo a guardare"', 28 April.

ISS (2020), 'Survey nazionale sul contagio COVID-19 nelle strutture residenziali e sociosanitarie, Epidemia COVID-19, Aggiornamento nazionale: 05 maggio 2020', available online at: https://www.epicentro.iss.it/coronavirus/pdf/sars-cov-2-survey-rsa-rapporto-finale.pdf

Istituto Ixè S.I. (2020), 'La situazione politica', 13 March, available online at: http://www.sondaggipoliticoelettorali

La Stampa. (2020) 'La Lega occupa il Parlamento, Salvini: "Basta autocertificazione e ripresa delle attività come nel resto d'Europa"', 30 April.

Lippi, A. (2012) *La politica degli intellettuali*, Bonanno editore, Acireale-Roma.

Longo, E. & Mobilio, G. (2016) 'Territorial government reforms at the time of financial crisis: the dawn of metropolitan cities in Italy', *Regional & Federal Studies*, vol. 26, no. 4, pp. 509–530.

Lupia, V. (2020) 'Visita a sorpresa del presidente Mattarella in una scuola di Roma. La preside: "Siamo una scuola simbolo di convivenza"', *La Repubblica*, 6 February.

Macciò, A. (2020) 'In Veneto nessun piano tamponi. Ci hanno salvato i miei reagenti', *Il Corriere del Veneto*, 25 May

Mapelli, F. (2012) *Il Sistema Sanitario italiano*, Il Mulino, Bologna.

Mari, L. (2020), '"Chiudere tutto, anzi no". Salvini e il COVID-19, la confusione del leader leghista sulla gestione dell'epidemia', *La Repubblica*, 16 April.

Ministero della Salute (2007) 'National plan for preparedness and response to an influenza pandemic', available online at: http://www.salute.gov.it/imgs/C_17_pubblicazioni_511_allegato.pdf

Ministero della Salute (2020) 'Informativa urgente del Ministro della Salute Roberto Speranza sulle iniziative per prevenire e contrastare la diffusione del nuovo coronavirus', 30 January, available online at: http://www.salute.gov.it/imgs/C_17_notizie_4033_0_file.pdf

Moschella, M. & Verzichelli, L. (forthcoming, 2021) 'L'Italia, l'Europa e il Recovery Fund. Contesto, attori, dibattito', *Rivista Italiana di Politiche Pubbliche*, March.

Neri, S. & Mori, A. (2017) 'Crisi economica, politiche di austerità e relazioni integovernative nel SSN. Dalla regionalizzazione al federalismo differenziato?', *Autonomie Locali e Servizi Locali*, vol. 40, no. 2, pp. 201–220.

Newell, J. L. (2020a) 'Italian politics: resisting the right-wing populist tide in 2020', *Contemporary Italian Politics*, vol. 12, no. 1, pp. 1–3.

Newell, J. L. (2020b) 'Italian politics in 2019 and their legacy: reactions to the coronavirus', *Contemporary Italian Politics*, vol. 12, no 1, pp. 109–111.

Openpolis (2020a) 'Coronavirus, chi decide durante lo stato di emergenza', available online at: https://www.openpolis.it/wp-content/uploads/2020/04/Report_Coronavirus_Le-mappe-del-potere.pdf

Openpolis. (2020b) 'L'attuazione dei decreti COVID19, una lunga e contorta strada', available online at: https://www.openpolis.it/lattuazione-dei-decreti-COVID19-una-lunga-e-contorta-strada

Pasquino, G. (2020) *Italian Democracy: How It Works*, Routledge, London.

Perone, G. (2021) 'The determinants of COVID-19 case fatality rate (CFR) in the Italian regions and provinces: an analysis of environmental, demographic, and healthcare factors', *Science of the Total Environment*, vol. 755, no. 142523, pp. 142523.

Perrone, M. (2020) '15 task force per combattere il virus: ripartenza a rischio caos', *24 Plus* (supplement of *Il Sole 24 Ore*), 19 April.

Pisano, G. P., Sadun, R. & Zanini, M. (2020) 'Lessons from Italy's response to coronavirus', *Harvard Business Review*, 27 March.

Ruiu, M. L. (2020) 'Mismanagement of Covid-19: lessons learned from Italy', *Journal of RiskResearch*, vol. 23, no. 7–8, pp. 1007–1020.

Sartori, G. (1982) *Teoria Dei Partiti E Caso Italiano*, Sugar & Co, Milan.

Sarzanini, F. (2020) 'Zone Rosse Alzano e Nembro, tre ore di interrogatorio per Conte', *Corriere della Sera*, 12 June.

Segatti, P. (2020) 'La popolarità del governo Conte', *Rivista il Mulino*, 9 June.

Terlizzi, M. (2019) *Health System Decentralization and Recentralization: Ideational and Institutional Dynamics in Italy and Denmark*, Palgrave Macmillan, London.

Termometro Politico. (2020), 'Sondaggio su elezioni politiche e coronavirus', 13 May, available online at: http://www.sondaggipoliticoelettorali

Vassallo, S. (2020) 'Il miracolo di Conte: ha convinto la sinistra', available online at: https://www.quotidiano.net/politica/conte-sondaggi-1.5149462, 15 May.

Vezzoni, C., Ladini, R., Molteni, F., Dotti Sani, G. F., Biolcati, F., Chiesi, A. M., Guglielmi, S., Maraffi, M., Pedrazzani, A. & Segatti, P. (2020) 'Investigating the social, economic and political consequences of the COVID-19 pandemic: a rolling cross-section approach', *Survey Research Methods*, vol. 14, no. 2, pp. 187–194.

World Bank (2020). 'Worldwide governance indicators', available online at: https://info.worldbank.org/governance/wgi/

OPEN ACCESS

The Limits of Power Concentration and Expert Knowledge in Emergency Management: Spain's Government Response during the First Phase of the Covid-19 Pandemic

Juan Rodríguez-Teruel, Eloísa del Pino and José Real-Dato

ABSTRACT
Focusing on the central government's response to the Covid-19 crisis during the first wave in Spain, the article analyses the executive's strategy of power concentration, and the factors that shape its implementation. We sketch how the crisis erupted, the main measures and strategies adopted by the national executive, the role of the experts, and the interaction with other political actors and institutions. We also explore the second phase and how the political reaction evolved towards a more consensual approach. Paradoxically, the consequences for the political actors were apparently less harmful than expected, since the governments did not lose political support, and the electorate continued to support the policy measures adopted to mitigate the pandemic.

Spain is a dramatic example of a country that quickly suffered severe consequences after its initial Covid-19 outbreak. By the end of the first phase of the crisis (June 2020), Spain had totals for deaths and infections that were among the highest in the world. Press reports labelled the situation a 'national failure', which could have been managed differently (The Economist 2020) – though this picture changed in subsequent waves.

Early accounts emphasised the unpreparedness of the country and the slow reactions of public institutions as key explanatory factors (Dubin 2021; Molina, Otero-Iglesias & Martínez 2020). However, from a comparative perspective, Spain could hardly be considered unprepared for such type of threats; nor was it simply slow in the stringent measures it adopted. Before the crisis, the national security and healthcare systems had taken steps to guarantee satisfactory levels of preparedness to cope with pandemic outbreaks, building on experience from previous episodes (2009 flu, 2014–2016 Ebola virus among the more recent).

Besides, Spain was also among the first to adopt measures against the threat. By the end of January 2021, when the first case was detected in the country, Spain had the highest level in Europe after Italy of 'stringency' in governmental response, as measured by the Oxford Covid-19 database (Hale et al. 2021a, 2021b). In mid-March, it was one of the countries to adopt the toughest lockdown measures, according to the same source. This lockdown was introduced when Spain had a similar number of detected infections and deaths to France or Britain (and lower than Italy) when they declared their own lockdowns (Rozenblum 2021; Vicentini & Galanti 2021; Williams, Rajan & Cylus 2021).

In this respect, Spain is an interesting case to illustrate how democratic governments face hard dilemmas and constraints when confronted with an exogenous shock (Greer, King & da Fonseca 2021, p. 4). In a context of urgency and high uncertainty, the balance between rationality, necessity, available resources and political legitimacy may be very difficult to achieve. Thus, although the Spanish government's response did not essentially differ from that of countries that enjoyed better results, like Portugal, Greece or France (Ladi, Angelou & Panagiotatou 2021; Rozenblum 2021; Silva, Costa & Moniz 2021), it was clearly not enough to avoid the high human and economic losses in the first months of the pandemic.

In order better to understand the Spanish case, this article analyses the central government's responses to the crisis, focusing on the main constraints that narrowed the choice of alternatives available. We limit our analysis to the first phase (between January and June 2020), the period which shows most clearly how the government should address these constraints without the 'golden time' necessary for more strategic decisions. This contrast with countries that had learned from previous failures in managing health pandemics, like South Korea (Moon 2020, p. 654).

Our analysis builds on previous studies that provide arguments to understand the motivations behind governments' crisis management (Boin et al. 2005; Lodge & Wegrich 2012), with particular attention to recent studies of the factors producing policy differentiation among countries during the Covid pandemics.[1]

In these exceptional situations, leaders and executives take decisions in a highly constrained environment, starting by giving meaning to the unfolding crisis (Boin et al. 2005, p. 13). Although emergency management might foster collaborative leadership strategies in public actors (Hattke & Martin 2020; Waugh & Streib 2014), a common feature of governments' reactions is power concentration, seeking to maximise the effectiveness of their decisions (Bolleyer & Salát 2021; Fleischer & Parrado 2010; Malandrino & Demichelis 2020). This was the case in Spain: once the containment strategy had failed to avoid the virus propagation, the national government adopted a strategy of policy centralisation.

In the following pages, we analyse how this power concentration was implemented and what obstacles it found. We observe this response in two dimensions. In policy terms, it involved intra-cabinet decisions, experts and policy advice, and coordination with the regional governments. In political terms, power concentration faced the polarisation of the parliamentary arena, bargaining with the main interest groups, and public opinion. Overall, this government response contributed to guaranteeing cohesion and effectiveness in public decisions, but it also became clear that the strategy was politically hard to sustain and suffered several policy pitfalls. Therefore, by the end of the first phase, the government decided to relax the policy centralisation.

The rest of the article offers evidence supporting this general argument. The next section introduces relevant aspects of the state's capacity and preparedness before the crisis and provides quantitative data about the impact of the pandemics. The third section assesses the government's policy response, the role of experts, and the relationship with the regions. The fourth section analyses the political dimension, focusing on the role played by the parliament and political parties, the interest groups, and public opinion. The final section provides an assessment of these variables and summarises the following phases of the crisis.

Crisis preparedness and state capacity

State capacity, particularly in terms of health services, and pandemic preparedness have been considered structural factors determining the government's reaction during the Covid outbreak (Capano 2020; Toshkov, Carroll & Yesilkagit 2021). The use of these resources is also conditioned by the multilevel structure of the country (Parrado & Galli 2021). Spain is a highly decentralised state, where most basic public services (including healthcare, education or social services) are under the jurisdiction of the 17 Autonomous Communities (*Comunidades Autónomas*, henceforth CAs), while the central government deals primarily with regulatory, planning, and evaluative tasks (Parrado 2020). Even if the central government centralises some powers on an extraordinary basis, as it did during the Covid-19 crisis between March and June, the implementation of its decisions would still depend on political collaboration with regional authorities. This collaboration may be particularly fragile with those CAs governed by parties that are in opposition in the national parliament (as was the case for Madrid, Catalonia, Andalusia, and Galicia, among others).

The National Health System (NHS) reflects this multi-level governance structure, with the 17 CAs managing 92.5 per cent of healthcare spending in the country (Ministry of Finance 2021). The Ministry of Health (MoH) is responsible for the regulation of the right to healthcare and the establishment of the basic elements of the organisation, coordination and financing of the NHS, designing training plans for health personnel, pharmaceutical policy and high-level inspection of the system. On the other hand, the regional governments use differing models of public/private collaboration to administer their networks of hospitals, specialised centres and primary care services (Alonso, Clifton & Díaz-Fuentes 2015; Gallego, Barbieri & González 2017).

This multilevel healthcare policy decision-making system is governed through the Interterritorial Council of the Spanish National Health Service (*Consejo Interterritorial del Sistema Nacional de Salud*, CISNS), a fundamental body linking the national and the regional healthcare ministries. The resulting framework has produced an intergovernmental distribution of roles and resources, with strong interdependence between the central government and the regions, which shapes the way in which decisions are made and implemented.

The Spanish NHS suffered from the economic recession (del Pino 2020), which reduced government health care expenditure from 6.8 to 6.2 per cent of GDP between 2009 and 2018. However, this did not substantially affect the Spanish NHS's capacity, which ranks in middle-to-top positions in the main indexes of health care capacity and efficiency.[2] The multi-level healthcare system therefore had a similar – if not better – level of preparedness than other countries in Southern Europe.[3]

Spain also had slightly more experience in dealing with epidemics, as it has been one of the European countries most affected by previous pandemic episodes in recent years (2009 swine flu, 2012 MERS-cov, 2014 Ebola). Set up by the MoH in 2004, the Centre for the Coordination of Health Alerts and Emergencies (*Centro de Coordinación de Alertas y Emergencias Sanitarias*, CCAES) is tasked with setting up preparedness and response plans to deal with public health threats including pandemics. The CCAES must also carry out a survey of the national capacity requirements set out in the International Health Regulations (WHO 2005) and work with the regions to ensure their implementation. Whenever a public health emergency arises, the ministry requests each region to organise a focal point who works with the CCAES.

Before the arrival of this coronavirus pandemic, the Ministry had preparedness plans and protocols that had been developed (and successively updated) to respond to the most dangerous detected viruses (H5N1, Ebola, Mers-Cov, dengue and zika). Spain had also participated in pandemic simulations organised by the European Commission in 2005. The central government was organising the first national preparedness exercise, which should have taken place in April 2020, in accordance with the National Security Strategy. Besides the CCAES, the National Centre of Epidemiology (CNE) coordinates the National Epidemiological Surveillance Network (RENAVE), created in 1995, to gather data about diseases and epidemics in cooperation with the regional governments. All these resources seem to indicate that Spain was a country relatively well prepared for early detection of epidemics.

However, these signals of preparedness could have contributed to fostering overconfidence among authorities and experts and an underestimation of the risks posed by the new virus – a psychological factor that has been largely ignored in previous policymaking studies (Maor & Howlett 2020, p. 229). For instance, focusing on the preparedness of the NHS implied diverting attention from other sectors that turned out to be crucial as the pandemic developed. This was the case for social care, and particularly nursing and care homes, whose residents accounted for about half of the Covid deaths (del Pino et al. 2020; Ministry of Social Rights and Agenda 2030 2020). A law – the Long-Term Care system – was passed in 2006 aiming to strengthen the quality of these services. However, the economic recession had a pronounced negative effect on its implementation and funding, producing lower development and professionalisation (for instance, keeping care home beds below the WHO recommendation) and significant regional variance in terms of equality. Further, coordination of the long-term care system with the NHS did not improve after the passing of the law, which also exacerbated the Covid crisis.

More generally, Spain faced the crisis with clearly limited state capacities in other key aspects, particularly economically. Despite averaging GDP growth of 2.8 per cent since 2015, unemployment remained high (13.8 per cent in January 2020, the second highest in the EU), the national debt was 97.9 per cent at the end of 2019, and the budget deficit averaged 3.5 per cent between 2015 and 2019.[4] These constraints became evident when the government needed to implement economic policies to mitigate the social consequences of the crisis.

The evolution of the pandemic in Spain

The first official Covid-19 case in Spain was detected on 31 January (a German tourist in La Gomera, Canary Islands). The early cases on the mainland were imported, with the first being reported on 26 February in Barcelona; the first death was reported on 3 March in Valencia, though it had actually occurred on 13 February, suggesting the virus had already been circulating in the country since the start of February (Gómez-Carballa et al. 2020). At the beginning of March, community spread occurred, and the numbers began to climb exponentially, particularly after 8 March. On the day the central government declared a state of emergency (13 March) the MoH reported more than 4,200 daily cases and 120 deaths.[5]

As seen in Figure 1(a), the government's policy reaction helped to reduce the contagion, since the peak of the curve of new daily cases was reached two weeks after the national lockdown (9,181 cases on 27 March). The maximum number of daily deaths came a week later (950 on 3 April), and two days later (5 April), Spain became the country in the world with the most deaths per million people (Figure 1(b). After that, the epidemic's curve started to

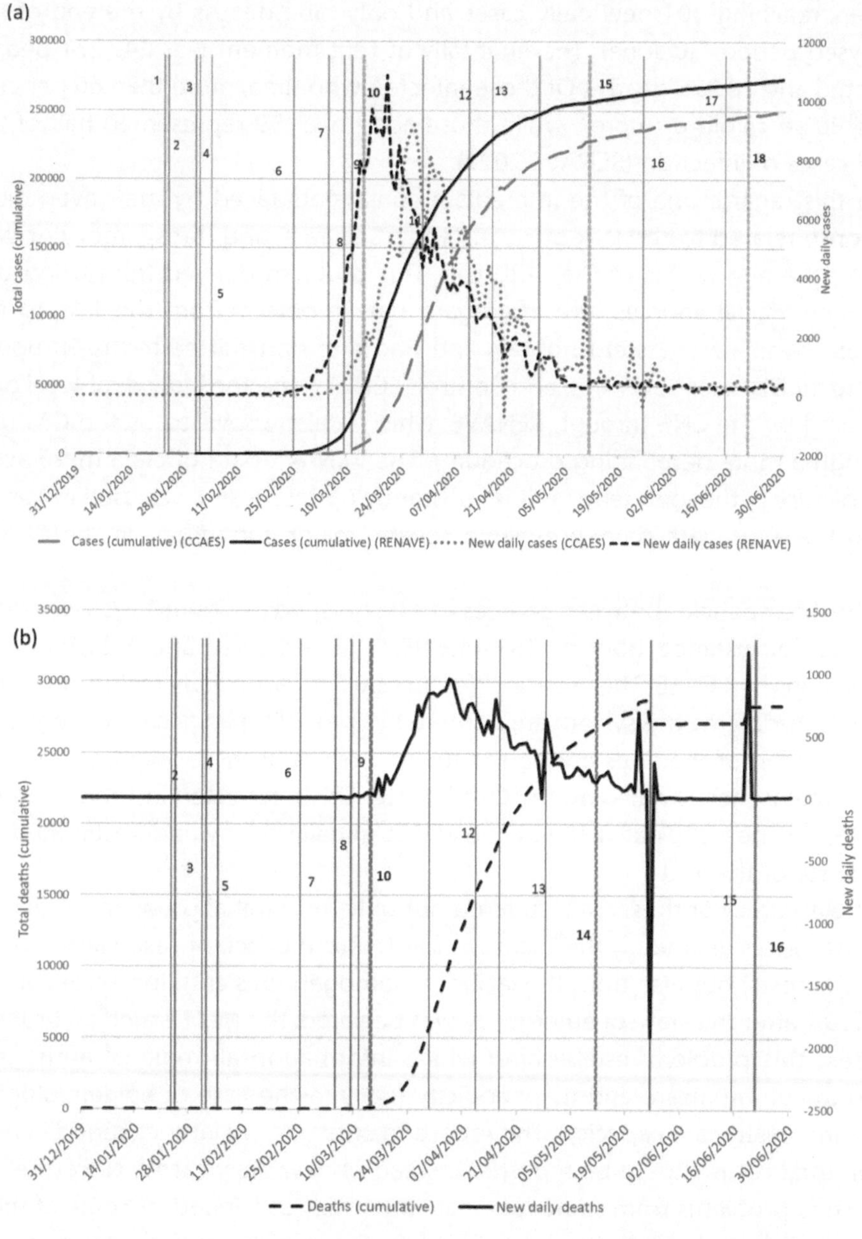

Figure 1. COVID-19 detected cases (a) and deaths (b) in Spain until 30 June 2020.
Sources: Own elaboration using data provided by the CCAES (MoH) to the ECDC (https://www.ecdc.europa.eu/en/publications-data/download-todays-data-geographic-distribution-covid-19-casesworldwide) and RENAVE data (https://cnecovid.isciii.es/covid19/#documentaci%C3%B3n-y-datos). Both accessed 12/08/2020.
Note: Vertical lines represent major events during the period: 1) The MoH establishes a monitoring committee (23/01/2020); 2) First detection protocol for COVID-19 (24/01); 3) WHO declares healthcare emergency (31/01): 4) First reported case (01/02); 5) First meeting of the CISNS (04/02); 6) Change in detection protocol (25/02); 7) First reported death (05/03); 8) Community transmission (09/03); 9) WHO declares pandemic (11/03); 10) State of alarm declared (14/03); 11) Total lockdown (29/03); 12) End of total lockdown (10/04); 13)

flatten, reaching 301 new daily cases and only nine deaths by the end of the analysed period (30 June). The final tally at that moment was 249,271 people infected and 28,355 deaths. Of those infected who died, more than 60 per cent were 80 years old or more,[6] while those aged over 59 represented half of the total cases of infection (RENAVE 2020).

In this regard, one of the immediate constraints faced by the government response related to the lack of consistency, accuracy and transparency of data during the first weeks of the outbreak. This problem derived from using two different official sources: the aggregate data reported from the CAs to the CCAES – which was faster to obtain and was later transmitted to the European Centre for Disease Prevention and Control (ECDC) – and the individual-level data gathered by the CNE through RENAVE, which is also provided by the CAs (but through a more demanding procedure). The RENAVE data offers a more accurate picture in the long term, as it is constantly updated, and was used in May to clean the aggregate data, provoking several major corrections in the CCAES' series.

The discrepancies between sources can be grasped in Figure 1(a,b), where we observe, for instance, how, by 30 June, RENAVE registered about 23,700 more cases than the CCAES. These data differences were particularly telling about the capacity problems the system encountered in providing an accurate diagnostic of the spread of the virus during the first moments of the epidemic, when the government mostly relied on the CCAES date. This is reflected in Table 1, where we observe how the data used by the CCAES initially clearly underestimated the incidence of the virus.

The accuracy of these data suffered not only from initial problems in detecting the illness (including the scarcity of PCR and the lack of reliability of other types of tests) but also from the lack of a homogeneous criterion across all the CAs. Just after the state of emergency was declared, the MoH issued an order to address this problem, establishing which information all regional authorities were to communicate and its periodicity (daily in the case of epidemiological data and healthcare capacity). The reporting criteria were later changed in mid-April (total cases should be reported instead of new daily cases). Nevertheless, reporting problems from some regional authorities continued, as some of them did not stick to the criterion established by the ministry to consider a case as Covid-19 positive. Additionally, the situation surpassed the daily statistical reporting capacity of Madrid and Catalonia, the most affected regions, and this affected the overall national figures (Linde et al. 2020).

Government passes plan for easing lockdown (28/04); 14) Phase 1 of easing plan starts; MoH changes criteria for case reporting (11/05); 15) First territories reach 'new normal' (Galicia) (15/06); 16) End of state of alarm. All territories in 'new normal' (21/06).

Table 1. Cumulative number of Covid-19 cases in Spain by Autonomous Community per 100,000 population at fortnightly intervals.

	28 February	6 March		13 March		7 April		11 May		21 June	
	RENAVE	RENAVE	CCAES	RENAVE	CCAES	RENAVE	CCAES	RENAVE	CCAES	RENAVE	CCAES
Andalusia	0.82	3.92	0.25	22.55	2.53	53.69	71.15	10.20	5.82	1.43	1.07
Aragon	1.28	6.47	0.45	35.97	6.06	143.07	200.26	31.31	26.91	13.17	10.69
Asturias (*)	0.29	3.04	0.49	30.23	6.55	66.65	90.54	5.60	7.72	0.29	0.68
Balearic Islands (*)	0.85	4.70	0.52	22.63	2.52	55.51	73.95	5.12	7.22	4.27	3.83
Basque Country	4.14	22.21	2.04	85.73	18.89	188.08	279.96	18.56	27.22	6.40	7.11
Canary Islands	1.15	4.97	0.51	22.21	2.97	24.47	51.31	1.75	3.76	2.07	2.09
Cantabria (*)	1.54	3.43	1.72	27.28	4.99	107.07	182.76	10.47	22.54	4.46	3.69
Castile and León	2.26	12.79	0.58	79.93	6.96	302.64	296.64	78.14	35.66	10.74	12.13
Castile-La Mancha	1.71	22.55	1.72	128.94	9.54	306.49	443.12	21.28	60.80	9.78	12.99
Catalonia	2.34	13.02	0.31	77.47	4.08	200.43	256.80	20.12	55.65	15.35	16.19
Ceuta (**)	0.00	3.58	0.00	19.08	0.00	66.79	88.47	14.31	16.51	0.00	0.00
Extremadura	2.16	7.24	0.56	40.52	3.65	123.92	135.06	54.82	15.73	3.01	2.72
Galicia	1.07	4.56	0.11	34.22	3.15	117.84	180.96	34.33	27.93	1.11	1.04
La Rioja (*)	9.07	68.20	9.15	209.60	76.71	393.86	638.58	9.70	35.04	2.50	3.79
Madrid (*)	9.31	53.52	2.06	231.40	29.79	223.22	418.00	25.20	43.46	14.46	18.08
Melilla (**)	0.00	2.30	0.00	34.45	2.31	55.12	63.59	2.30	5.78	4.59	2.31
Murcia (*)	1.13	4.77	0.00	28.99	2.34	32.36	56.83	6.16	2.81	1.72	1.67
Navarra (*)	3.78	22.55	0.46	144.65	19.87	328.80	346.98	55.68	49.22	10.14	8.10
Valencian Community	2.12	7.91	0.60	43.29	1.72	64.10	100.70	14.78	10.71	2.04	2.84
SPAIN	*2.86*	*15.97*	*0.78*	*78.89*	*8.99*	*145.68*	*210.69*	*21.61*	*27.93*	*7.30*	*8.08*

Source: RENAVE data: https://cnecovid.isciii.es/covid19/#documentaci%C3%B3n-y-datos, accessed 12/08/2020; CCAES data: Daily reports (available at https://www.mscbs.gob.es/profesionales/saludPublica/ccayes/alertasActual/nCov-China/situacionActual.htm, accessed 17/08/20.

Note: (*) One-province Autonomous Community; (**) Autonomous city. The RENAVE data correspond to the data consolidate by 12 August. The CCAES data have been extracted from the daily reports issued on each date.

Furthermore, there was also criticism with respect to the MoH's transparency. For instance, the MoH established in April that CAs should provide information twice a week on the number of deaths in nursing homes. However, this information was not released until November 2020. According to a report of the Ministry of Social Rights and Agenda 2030 (2020), the total number of COVID-related deaths in nursing home facilities during the first wave was almost 20,300 people (including those who died with symptoms associated with Covid-19 but who were not diagnosed) which might represent around 47–50 per cent of confirmed Covid-19 deaths (Ministry of Social Rights and Agenda 2030 2020, p. 13).

Finally, several studies comparing deaths during the pandemic period with similar periods in previous years have also questioned the Covid-19 death toll reported by the public authorities. The CNE calculated an excess of mortality from 10 March to 9 May of 43,617 deaths, while the cumulative number of Covid-19 deaths during the period reported by the MoH was 26,473 (CNE 2020).

The policy response: centralisation and expertise

Centralising the allocation of power

Two weeks before the first case was detected in Spain, the first multi-party cabinet at national level since the return of democracy in 1977 was formed by the PSOE (*Partido Socialista Obrero Español* – Spanish Socialist Workers' Party) and the radical left-wing UP (*Unidas Podemos* – United We can). The pandemic therefore provided a significant test of the functioning of the brand-new executive. While traces of departmentalism and internal coordination problems are not uncommon in Spanish cabinets (Rodríguez-Teruel 2020a), such an unprecedented crisis potentially threatened the effectiveness of cabinet decision-making and the prime minister's authority. Moreover, the resulting portfolio allocation split the departments that would be most concerned with managing the crisis between the two coalition partners. Hence, the socialist Salvador Illa was appointed as Minister of Health, and Social Services were allocated to the Ministry of Social Rights and Agenda 2030, headed by the deputy prime minister Pablo Iglesias, leader of Podemos. Besides, the Ministry of Labour was assigned to the radical left-wing Yolanda Díaz (appointed by Podemos), while the core departments of Defence and Interior were allocated to non-partisan ministers close to prime minister Pedro Sánchez.

These internal problems did not arise during the first stage of the crisis. Between January and the beginning of March, the government implemented a containment strategy, based on updating the crisis protocols, increasing control over critical infrastructure (airports, policies, etc), and prevention measures addressed to the NHS. The management of these actions was led exclusively by the abovementioned Minister of Health, Illa, and the CCAES director,

Fernando Simón, in coordination with the regional health ministers. On 23 January, the MoH reported the elaboration of a protocol to deal with potential cases of the new coronavirus, whose evolution had already been followed by a daily ad hoc crisis committee meeting in the ministry. In parallel, the CCAES had started to produce daily reports analysing the situation in China and assessing Spain's exposure to the risk, according to the analysis offered by the WHO and the ECDC, in order to provide the MoH with scientific criteria for policy measures.

This progressive, moderate reaction reflected leaders' overconfidence, but was also conditioned by the lack of accurate data during the early weeks. Indeed, the decision makers were ignorant of the fact that the virus had already been circulating in Spain since January (Gómez-Carballa et al. 2020). Therefore, the few preventive measures adopted in these first weeks, which were built upon an underestimation of the actual impact of the virus, prioritised controlling popular alarm over more preventive stringent actions. On 24 February the CCAES reported a medium-level risk for Spain, concluding that the healthcare system was sufficiently prepared to deal with outbreaks like those in Italy (CCAES 2020). Accordingly, the government maintained its role of centralising information and promoting coordination with the regional governments, while no substantive decisions under its area of competence were taken: flights from China and Italy were not restricted and mass events, including football matches and mass demonstrations, like those on International Women's Day, continued to be allowed.

However, as a consequence of the deterioration of the situation after 8 March and the failure of the containment strategy, the differing reactions of the regional governments demonstrated the limits to providing a coordinated response within the NHS. Besides this, internal divergences among cabinet ministers started to arise, reflecting different approaches to 'making sense' of the situation. The economic ministers (particularly Nadia Calviño, a non-partisan cabinet member recruited from the EU administration) claimed the crisis was a temporary shock that should not be overestimated, were the most reluctant within the cabinet to implement a lockdown, and defended a more business-friendly approach. On the contrary, other ministers (including UP cabinet members) worried increasingly about the social effects of the crisis and demanded more anticipatory actions (Linde et al. 2020, p. 70).

In the second stage of the crisis, a mitigation strategy started on 13 March, when the prime minister announced draconian measures that not only meant an important increase in the stringency of the government's response, but also a new approach, based on centralising power. The main tool for this policy centralisation was the 'state of emergency',[7] an unprecedented decision through a constitutional disposition that allows the executive to order exceptional measures provided they do not affect fundamental rights (such as freedom of speech or the right to demonstrate).[8] It can only be implemented for a limited period of time (15 days), and its extension requires a parliamentary majority. The 'state of emergency' was extended every 15 days for almost four months until 21 June, having been approved by parliament in six different votes (see the following section on the political response). Under this *constitutional umbrella*, the central government adopted a flood of measures at various levels.

First, it centralised cabinet-delegated authority to four ministers (Health, Internal Affairs, Defence, and Transport, Mobility and Urban Agenda). The Minister of Health was given special relevance, since he also assumed delegated responsibility for the rest of the policy areas of the government. These four ministers (and some of the key top officials in their departments) formed the Technical Committee for the Management of the Coronavirus (TCMC), a sort of reduced informal cabinet, headed by the prime minister, which met on a daily basis to coordinate actions and take decisions according to the evolution of the situation. They were also assisted by the Situation Committee (*Comité de Seguimiento sobre la situación del COVID-19*), a collective deliberative body for emergency situations, formed by several ministers involved in those areas related to the management of the crisis. Beside these intra-cabinet groups, the executive undertook intensive political activity during the lockdown period: the full cabinet held 24 meetings (ten of them as extraordinary meetings) – an average of one meeting every four days.

One relevant aspect of this internal reorganisation was the absence of UP ministers from the new core executive, with the sole exception of Pablo Iglesias, who was a member of the Situation Committee. Even if this decision was consistent with the initial portfolio allocation, where Podemos did not hold key ministries related to the pandemic, it constrained UP's role in the executive's management of the crisis. Although these decisions apparently increased coordination within government, they also caused friction between the coalition partners concerning decisions regarding social and economic issues, such as the minimum income scheme or the preparation of plans for the easing phase.

Second, and more critically, the executive centralised the regional powers necessary for the management of the crisis: the MoH formally took over responsibility for decision-making and the coordination of health policy decisions from its regional counterparts. This created some tensions with regions led by parties that were in opposition nationally (see next section on the impact of the state structure).

Finally, the executive launched a flood of measures. An emergency decree initiated a series of health policy measures (see Table 2), including a total national lockdown. On the economic and social fronts, the government attempted to ameliorate the social costs of the lockdown and the economic downturn by, among other measures, providing income support for those who could not work or had to remain at home and promoting temporary employment adjustment schemes – through an existing mechanism, the Temporary Employment Regulatory File (*Expediente de Regulación Temporal de Empleo*,

Table 2. Main policy measures implemented by the central government during the first phase of the Covid-19 crisis, January–June 2020.

Date	Norm	Policy area	More relevant policy measure implemented at the national level
			Containment strategy
24 January	Announcement	Public health	Development of a protocol for action in the event of the appearance of possible suspected cases of coronavirus.
4 February	Announcement	Public health	Creation of the Interministerial Coordination Committee to deal with the coronavirus threat.
3 March	Agreement	Public health	Cancellation of at-risk events where health professionals are involved; recommendation for holding behind closed doors large scale sport events such as soccer with a high chance of people attending from at risk areas.
10 March	Order	Public health	Cancellation of all direct flights from Italy to Spain (with some exceptions).
	RDL 6/2020	Socio-economic	Increased sick pay for coronavirus infected workers or those quarantined, paid by the social security budget. (EUR 1.4 billion).
12 March	RDL 7/2020	Socio-economic	Budget increase for attending emergencies related to Covid (EUR 18,225 millions). Transfers to regional governments to manage new costs related to Covid. 50 per cent exemption from employers' social security contributions, from February to June 2020, for workers with permanent discontinuous contracts in the tourism sector and related activities. Flexibility for changing/cancelling public trains tickets.
			Mitigation strategy
14 March	RD 463/2020	Public health	State of emergency. Full lockdown with some exceptions for different professions (RD 463/2020). Centralisation of all policy competences related to Covid mitigation. Cabinet authority delegation to the ministers of Health, Defence, Interior, and Transports, Mobility and Urban Agenda. All forces of public order are allocated under the authority of the Minister of Interior.
			Restrictions of free movement with some exceptions. Civil requisition of goods necessary to combat the epidemic. Retail establishments closure with some exceptions. Shutdown of all educational establishments (online teaching). Closure of museums, archives, libraries, monuments. Hotel and restaurant activities are suspended, and home delivery services can be exclusively provided. Festivals, parades and popular festivals are also suspended. Suspension of religious ceremonies/services. Reduction of public transport capacity. Suspension of deadlines for judicial and administrative procedures.
6 March	Order	Public health	Land border controls.
17 March	RDL 8/2020	Socio-economic	First economic package, including a new line of guarantees via the national development bank (ICO) of up to EUR 100 billion. Additional flexibility for local authorities to use their 2019 budgetary surplus to fund social services and primary assistance to dependent persons (EUR 300 million). Six-month suspension of social security contributions for the self-employed (for the period May–July) and companies (for the period April–June) without interest (EUR 359 million), among others.
19 March	Order	Public health	Closure of all touristic hotels and residences.
	Order	Public health	Measures regulating nursing home services.
22 March	Order	Public health	Temporary restrictions to the entry to the EU/Schengen area from external visitors.
27 March	RD 476/2020	Public health	Renewal of the state of emergency.
	RDL 9/2020	Socio-economic	Second economic package of measures aimed to increase labour protection. Adoption of urgent procedures for public contracts.

(*Continued*)

Table 2. (Continued).

Date	Norm	Policy area	More relevant policy measure implemented at the national level
29 March	RDL 10/2020	Socio-economic	The full lockdown is tightened, now with all non-essential workers in Spain compelled to remain at home. Adoption of a recoverable paid leave for private employees.
1 April	RDL 11/2020	Socio-economic	Third economic package, budget flexibility to enable transfers between budget lines and for local governments to use budget surplus from the previous years for supporting measures in the area of housing.
7 April	RDL 13/2020	Socio-economic	Measures aimed to favour temporary employment in the agricultural sector.
10 April	RD 487/2020	Public health	Renewal of the state of emergency.
13 April	Announcement	Socio-economic	Guidelines of the economic package amounting to around EUR 138.2 billion funded by the EU.
21 April	RDL 15/2020	Socio-economic	Fourth economic policy package, including measures to align the tax bases to the current situation. Reduction of VAT applicable to the supply of medical equipment from national producers to public entities, non-profit organisations and hospital centres to 0 per cent Reduction of VAT on electronic books and newspapers, among others.
24 April	RD 492/2020	Public health	Renewal of the state of emergency.
			Easing strategy
28 April	Executive agreement	Socio-economic	Adoption of the de-escalation scheme (Plan for the Transition towards a New Normality).
	RDL 16/2020	Socio-economic	Package of measures for the recovery of activity under Covid.
5 May	RDL 17/2020	Socio-economic	Package of economic measures to support the cultural sector, establishing investments and subsidies, as well as labour and tax measures, and other incentives. Third tranche of the public guarantees for lines of credit for the sum of 24.5 billion euros to guarantee liquidity of companies and the self-employed.
	RD 514/2020	Public health	Renewal of the state of emergency.
12 May	RDL 401/2020	Socio-economic	Extension of temporary lay-off plans (ERTE) due to force majeure until 30 June.
	Order	Public health	Quarantine for 14 days after arrival of those people arriving from abroad – except those performing cross-border work, hauliers, crew and healthcare professionals. Temporarily re-establishment of air and sea border controls (until 24 May).
16 May	Order	Public health	Measures for extending easing measures to those regions acceding to Phase 2 of the de-escalation plan.
22 May	RD 537/2020	Public health	Renewal of the state of emergency.
26 May	RDL 19/2020	Socio-economic	Extraordinary credit of 14 billion euros to the social security system, as well as a maximum loan of 16.5 billion euros, interest-free. Incentive for moratoriums on mortgage loans and other loans that extends the number of beneficiaries that can defer loans. Extension of some previously adopted economic measures.
29 May	RDL 20/2020	Socio-economic	Approval of a Minimum Living Income.
5 June	RD 555/2020	Public health	Last renewal of the state of emergency.
9 June	RDL 21/2020	Public health	Package of measures governing after the end of the state of emergency and the de-escalation process (due on 21 June).
16 June		Socio-economic	Creation of a Covid funding scheme amounting to 16 billion to be transferred to the regions to finance the cost of the pandemic.
26 June			Extension of the ERTE programme. Increase of the social security exemptions for private companies.

Source: OECD (https://www.oecd.org/coronavirus/en/policy-responses), Coronanet (https://www.coronanet-project.org), ACAPS (https://data.humdata.org/dataset/acaps-covid19-government-measures-dataset) and the Spanish Government (www.lamoncloa.gob.es). For more detailed measures, see OCDE Country Policy Tracker. Link: https://www.oecd.org/coronavirus/country-policy-tracker/.

ERTE), that aimed to reduce the number of workers moving directly into unemployment. By 30 June, workers in the ERTE scheme numbered 1.83 million, 40 per cent less than at the end of May (according to the Ministry of Inclusion, Social Security and Migrations).

The centralisation of power at the apex of the executive helped the effectiveness of many of these measures, managing to flatten the epidemiological curve and reduce deaths in April. But it also made clear important failures of policy coordination, not only between different levels of government (see the section on state structure), but also within the government (del Pino et al. 2020). The urgency of decision-making downgraded the role of formal actors preparing the work of the cabinet meeting (like the General Commission of State Secretaries and Undersecretaries). As a result, the rest of the cabinet did not participate in, and were not informed of, important measures until the Council of Ministers meeting. The absence of the UP ministers from the new core executive did not help with this. Besides, the pre-eminence of the healthcare approach in the measures, and the division of healthcare and social services among different ministries in the national and most regional administrations, contributed to a failed public response regarding nursing and care homes.

Aiming to solve these problems, the executive relaxed centralisation as the lockdown eased. The prime minister also allowed UP ministers (and other cabinet members) more say in the management of the crisis. The TCMC had already been expanded in April to include Pablo Iglesias, the Minister of Labour (UP) and the three other deputy prime ministers (all from PSOE). In parallel, the central government pursued a more cooperative approach towards the regions, reintroducing opportunities for adapting measures to the local context of the pandemic. In practice, the return to the 'new normal'[9] after 21 June reduced the role of the central government in managing the pandemic and returned key policy responsibilities to the regional administrations.

The role of experts

In policy terms, the centralisation of executive powers entails necessarily placing boundaries on external sources of specialist knowledge in the decision-making process. In Spain, this was not problematic, since central government has traditionally excluded external experts (from consultancy firms, think tanks, or academia) from public decisions (Parrado 2020, p. 249). However, the nature of the Covid-19 crisis put experts in the limelight during this period, although the actual influence of experts on policymaking depended on their hierarchical position and access to government decision-makers (OECD 2017; see also Halligan 1995). As seen in Table 3, there were three structures at play here.

In a context of policy centralisation, intramural experts working inside the government, like the CCAES, were more likely to have close access to decision makers and, hence, to influence policy decisions, particularly when the technical aspects dominated. From the first moments of the crisis, the CCAES monitored the evolution of the pandemic, issuing daily reports (as of 30 June, 152 reports had been released). The daily press conferences of its director also made him a public celebrity. The CCAES' relevance was also evident in the planning and decision-making during the successive easing phases.

In addition, two public advisory bodies 'at arms' length' from the government were set up after the implementation of the state of emergency. The first (the Covid-19 Scientific Committee) started as an informal group of public experts aimed at providing policy advice to the prime minister. The second was a technical committee focused on advising the preparation of the transition plans for the easing strategy to return to the 'new normal'. Almost all the regional governments also created their own groups of experts on health and economic advice. With respect to these ad hoc advisory committees, the available evidence runs against the idea that decisions fully adjusted to expert input. For instance, one key member of the Covid-19 Scientific Committee publicly declared that the government had not consulted the committee regarding its decision to resume non-essential productive activities. Whether the regional committee created in Madrid in the early moments of the crisis actually played a role in policy decisions has also been brought into question (Mateo 2020).

Another type of expertise came from international public health monitoring schemes: Spain is internationally integrated through liaison between the CCAES, the WHO and the ECDC. The MoH has reiterated that it follows these organisations' recommendations, and the WHO has praised the behaviour of the Spanish government. However, some critical press and opposition parties questioned Spanish authorities' compliance with the guidelines from international organisations, particularly in the first weeks of the pandemic (Mercado 2020).

Finally, the Spanish media have paid a lot of attention to external experts (who are not formally linked to the government), not only as a source of information and opinions about the pandemic, but also to provide a contrasting view of government measures. In some cases, external experts were granted close access to decision-makers, and not only for policy reasons. This was the case with the appointment of Oriol Mitjà, a reputed scientist who, as the personal advisor to the pro-independence regional Catalan president, had strongly criticised the national government's approach to the outset of the pandemic (Segura 2020). Mitjà illustrates the contentious style of expert interventions, as it was frequently the case that governmental expert-based decisions were criticised by external experts or even by other governmental experts, sometimes with inaccurate or contradictory statements.

These public disagreements, and the role of experts in promoting overconfidence among public authorities during the first stages of the crisis, helping to downplay the risk for public health,[10] contributed to lowering citizens'

Table 3. The most relevant groups of experts involved in policy advice to governments in Spain during the first phase of the Covid-19 crisis.

	Type of expert	Composition	Time of creation	Function
CCAES	Intramural	Eight civil servants, including the director	From the beginning	Coordination of the monitoring of public health threats and the elaboration of prevention and reaction plans. Technical assessment to implement the easing phase. Liaison with international public health organisations (WHO, ECDC)
Covid-19 Scientific Committee	Advisory body 'at arm's length'	Six healthcare experts (mostly directors at public health research centres)	March (informally), April (formally)	Policy advice for the prime minister in the management of the lockdown
Technical Committee for Lockdown Easing	Advisory body 'at arm's length'	50 experts (mostly intramural experts, also including public officers) from several disciplines	April	Policy advice for the government to prepare the transition plans to the 'new normal'
Ad hoc committees for the regional governments (except Cantabria and Catalonia)	Advisory body 'at arm's length'	Different composition: predominance of healthcare experts, with economists and other experts occasionally	March–April	Policy advice to deal either with the pandemic (five regions) or with the easing phase (ten regions). Policy advice on economic consequences (Galicia, Murcia, Madrid)

Source: Own elaboration.

confidence in scientists during the pandemic. By the end of April, only 21 per cent of Spanish respondents to an international survey expressed trust in experts and government (Dennison et al. 2020).

The impact of the multilevel state structure

As mentioned in the introduction, Spain's decentralised state structure has strongly shaped the government's response to the Covid-19 crisis. According to the national law on health emergency situations and the design of the system for epidemiological monitoring, the response to health crises should occur in coordination with the regional governments. During the first phase, the multi-level dynamics between the state and the regions were characterised by a combination of an intensive period of centralisation in decision-making with simultaneous coordination efforts to assess the evolution of the pandemic and to implement the policy response. The paradoxical outcome was that, while most regions accepted the need to place the responsibility on the central government, this also resulted in some institutional frictions, which had to do with the very nature of the state of emergency as an instrument that curtailed regional political autonomy. However, in spite of the veto power that regions had during the whole period, it seems that they did not stand in the way of the national government's response (Parrado & Galli 2021, p. 15).

Coordination between national and regional governments took place at the highest level, with two main collective arenas. The more effective was the already mentioned CISNS (formed by the regional and national ministers of health), which held 35 meetings between February and June – compared to only five in 2019.[11] The other was the Conference of Presidents (*Conferencia de Presidentes*), the highest-level coordination body between the national and regional governments, which brings together the Spanish PM and the presidents of the various CAs and autonomous cities. The Conference held 14 meetings during the first phase – while before the pandemic, it had met only six times since its inception in 2004. Below these high bodies, the regional health systems operated mostly as isolated political units, which narrowed the opportunities for interregional collaboration. For instance, regions in a better situation did not usually transfer resources or assistance to nearby regions that faced more complicated situations (Linde et al. 2020, p. 163).

The crisis, then, represented a critical test of the main structures of policy coordination in the Spanish multi-level framework. Although some pitfalls and frictions proved unavoidable (see later), these arenas of coordination contributed satisfactorily to the cohesion of the response and to policy diffusion. Particularly important were the CISNS and its internal body, the Forum of Alerts and Preparedness and Response Plans (*Ponencia de Alertas y Planes de Preparación y Respuesta*, PAPP), consisting of technical representatives of the national and regional health services. The CISNS deliberated and prepared the implementation of the policy decisions; PAPP delivered reports detailing how to conduct this implementation. Examining the content of the CISNS' meetings,[12] we can grasp the evolution of the measures agreed by regional and central governments, which reflect a progressive, smooth intensification of the measures in reaction to the spread of the virus until March (see Table 4).

However, before the centralisation of powers, the CISNS' agreements only applied to a limited number of measures, and only a few of them (suspension of educational activities, limitation of public events) implied the use of compulsory instruments. In contrast, existing evidence demonstrates the heterogeneity of regional responses in the first weeks of the crisis, with CAs adopting different levels of stringency. Besides this, the much less intense intergovernmental coordination in the area of social services, at least at the highest level, must also be noted. For instance, the main coordination body between national and regional

Table 4. Measures agreed within the Interterritorial Council of the Spanish National Health Service in the first weeks of the crisis.

Date of meeting	Agreed measure
4 February	Reassuring citizens that monitoring actions and coordination within the NHS (between state and regional governments) were working properly.
27 February	Increasing the sensitiveness of the monitoring system by widening the definition of 'COVID-19 case', following a ECDC agreement.
3 March	Recommendation that sports competitions with presumed presence of public from risk areas (particularly those in Italy) be held behind closed doors.
9 March	Suspension of face-to-face activities in education and public events above 1,000 people in areas with a strong community transmission (the regions of Madrid and La Rioja, and some areas of the Basque Country), and additional recommendations regarding hygiene, care of the aged, travelling and behaviour in work centres.
10 March	Sports events to be held behind closed doors.
12 March (*)	Generalisation of measures to the whole territory (12 March). In this respect, many regions increased the stringency of the agreed measures.

Source: Own elaboration. (*) The WHO declared the pandemic on 11 March.

ministers in that area (the Territorial Council for Social Services, *Consejo Territorial de Servicios Sociales*, equivalent to the CISNS) did not meet before the state of emergency was declared, and met only twice afterwards (20 March and 18 June).

In the state of emergency period, the centralisation of powers meant complete policymaking authority for the Ministry of Health, yet it needed regional authorities and administrations to implement its decisions. Significantly, the CAs kept their competences in those aspects not limited by the state of emergency. Therefore, a total of 1,375 Covid-related regional legal acts (including 71 decree-laws and laws) were passed during this period. In spite of the increased effectiveness of the response during the period of concentration of powers, frictions between national and subnational authorities were also frequent, particularly once the most critical period of infections had passed.

In the policy dimension, CAs criticised the hierarchical style of decision-making of the national executive, where regional executives were excluded from the policy formulation. This was particularly obvious in the way the Conference of Presidents operated: the prime minister used to announce the main political initiatives unilaterally to the public just before the start of the Conference, at which he simply explained those decisions to the Presidents in more detail. Moreover, regional governments also complained about the design of central government decisions, which were frequently deemed to be 'confusing' or too top-down in their implementation.

For instance, one of the first criticisms faced by the government referred to the MoH's initial decision to centralise the purchase of basic medical supplies: not only was this considered to be ambiguous, but also the MoH lacked the administrative capacity to take on the task. Some days later, the government had to clarify that regions were authorised to make their own purchases. Similarly, during the preparation of the easing plan, some regions criticised the plan's lack of clarity and the use of the province as the territorial unit of implementation instead of smaller areas – a point that was finally taken by the government. During the design and, particularly, the implementation of the easing plan in May, these criticisms increased as the central government still had the last word in deciding which regions would move ahead to the next phase.

These policy frictions between central and regional governments frequently became entangled in political confrontation. Thus, those CAs governed by the main national opposition party, the PP (*Partido Popular* – People's Party), tended to be more critical of the government, though not all with the same intensity. Here, the regional government of Madrid stood out among the other PP regions, particularly during the easing phase. The pro-independence Catalan government also maintained a confrontational stance during most of the state of emergency, in order to reaffirm the political autonomy of the region and its ability to cope with the crisis without the assistance of the central government. Indeed, the speaker of the Catalan government claimed that an independent Catalonia 'would have reacted earlier and would not have had so many deaths' (Ríos 2020).

The political response: personalisation, weak rally-around-the-flag

Parties and parliament

In the years leading up to the Covid-19 outbreak, the Spanish party system had undergone changes resulting in intense party fragmentation and ideological polarisation, with the rise of new radical right-wing and left-wing forces (Orriols & León 2020; Rodríguez-Teruel 2020b). The result had been the increase of adversarial politics, narrowing the boundaries for agreements among political opponents. This trend had been reinforced by the formation of the first multi-party coalition cabinet at the national level in January 2020. In such contexts, parties may have less incentives to collaborate at times of crisis, preferring instead to adopt blame-game strategies to limit their exposure to risk (Hood 2011).

Interestingly, the centralisation of executive powers implemented during the state of emergency did not necessarily imply side-lining the polarised parliament. Even if recent studies have suggested that Covid-19 may have favoured *executive aggrandisement* (Bolleyer & Salát 2021) as the executive sought greater autonomy, there are only limited traces of increased predominance of the executive to the detriment of the parliament in this first phase. On the one hand, parliament drastically reduced its activity for one month (between 14 March and 13 April), cancelling ordinary legislative procedures and sessions dedicated to scrutinising the government. During this period, it actually met only to pass urgent Covid legislation and to renew the state of emergency. On the other hand, the executive continued to employ rapid legislative procedures through royal decree-laws

– an exceptional procedure to pass legislation that substantially reduced the time for parliamentary discussion to less than a month. In 2020, 72.2 per cent of laws passed by the parliament followed this procedure (Table 5).

Nevertheless, some obstacles limited the opportunities for *executive aggrandisement*. First, the minority status and the multiparty composition of the Spanish executive are factors that help to maintain intra-governmental checks and balances (Bolleyer & Salát 2021, p. 1106). Moreover, the prime minister's party attempted (unsuccessfully) to capitalise on the crisis as an opportunity to include the centrist *Ciudadanos* party in the parliamentary coalition. Further, the need to maintain collaboration with the regional governments, some of the more important of which were run by the PP, produced incentives not to alter parliament's policy-making power. Finally, the Constitutional Court also contributed to preserving parliamentary power, after the radical right-wing party Vox appealed to the Court regarding the state of emergency and the decision to reduce parliamentary activity. One year later, the Court declared both decisions to be unconstitutional. In this respect, the judicialisation of politics set limits to executive predominance.

In this context, the prime minister could hardly adopt a 'go it alone' strategy, based on imposing the government's view on the other political actors (Cox & Kernell 1991). Yet Sánchez tried to maintain a central position in this process, particularly in terms of communication. During the state of emergency, he delivered an institutional declaration and 18 press conferences (at least one per week), usually held before the online Conference of Regional Prime Ministers. The national executive held a total of 181 press conferences, in which it answered more than 1,660 questions. Most of the press conferences were headed by the Minister of Health and the CCAES director, often accompanied by members of the police and the military. In his speeches, Sánchez also adopted military rhetoric, with a strong emphasis on national unity, insisting on the international dimension of the crisis, and framing the executive response as a science-based and evidence-led approach (Castillo-Esparcia, Fernández-Souto

Table 5. Types of legislative initiative passed by the Spanish parliament, 2011–2020.

	Laws (ordinary procedure)	Organic laws (reinforced procedure)	Royal Decree-Law (urgent procedure)	Legislative decrees (executive-issued procedure)	Total legislative initiatives
2011	38	12	20	3	73
2012	17	8	29	0	54
2013	27	9	17	1	54
2014	36	8	17	0	61
2015	48	16	12	8	84
2016	0	2	7	1	10
2017	12	1	21	0	34
2018	11	5	28	0	44
2019	5	3	18	0	26
2020	11	3	39	1	54

Source: Own elaboration with data obtained from the Spanish parliament (www.congreso.es).

& Puentes-Rivera 2020). However, the prime minister had to adopt a more pluralistic strategy over time as parliamentary groups became increasingly reluctant to support the renewal of the state of emergency.

Hence, as the toughest moments of the first phase were left behind, political parties made more demands in exchange for their vote. As seen in Table 6, the last three renewals of the state of emergency were passed with narrow majorities, with parties progressively moving towards abstention or rejection. Those parties that had given support to the minority cabinet from the beginning – such as PNV (Partido Nacionalista Vasco – Basque Nationalist Party) and small regionalist forces – combined criticism with loyal support. Some ended by rejecting the state of emergency. This was the case, for example, of the Valencian *Compromís* (Engagement), which rejected the last two votes. The exception was the left-wing Catalan secessionist ERC (Esquerra Republicana de Catalunya – Catalonia's Republican Left), which maintained its position against the centralisation of powers throughout the period and did not support any of the state of emergency votes. Although the measures adopted were not substantially criticised, the political debate focused on the unilateral mode used by the government during the policy centralisation period. In contrast, Ciudadanos was a key source of parliamentary support for the government in the first phase, despite having voted against the investiture of the prime minister two months earlier (Simón 2020, p. 554).

In contrast, the two main opposition parties – PP and Vox – took stronger positions against the government. Both parties criticised the government's competence in crisis management in general and its dramatic effects on the economy, without entering into debates about specific policies. Both also denounced the increase in executive power and the attempts by the government to produce 'a change of regime' (in the words of PP's leader, Pablo Casado). While the PP fluctuated between critical support (in the first three votes) and pragmatic rejection afterwards, Vox supported only the first vote, and expressed increasingly harsh criticism, considering the government to be 'illegitimate' and 'criminal' due to all the Covid-19 deaths. In June, Vox called a vote of no-confidence against the executive, to be held after the summer. Vox's contentious tone forced the PP to adopt an inconsistent position in the last weeks of the lockdown: while the party opposed extending the state of emergency in the national parliament, most of its representatives in regional governments demanded the tough measures taken to control the crisis be maintained.

Interest groups and public opinion

Theoretically, the centralisation of executive powers could have entailed some changes in the societal arena. Potentially, it could have reduced the role of interest groups in the policymaking process to the benefit of the government

Table 6. Votes in the lower chamber to extend the state of emergency.

	Support	Reject	Abstention
1st extension (25 March)	321	0	28
	PSOE, UP, Ciudadanos, Vox, PNV, MP, CC, PRC, TE, UPN, NC, PP, Compromís, Foro	-	ERC, JxC, Bildu, BNG, CUP
2nd extension (9 April)	270	54	25
	PSOE, UP, Ciudadanos, PNV, MP, CC, PRC, TE, UPN, NC, PP, Compromís, Foro	Vox, CUP	ERC, JxC, Bildu
3rd extension (22 April)	269	60	16
	PSOE, UP, Ciudadanos, PNV, MP, CC, PRC, TE, UPN, NC, PP, Compromís, Foro	Vox, CUP, JxC,	ERC, Bildu
4th extension (6 May)	178	75	97
	PSOE, UP, Ciudadanos, PNV, MP, CC, PRC, TE, NC, Compromís,	Vox, ERC, JxC, Foro, CUP	PPBildu, BNG, UPN
5th extension (20 May)	177	162	11
	PSOE, UP, Ciudadanos, PNV, MP, CC, PRC, TE	PP, Vox, ERC, JxC, Foro, CUP, Compromís	Bildu, BNG, UPN, NC
6th extension (3 June)	177	155	18
	PSOE, UP, Ciudadanos, PNV, MP, CC, PRC, TE, NC	PP, Vox, JxC, Foro, CUP, Compromís, UPN	ERC, Bildu, BNG,

Source: www.congreso.es.

Note: Key to political parties: PSOE (Partido Socialista Obrero Español, Spanish Socialist Workers' Party), PP (Partido Popular, People's Party), UP (Unidas Podemos, United We can), MP (Más País, More Country), CC (Coalición Canaria, Canarian Coalition), PRC (Partido Regionalista Cántabro, Cantabrian Regionalist Party), TE (Teruel Existe, Teruel Exists), UPN (Unión del Pueblo Navarro, Navarra People's Union), NC (Nueva Canaria, New Canary), Foro (Forum), JxC (Junts per Catalunya, Together for Catalonia), Bildu (Gather), BNG (Bloque Nacionalista Gallego, Galicia Nationalist Bloc), CUP (Candidatura d'Unitat Popular, Popular Unity Candidacy).

(Hattke & Martin 2020). It might also have intensified leadership personalisation in search of the rally-around-the-flag effect (Kritzinger et al. 2021). As we have previously explained, Prime Minister Sánchez overwhelmingly attempted to seize upon the opportunity to project his leadership and his power over executive decision-making in the first phase.

However, in contrast with the highly polarised political environment, the dialogue between the government and the economic and social actors found stronger incentives for collaboration and agreement on common ground. In particular, the severe consequences of the Covid crisis and the mitigation policies for business and the labour market produced a permanent trade-off between health and economic goals. This had internal and external implications for the executive's management of the pandemic. Sánchez took special care of the government's relationship with the main business organisations (like the CEOE) and the unions, putting in practice what scholars have called 'Covid Corporatism' (Coulter 2020). The previously mentioned ERTE scheme for temporary employment was fundamental to this. Hence, from the early stages of the crisis, the CEOE expressed their support of the government policies, particularly the stimulus package, in exchange for influence over its implementation. Similarly, the dialogue between the unions, the CEOE and the government to maintain the ERTE scheme was continuous and largely without conflict. As a consequence, the main interest groups did not lose access to the executive in the policy-making process, although they did not improve their influence in the parliamentary arena either (Chaqués-Bonafont & Medina 2021).

In terms of public opinion, this strategy of collaboration with the main economic interest groups contributed to reducing the risk of social conflict, despite the severe costs paid by the population – and notwithstanding the low levels of trust in politicians existing during the preceding months. As seen in Table 7, public perception of the political situation was initially worse than public perception of the economy. The crisis produced a general perception of concern across different social groups, which was initially focused on health rather than economics, and entailed wide support for the severe measures adopted. In May, when asked which consequences of the pandemic caused more concern, 52.9 per cent said the effects on health, while 23.3 per cent worried more about the effects on the economy and employment (source: CIS Survey 3,281).

Interestingly, the government's centralisation of power at the expense of the regional administrations received widespread support (three out of four individuals in March, see Table 7), although this cannot be interpreted as significant criticism towards devolution. Later, in September, 72.3 per cent preferred collaboration among different administrations to giving predominant crisis management powers either to the central government (15.8 per cent) or to the regions (4.9 per cent) (source: CIS Survey 3,292).

Table 7. Public opinion during the Covid-19 pandemic in Spain, 2020.

	Jan.	Feb.	March	April	May	June	July	Sept.	Oct.	Nov	Dec
Trust and Rating											
Trust in prime minister (%)	25.9	31.0	28.3	39.0	37.0	33.6	32.6	30.1	29.6	26.9	28.3
Prime minister's rating (0–10, sd)	4.2 (2.6)	4.5 (2.6)	4.4 (2.6)	5.2 (2.6)	5.0 (2.6)	4.9[1] (2.8)	5.1[1] (2.7)	4.6 (2.7)	4.5 (2.8)	4.4 (2.6)	4.4 (2.7)
Leader of the opposition's rating (0–10, sd)	3.3 (2.3)	3.7 (2.3)	3.5 (2.3)	4.2 (2.1)	3.6 (2.0)	3.4[1] (2.1)	3.5[1] (2.1)	3.2 (2.0)	3.1 (2.1)	3.2 (1.9)	3.4 (2.1)
Vox leader's rating (0–10, sd)	2.6 (2.4)	2.8 (2.6)	2.6 (2.4)	2.8 (2.3)	2.4 (2.1)	2.3 (2.1)	2.5 (2.1)	2.3 (2.0)	2.4 (2.2)	2.1 (1.9)	2.3 (2.1)
Economic and Political Assessment											
Bad assessment of the economic situation (%)	46.5	46.0	40.3	32.9[2]	40.5[2]	86.4	73.8	78.9	86.7	88.3	85.0
Bad assessment of the political situation (%)	62.6	57.0	53.4	-	-	-	-	-	-	-	-
Opinions on Government Response to COVID-19											
Trust in government's management of the crisis (%)	-	-		46.5	46.0	-	-	31.6	-	-	-
Central government should take the decisions to deal with the crisis (%)	-	-	73.3	55.9	-	-	-	15.8[3]	16.6	18.1	16.7
Regional governments should take the decisions to deal with the crisis (%)	-	-	20.7	36.6	-	-	-	4.9[3]	5.9	5.2	6.3
Both levels of governments should collaborate (%)	-	-	-	-	-	-	-	72.3[3]	69.1	69.3	70.3

Source: Own elaboration with data obtained from the CIS Databank (http://www.analisis.cis.es).

Note: (1) The wording of the question was changed in April ('How would you rate these political leaders according to what they are doing regarding the Covid-19'). (2) The wording of the question was changed in April ('Letting aside the Covid-19, how would you assess the economic situation in Spain'). (3) Preference about which level of government should take decisions were separated in March and April, and then merged in one single question after September.

In this context, the government benefited from a temporary 'rally around the flag' effect, which increased trust in the prime minister, in contrast with opposition leaders. Asked about political accountability, 87.8 per cent of respondents (in April) and 74.9 per cent (in May) said it was time to support the central government and postpone political criticism (source: CIS Survey 3,279/3,281). Accordingly, 95.2 per cent of the individuals considered that the measures adopted by the government to deal with the pandemic had been necessary, and 60.4 per cent defended the maintenance of a strict lockdown for longer if needed (source: CIS Survey 3,281).

However, the personalisation of the government response did not produce a substantial improvement in the prime minister's support. Although Sánchez was the only politician with public approval during the lockdown (Table 7), this effect quickly vanished by the end of the period. In contrast, the bad rating of the main opposition leader, Pablo Casado, substantially below Sánchez, made evident the lack of support for his confrontational style of opposition. Finally, Santiago Abascal, leader of Vox, remained the lowest rated leader, without any significant variation over the period. Similarly, the ruling parties, PSOE and UP, maintained their electoral support across the period,[13] while the official opposition PP benefited from Ciudadanos' collapse and Vox's stagnation in the polls.

Conclusions

In the first phase of the Covid-19 pandemic, Spain was often cited as a case of a failed governmental response to the crisis because of the high number of deaths and infections. This article has analysed this response, arguing that the executive did not act substantively differently, in terms of timing or stringency, to other comparable countries in continental or Southern Europe. We have seen that the combination of some contingent factors and moderate state capacities quickly overcame the government response, led by a government and political actors who were too self-confident. In particular, structural factors like the country's exposure to this type of threat, poor capacities in virus detection (and the difficulty of providing accurate diagnostics during the crisis' first weeks), and the structural problems in the nursing and care home sector all played a role in turning the containment strategy into a policy failure.

In contrast, once the containment phase was replaced by a mitigation strategy, the government's centralisation of powers enabled it to reconfigure the situation through a more cohesive response. This reaction was controversial in the context of a recently formed cabinet coalition, in a multi-level political system where regional governments kept their competences to implement health policies, and in a context of deep parliamentary polarisation. However, we have seen that the executive and the prime minister quickly adapted to the situation, especially after the worst period of the first phase.

Power concentration also had limitations in terms of the policy-making process (too focused on intramural expertise, lacking horizontal coordination between regions, and with some evidence of departmentalism in the national cabinet). But these problems cannot adequately account for the initial impact after the outbreak, since they were fixed factors that were also present in the following stages of the pandemic, when Spain's Covid situation improved. Our analysis may even suggest that the government's response contributed to countervail the more vulnerable capacities, particularly after implementing a more pluralistic approach with the regions, once their powers were fully restored. This supports those analyses which defend coordination and fragmented authority as sources of successful responses to the pandemic (Hattke & Martin 2020).

In political terms, the results are consistent with this interpretation. The complicated context of the first phase became a successful test for the new cabinet coalition. For instance, in internal policy disagreements the divide was not strictly partisan, since some key PSOE ministers also backed UP positions against the economic ministers. Besides, the intense political polarisation also contributed to limiting executive predominance, and paradoxically curbed the potential negative effects of the crisis on the government's support. It is interesting to note that the polls conducted during the first semester of 2020 were the most stable since the breakthrough of new political forces in the Spanish party system in 2014. Nevertheless, the political tensions between the national government and the Madrid region, ruled by the PP and Ciudadanos, combined with the competitive incentives produced by the de-escalation process, anticipated problems that would arise in the following waves of the pandemic.

What happened after the first phase?

Although Spain had experienced five new Covid-19 waves by the end of 2021, their health impact was less severe than elsewhere in Southern Europe. Countries that appeared more successful in the first wave, like Portugal or Greece, had a worse time of it afterwards. In Spain, each wave resulted in fewer deaths than the first, despite each having a higher number of infections. This suggests that the data on the first phase underestimated the real impact. In the subsequent phases, changes were implemented in the government's response. The main difference was the end of the power concentration strategy, even under the new state of emergency.

In policy terms, the end of the first lockdown opened the door to a period that was labelled 'co-governance' – coordination between the national and regional levels. Although this coordination continued to operate through the CISNS, the new approach placed most of the responsibility for designing measures in the hands of the regional executives. Meanwhile, the national government focused on the allocation of resources among the regional administrations, in parallel with efforts to ensure some degree of cohesiveness among the different measures which the regions adopted. In the absence of the legal coverage of the state of emergency, the judiciary achieved critical influence, since the regional courts had to approve any measures that could curtail individual rights. In some decisions, this led to a clash between the executive's initiatives based on health expertise and the judiciary's interpretations aimed at preserving fundamental rights. In order to reduce problems with the judiciary, the national government approved a second state of emergency in October 2020, with Vox voting against. This time, the new decree of emergency was implemented for a period of six months, in order to reduce the political costs of each renewal. But it did not include any reallocation of powers among administrations, as the only goal was to provide a constitutional cover for the regional restrictive measures. The Constitutional Court also gained relevance with its decisions to declare the two states of emergency unconstitutional, though this did not have real consequences as the rulings came after the end of these periods.

The consequence of the end of the power concentration strategy was the implementation of alternative responses launched at the regional level. Madrid took the lead (sometimes in isolation) in opposing restrictive measures proposed by the national government. In this respect, the management of the Covid-19 crisis became instrumental for Madrid's regional president from the PP, Isabel Díaz Ayuso, in her attempt to gain political exposure at the national level, to the detriment of Casado, the national party leader.

The more recent waves of the pandemic were managed in a more contentious political context, starting with the failed no-confidence vote against the executive called by Vox and held on 22 September 2020. Despite attempts to broaden the executive's parliamentary support, the PSOE finally had to give up its efforts to include Ciudadanos as a stable partner and returned to the original coalition that had voted for the investiture of Sánchez. The subsequent phases of the pandemic saw the decline of Ciudadanos' support in the opinion polls, to the benefit of PP. In this respect, mainstream political parties were not punished electorally for their management of the pandemic. In the four regional elections held after the first wave (Galicia and the Basque Country in July 2020, Catalonia in February 2021, and Madrid in May 2021), the ruling parties largely maintained their electoral support and were able to keep their positions in the regional executives.

Notes

1. See, among others, Cheibub, Hong and Przeworski (2020), Engler et al. (2021), Maor and Howlett (2020), Sebhatu et al. (2020) and Toshkov, Carroll and Yesilkagit (2021).

2. For instance, Spain ranked 15th in the 2019 Global Health Security Index; 19th in the 2016 Health Access and Quality Index (The Lancet); 1st in the Health Pillar of the 2019 Global Competitive Report; 19th in health expenditure (as a share of GDP) in 2019 (OECD); 16th in critical care beds (2012); 3rd in the 2018 Bloomberg Health Care Efficiency Index; and the 1st in the 2019 Bloomberg Healthiest Country Index. Sources: GHS Index (https://www.ghsindex.org), The Lancet (https://www.thelancet.com/journals/lancet/article/PIIS0140-6736%2818%2930994-2/fulltext#seccestitle190%20), WEF (http://www3.weforum.org/docs/WEF_TheGlobalCompetitivenessReport2019.pdf), beds (Rhodes et al. 2012); Bloomber indexes https://www.bloomberg.com/news/articles/2018-09-19/u-s-near-bottom-of-health-index-hong-kong-and-singapore-at-top and https://www.bloomberg.com/news/articles/2019-02-24/spain-tops-italy-as-world-s-healthiest-nation-while-u-s-slips (last accessed 12th August 2021).
3. See in this volume Kemahlıoğlu and Yeğen (2021), Ladi, Angelou and Panagiotatou (2021), Silva, Costa and Moniz (2021) and Vicentini and Galanti (2021).
4. Source: Eurostat's database (https://ec.europa.eu/eurostat/). Accessed in 10 July 2020.
5. Unless any other source is mentioned, this and the following figures in this section correspond to the data provided by the CCAES (MoH) to the ECDC and available at this organisation's website by 12 August 2020 (https://www.ecdc.europa.eu/en/publications-data/download-todays-data-geographic-distribution-Covid-19-cases-worldwide). We discuss the reliability of these figures below.
6. Due to changes in data gathering (see below) until 10 May the percentage was 63 percent. Between 11 May and 15 July the corresponding figure is 65 per cent.
7. Spanish Royal Decree 463/2020, of March 14th, 2020, declaring the state of emergency in Spain to manage the health crisis situation caused by Covid-19.
8. It must be noted that the use of the 'state of emergency' to order policies constraining some citizens' freedoms was intensively debated among lawyers during these months, particularly between those defending the measures adopted, others who argued a 'state of exception' was needed (as the Constitutional Court finally ruled) and those arguing against the unnecessary accumulation of power in the hands of the government.
9. The *new normal* was defined by the Spanish Decree-law 21/2020 on urgent prevention, containment and coordination measures to deal with the health crisis caused by Covid-19 which was passed by the cabinet on 9 June and ratified by the parliament on 25 June.
10. See, for instance, the public statement by the director of the CCAES on 31 January, who maintained that 'Spain will have at most some few diagnosed cases' (ABC 2020), or that of the later advisor of the Catalan president on 11 February, who stated that 'The coronavirus causes alarm because it's new, not because it's serious' (La Vanguardia 2020).
11. See the CISNS's website (https://www.mscbs.gob.es/organizacion/consejoInterterri/ordenes.htm, accessed 31/08/2020). MPFTF (Ministerio de Política Territorial y Función Pública) (2020) Meetings of Sector Conferences, https://www.mptfp.gob.es/portal/politica-territorial/autonomica/coop_autonomica/Conf_Sectoriales/Conf_Sect_Reuniones.html, accessed 07/09/2020.
12. The minutes are still not available at the time of writing. We have relied mostly on the Ministry of Health press releases after the meetings (available at https://www.mscbs.gob.es/profesionales/cargarNotas.do?time=1583017200000, accessed 31/08/2020), public declarations by the minister, and newspapers' accounts of these meetings.

13. See the series of surveys published in Spain during the first semester of 2020 in https://elelectoral.com/encuesta-media/ (last accessed: 15 October 2020).

Acknowledgments

The authors thank the editors and the two reviewers for their valuable comments.

Disclosure statement

No potential conflict of interest was reported by the author(s).

Funding

This work was supported by Ministerio de Ciencia, Innovación y Universidades [CONESPOL Project PGC2018-098319-B-C21 and PGC2018-098319-B-C22].

ORCID

Juan Rodríguez Teruel http://orcid.org/0000-0002-7112-986X
Eloísa del Pino http://orcid.org/0000-0001-5497-1302
José Real-Dato http://orcid.org/0000-0001-9734-0850

References

ABC (2020) 'España no va a tener, como mucho, más allá de algún caso diagnosticado', January 31, available online at: https://www.abc.es/espana/abci-fernando-simon-espana-no-tener-como-mucho-mas-alla-algun-caso-diagnosticado-202001311357_video.html.

Alonso, J. M., Clifton, J. & Díaz-Fuentes, D. (2015) 'The impact of new public management on efficiency: an analysis of Madrid's hospitals', *Health Policy*, vol. 119, no. 3, pp. 333–340.

Boin, A., t' Hart, P., Stern, E. & Sundelius, B. (2005) *The Politics of Crisis Management: Public Leadership under Pressure*, Cambridge University Press, Cambridge.

Bolleyer, N. & Salát, O. (2021) 'Parliaments in times of crisis: COVID-19, populism and executive dominance', *West European Politics*, vol. 44, no. 5–6, pp. 1103–1128.

Capano, G. (2020) 'Policy design and state capacity in the COVID-19 emergency in Italy: if you are not prepared for the (un)expected, you can be only what you already are', *Policy and Society*, vol. 39, no. 3, pp. 326–344.

Castillo-Esparcia, A., Fernández-Souto, A.-B. & Puentes-Rivera, I. (2020) 'Comunicación política y Covid-19. Estrategias del Gobierno de España', *El Profesional de la Información*, vol. 29, no. 4, pp. 1–22.

CCAES (2020) 'Neumonía por nuevo coronavirus SARS-CoV-2 (24 February)', Madrid, available online at: https://www.mscbs.gob.es/profesionales/saludPublica/ccayes/alertasActual/nCov/documentos/Evaluacion_de_riesgo_y_medidas.pdf.

Chaqués-Bonafont, L. & Medina, I. (2021) 'The representation of business interests during the COVID-19 pandemic in Spain', *Revista Espalola de Ciencia Política*, no. 57, pp. 21–44.

Cheibub, J. A., Hong, J. Y. & Przeworski, A. (2020) 'Rights and deaths: government reactions to the pandemic', *SSRN Electronic Journal*. doi:10.2139/ssrn.3645410.

CNE (2020) 'Vigilancia de los excesos de mortalidad por todas las causas. MoMo', *Situación a 13 de agosto de 2020*, Madrid.

Coulter, S. (2020) 'All in it together? The unlikely rebirth of Covid corporatism', *Political Quarterly*, vol. 91, no. 3, pp. 534–541.

Cox, G. W. & Kernell, S. (1991) 'Conclusion', in *The Politics of Divided Government*, eds G. W. Cox & S. Kernell, Westview Press, Boulder, CO, pp. 239–249.

del Pino, E. (2020) 'Welfare state', in The Oxford Handbook of Spanish Politics, eds D. Muro & I. Lago, Oxford University Press, Oxford, pp. 525–541.

del Pino, E., Moreno-Fuentes, F. J., Cruz-Martínez, G., Hernánez-moreno, J., Moreno, L., Pereira-Puga, M. & Perna, R. (2020) Gestión Institucional y Organizativa de las Residencias de Personas Mayores y COVID-19: dificultades y aprendizajes, CSIC, Madrid.

Dennison, S., Zerka, P., Ciulla, W. M., Coratella, T., Franco, L., Hobbs, C., Puglierin, J., Riedel, M., Söderström, J., Sørensen, C., Tcherneva, V. & Torreblanca, J. I. (2020) 'Together in Trauma: Europeans and the World after Covid-19', European Council on Foreign Affairs Policy Brief, available online at: https://ecfr.eu/publication/together_in_trauma_europeans_and_the_world_after_covid_19/.

Dubin, K. A. (2021) 'Spain's response to Covid-19', in *Coronavirus Politics. The Comparatuve Politics and Policy of Covid-19*, eds S. L. Greer, E. J. King, E. M. da Fonseca & A. Peralta-Santos, University of Michigan Press, Ann Arbor, pp. 339–360.

The Economist (2020) 'Spain's poisonous politics have worsened the pandemic and the economy', 3 October.

Engler, S., Brunner, P., Loviat, R., Abou-Chadi, T., Leeman, L., Glaser, A. & Kübler, D. (2021) 'Democracy in times of the pandemic: explaining the variation of public health policies against Covid-19 across European democracies', *West European Politics*, vol. 44, no. 5–6, pp. 1077–1102.

Fleischer, J. & Parrado, S. (2010) 'Power distribution in ambiguous times: the effects of the financial crisis on executive', *Der Modern Staat*, vol. 3, no. 2, pp. 361–376.

Gallego, R., Barbieri, N. & González, S. (2017) 'Explaining cross-regional policy variation in public sector reform: institutions and change actors in the health sector in Spain', *Public Policy and Administration*, vol. 32, no. 1, pp. 24–44.

Gómez-Carballa, A., Bello, X., Pardo-Seco, J., Luisa Pérez del Molino, M., Martinón-Torres, F. & Salas, A. (2020) 'Phylogeography of SARS-CoV-2 pandemic in Spain: a story of multiple introductions, micro-geographic stratification, founder effects, and super-spreaders', *Zoological Research*, vol. 41, pp. 1–16.

Greer, S. L., King, E. J. & da Fonseca, E. M. (2021) 'Introduction. Explaining pandemi response', in *Coronavirus Politics. The Comparatuve Politics and Policy of COVID 19*, eds S. L. Greer, E. J. King, E. M. da Fonseca & A. Peralta-Santos, University of Michigan Press, Ann Arbor, pp. 3–33.

Hale, T., Anania, J., Angrist, N., Boby, T., Cameron-Blake, E., Di Folco, M., Ellen, L., Goldszmidt, R., Hallas, L., Klra, B., Luciano, M., Majumadar, S., Nagesh, R., Petherick, A., Phillips, T., Tatlow, H., Webster, S., Wood, A. & Zhang, Y. (2021a) 'Variation in government responses to COVID-19, version 12.0', *BSG Working Paper Series*, available online at: https://covidtracker.bsg.ox.ac.uk/stringency-scatter.

Hale, T., Webster, S., Petherick, A., Phillips, T. & Kira, B. (2021b) *Oxford COVID-19 Government Response Tracker*, Blavatnik School of Government, Oxford.

Halligan, J. (1995) 'Policy advice and the public service', in *Governance in a Changing Environment*, eds B. G. Peters & D. J. Savoie, Canadian Centre for Management Development/McGill-Queen's University Press, Montreal, pp. 138–172.

Hattke, F. & Martin, H. (2020) 'Collective action during the Covid-19 pandemic: the case of Germany's fragmented authority', *Administrative Theory and Praxis*, vol. 42, no. 4, pp. 614–632.

Hood, C. (2011) *The Blame Game. Spin, Bureaucracy, and Self-Preservation in Government*, Princeton University Press, Princeton, NJ.

Kemahlıoğlu, Ö. & Yeğen, O. (2021) 'Surviving the Covid-19 pandemic under right-wing populist rule: Turkey in the first phase', *South European Society & Politics*, pp. 1–30. doi:10.1080/13608746.2021.1985497

Kritzinger, S., Foucault, M., Lachat, R., Partheymüller, J., Plescia, C. & Brouard, S. (2021) '"Rally round the flag": the Covid-19 crisis and trust in the national government', *West European Politics*, vol. 44, no. 5–6, pp. 1205–1231.

La Vanguardia (2020) 'El coronavirus crea alarma porque es nuevo, no por su gravedad, según experto', February 11, available online at: https://www.lavanguardia.com/vida/20200211/473455536988/el-coronavirus-crea-alarma-porque-es-nuevo-no-por-su-gravedad-segun-experto.html.

Ladi, S., Angelou, A. & Panagiotatou, D. (2021) 'Regaining trust: evidence-informed policy-making during the first phase of the Covid-19 crisis in Greece', *South European Society & Politics*, pp. 1–26. doi:10.1080/13608746.2021.1983932

Linde, P., Rejón, R., Sánchez, C. & Sevillano, E. (2020) *Estado de alarma. Los cien días que pusieron a España en jaque*, Península, Barcelona.

Lodge, M. & Wegrich, K. (eds.) (2012) *Executive Politics in Times of Crisis*, Palgrave Macmillan, Basingstoke.

Malandrino, A. & Demichelis, E. (2020) 'Conflict in decision making and variation in public administration outcomes in Italy during the Covid-19 crisis', *European Policy Analysis*, vol. 6, no. 2, pp. 138–146.

Maor, M. & Howlett, M. (2020) 'Explaining variations in state Covid-19 responses: psychological, institutional, and strategic factors in governance and public policy-making', *Policy Design and Practice*, vol. 3, no. 3, pp. 228–241.

Mateo, J. J. (2020) 'El grupo de expertos convocado en enero por Ayuso para luchar contra el coronavirus ya está inactivo', *El País*, May 19.

Mercado, F. (2020) *Una pandemia de errores*, Deusto, Barcelona.

Ministry of Finance (2021) 'Mecanismos de financiación de las Comunidades Autónomas y las Entidades Locales', available online at: https://www.hacienda.gob.es/es-ES/CDI/Paginas/SistemasFinanciacionDeuda/InformacionCCAAs/Mecanismosdefinanciacion.aspx.

Ministry of Social Rights and Agenda 2030 (2020) Informe del Grupo de Trabajo 'Covid-19 y residencias', version 24 November 2020 (final), Madrid, available online at: https://www.imserso.es/InterPresent2/groups/imserso/documents/binario/gtcovid_residencias_vf.pdf.

Molina, I., Otero-Iglesias, M. & Martínez, J. P. (2020) Has Spain's Management of Covid-19 Been a Failure? Errors, Lessons and Recommendations, No. 16, Real Instituto Elcano, Madrid.

Moon, M. J. (2020) 'Fighting Covid-19 with agility, transparency, and participation: wicked policy problems and new governance challenges', Public Administration Review, vol. 80, no. 4, pp. 651–656.

OECD (2017) *Policy Advisory Systems: Supporting Good Governance and Sound Public Decision Making*, OECD, Paris.

Orriols, L. & León, S. (2020) 'Looking for affective polarisation in Spain: PSOE and Podemos from conflict to coalition', *South European Society & Politics*, vol. 25, no. 3–4, pp. 351–379.

Parrado, S. (2020) 'Public administration and its problem-solving capacities', in The Oxford Handbook of Spanish Politics, eds D. Muro & I. Lago, Oxford University Press, Oxford, pp. 240–257.

Parrado, S. & Galli, D. (2021) 'Intergovernmental veto points in crisis management: Italy and Spain facing the Covid-19 pandemic', *International Review of Administrative Sciences*, vol. 87, no. 3, pp. 576–592.

RENAVE (2020) *Report Panel Covid-19 (Daily update*), Madrid, available online at: https://cnecovid.isciii.es/covid19/#documentación-y-datos.

Rhodes, A., Ferdinande, P., Flaatten, H., Guidet, B., Metnitz, P. G. & Moreno, R. P. (2012) 'The variability of critical care bed numbers in Europe' Intensive Care Medicine, vol. 38, no. 10, pp. 1647–1653.

Ríos, P. (2020), 'La Generalitat sostiene que en una Cataluña independiente "no habría tantos muertos"', *El País*, April 20.

Rodríguez-Teruel, J. (2020a) 'Executive politics in Spain', in *The Oxford Handbook of Spanish Politics*, eds D. Muro & I. Lago, Oxford University Press, pp. 189–209.

Rodríguez-Teruel, J. (2020b) 'Polarisation and electoral realignment: the case of the right-wing parties in Spain', *South European Society & Politics*, vol. 25, no. 3–4, pp. 381–410.

Rozenblum, S. D. (2021) 'France's multidimensional Covid-19 response. Ad hoc committees and the sidelining of public health agencies', in *Coronavirus Politics. The Comparative Politics and Policy of COVID.19*, eds S. L. Greer, E. J. King, E. Massard-da-Fonseca & A. Peralta-Santos, University of Michigan Press, Ann Arbor, pp. 264–279.

Sebhatu, A., Wennberg, K., Arora-Jonsson, S. & Lindberg, S. I. (2020) 'Explaining the homogeneous diffusion of Covid-19 nonpharmaceutical interventions across heterogeneous countries', *Proceedings of the National Academy of Sciences of the United States of America*, vol. 117, no. 35, pp. 21201–21208.

Segura, C. (2020) 'Oriol Mitjà, el científico de cabecera deTorra', *El País*, April 11

Silva, P., Costa, E. & Moniz, J. (2021) 'A Portuguese miracle: the politics of the first phase of Covid-19 in Portugal', *South European Society & Politics*, pp. 1–29. doi:10.1080/13608746.2021.1979741

Simón, P. (2020) 'Two-bloc logic, polarisation and coalition government: the November 2019 general election in Spain', *South European Society & Politics*, vol. 25, no. 3–4, pp. 533–563.

Toshkov, D., Carroll, B. & Yesilkagit, K. (2021) 'Government capacity, societal trust or party preferences: what accounts for the variety of national policy responses to the COVID-19 pandemic in Europe?', *Journal of European Public Policy*, pp. 1–20. doi:10.1080/13501763.2021.1928270

Vicentini, G. & Galanti, M. T. (2021) 'Italy, the sick man of Europe: policy response, experts and public opinion in the first phase of Covid-19', *South European Society & Politics*, pp. 1–27. doi:10.1080/13608746.2021.1940582

Waugh, W. L. & Streib, G. (2014) 'Collaboration and leadership for effective emergency management', *Public Administration Review*, vol. 66, no. S1, pp. 131–140.

WHO (2005) International health regulations, World Health Organization, Geneva, 3rd ed.

Williams, G. A., Rajan, S. & Cylus, J. D. (2021) 'Covid-19 in the United Kingdom. How austerity and a loss of state capacity undermined the crisis response', in *Coronavirus Politics. The Comparative Politics and Policy of Covid-19*, eds S. L. Greer, E. J. King, E. Massard-da-Fonseca & A. Peralta-Santos, University of Michigan Press, Ann Arbor, pp. 215–234.

A Portuguese Miracle: The Politics of the First Phase of Covid-19 in Portugal

Patrícia Silva, Edna Costa and João Moniz

ABSTRACT

Facing the first phase of the pandemic with exceptionally low casualties, Portugal was internationally praised as an outstanding example, particularly when compared to other Southern European countries. This article depicts how the pandemic crisis erupted in Portugal and how the Socialist government, the opposition and, to an important degree, the head of state responded to its demands, curbing the initial spread of the infection. The government ensured considerable levels of support from citizens and from other parties. The official opposition maintained its pragmatic and conciliatory tone during the confinement stages of the pandemic. It is argued that lower levels of political polarisation and a climate of cross-party collaboration are key factors in understanding the 'Portuguese miracle'.

At the beginning of March 2020, one month after coronavirus appeared in Spain and Italy, Portugal registered its first cases of the disease. Two days after reporting the first death, Portugal implemented tighter restrictions and enacted the state of emergency as a strategy to avoid further spread of the virus. Eight weeks after the first case, its coronavirus mortality rate hovered just above 4 per cent (Statista 2020), a figure considerably lower than the figures reported in neighbouring countries – particularly Italy and Spain which reported the highest fatality rates in the region (Moreira et al. 2021).

As the devastating scenes in Europe unfolded, Portugal scrambled to avoid the same course. While the timing and geographic position of the country allowed for a rapid response, these are certainly only two among other relevant variables that explain the evolution of the pandemic. In this article we seek to describe and explain the political conditions that determined its development in Portugal.

The pandemic erupted in a country with political stability and a welfare system under stress. As a country hard-hit during the eurozone crises, Portugal presented a health system with low capacity and efficiency, particularly regarding long-term care facilities. The positive Portuguese macroeconomic condition had been fuelled by the rampant growth in tourism, which faced immediate and unprecedent shock. Moreover, as the preceding legislature of 2015–2019 wore on, the tension between ending austerity and maintaining budgetary consolidation also became evident, reflected *inter alia* in a wave of strikes, particularly in the health sector – one of the areas most affected by low levels of public investment. While seeking to contain discontent, the Socialist government often resisted meeting public sector workers' demands, despite protracted and very public strikes by key sectors. In the 2019 election, the macroeconomic scenario benefitted the governing socialists, who emerged as the leading party, although with modest electoral gains. Falling short of a majority, prime minister António Costa now formed a minority government, without the formal parliamentary entente enjoyed during the preceding mandate.

The political scenario and, particularly, the inefficient resource allocation in the public sector and the associated health access inequalities would provide a difficult setting to deal with a global pandemic. However, by having faced the first phase of the pandemic with exceptionally low casualties, Portugal emerged as an outstanding example, particularly when compared to other South European countries, considering the number of cases of the coronavirus disease and the case fatality rate. Beyond the proactiveness and centralisation of policy responses – focused on flattening the epidemic curve to avoid overloading hospitals and to preserve jobs and family income – party politics and the social dynamics were also relevant variables. In fact, the low levels of political polarisation over the government's handling of the sanitary crisis and a climate of cross-party collaboration – strongly influenced by the President of the Republic (PR) – suggest that the Portuguese handling of the first stages of the pandemic resonates the 'rally-round-the-flag' effect.

The article seeks to present and discuss the first phase of the Covid-19 crisis, centred around the events and policies from March to June 2020, when Southern Europe seemed to have controlled the spread of the virus (Moreira et al. 2021). The article is divided into three sections. The first begins by charting how prepared the country was to deal with the spread of the virus and depicts how the pandemic unfolded during its first phase. Then, it presents the policy response to the pandemic, which has proven to be a challenging task and a strong reminder of the hardships experienced during the Great Recession. The third section discusses the party politics of Covid-19 in Portugal and the social dynamics of the crisis and how it echoes the 'rally-round-the-flag' effect.

Country background

Crisis preparedness and state capacity

António Costa's first mandate (2015–2019) – and the unprecedented cooperation between the parties on the left, dubbed the Geringonça (Contraption) – sought to rollback austerity. Macroeconomic indicators prove this goal was successfully achieved: the yearly GDP growth rate was kept well above two per cent and unemployment rates were low (6.5 per cent in 2019) (Eurostat 2020b). This stands in stark contrast with the preceding two legislatures, under bailout conditionality. The budget deficit averaged 2.4 per cent in the years 2015–2018, with a record low of 0.4 per cent in 2018 – the lowest within the democratic period (Eurostat 2020a).

The PS (Partido Socialista – Socialist Party) was largely credited with the macroeconomic achievements and was rewarded at the 2019 elections, reinforcing its position in Parliament, and forming a minority government. While the entente between the PS, the PCP (Partido Comunista Português – Portuguese Communist Party) and the BE (Bloco de Esquerda – Left Bloc) was popular, it was not re-established after the 2019 election. Nonetheless, unlike the intense government formation processes in Spain and Italy, the political situation in Portugal was relatively stable before the pandemic crisis. To some extent, the conciliatory and pragmatic tone of the leader of the main party in opposition, the PSD (Partido Social Democrata – Social Democratic Party) also explains this stability. Despite internal conflict, Rui Rio collaborated with the government by supporting important structural reforms.

The government's strategy for fiscal consolidation was, however, achieved through a reduction in public sector investments (Moury, de Giorgi & Barros 2020). The sovereign debt crisis acted as a catalyst for structural reforms targeting specific deficiencies of the Portuguese healthcare system, which accelerated the pace and enlarged the scope of market-enhancing reforms (Pereirinha & Murteira 2019). The consequences for the NHS (National Health Service) were clearly negative.

The NHS was reported as ill-equipped and underfunded and the average government expenditure declined after 2015. Whereas across OECD countries, a substantial proportion of health spending is funded through the state's budget (73.8 per cent), this percentage (66.5 per cent) is lower in Portugal, which emerges as the \EU country with the third lowest share of public healthcare spending. Critical care capacity measured by the number of intensive care beds available, has also been identified as a major pitfall. The country has the lowest ratio of beds per 100,000 inhabitants in Europe: a ratio of 4.2, considerably lower than the EU average (11.5) (Rhodes et al. 2012, p. 1651). Additionally, following the Memorandum of Understanding signed with the Troika of international lenders in 2011, the Health Service witnessed a sharp increase in its debts to suppliers, threatening the quality of the health supply (Oliveira 2019), with cuts in operational costs and drugs purchases (Pereirinha & Murteira 2016). Austerity policies also had a negative impact on human resources and lack of specialisation (Ministério da Saúde 2019). Finally, fiscal consolidation measures through hiring and salary freezes led to the demotivation of health professionals and to a significant series of strikes.

Strict austerity in the health sector also stimulated the transfer of health care activities to non-profit institutions, traditionally relevant players in social care activities, particularly in long-term care (Pereirinha & Murteira 2019). Despite the existence of long-term care facilities outside the network, mainly operated by the private sector, there is a clear insufficient national coverage (Joël, Dufour-Kippelen & Samitca 2010).

While the supply side of care had been suffering from structural problems, the health system faced considerable demand, with Portugal standing out as the major emergency services user per capita within the OECD (Santana et al. 2020). This pattern resulted in citizens increasingly concerned about its response capacity. On the verge of the pandemic, 52.2 per cent of respondents perceived the national health service as incapable of containing the infection and protecting citizens (Aximage 2020).

Throughout the first phase of the pandemic crisis, the prime minister (PM) consistently stressed that the NHS was technically prepared to face the pandemic, but health professionals regularly reported otherwise (Bastos 2020). The shortage of both personal protective equipment and swabs used to test patients was also reported, thus limiting testing capacity, particularly in the most affected regions. The SNS24 health line, the primary channel for potentially infected patients into the NHS, registered an exponential increase in communications, for which there was insufficient human resources capacity (Campos & Carvalho 2020).

The scarcity of resources is not exclusive to the NHS. While Portuguese government effectiveness – following the World Bank's indicator on the quality of policy-making formulation and implementation – is in line with other EU economies, it is the inefficient resource allocation that has been identified as the major issue in the public sector (Baer, Dias & Duarte 2013).

The evolution of Covid-19 in Portugal

The first Portuguese patient was diagnosed on 2 March 2020 and the first death occurred 14 days later. As depicted in Figure 1 the number of cases and reported daily deaths increased until the third renewal of the state of emergency, when a declining trend became perceptible.

At the beginning of May, with a total of 1,007 deaths reported, a relatively high testing rate and sufficient supplies of protective equipment, authorities decided to gradually lift lockdown measures. As depicted in Table 1, the first and second deconfinement stages ran smoothly, with declining levels of deaths and cases, a pattern that did not hold during the latter stage.

Long-term care facilities were one of the central concerns. During the first phase, under 10 per cent of the retirement homes reported cases of infection (Visão 2020a). With an overall number of 1,512 deaths, Portugal faced the first phase of the pandemic with a comparatively low death-toll, backed up by one of

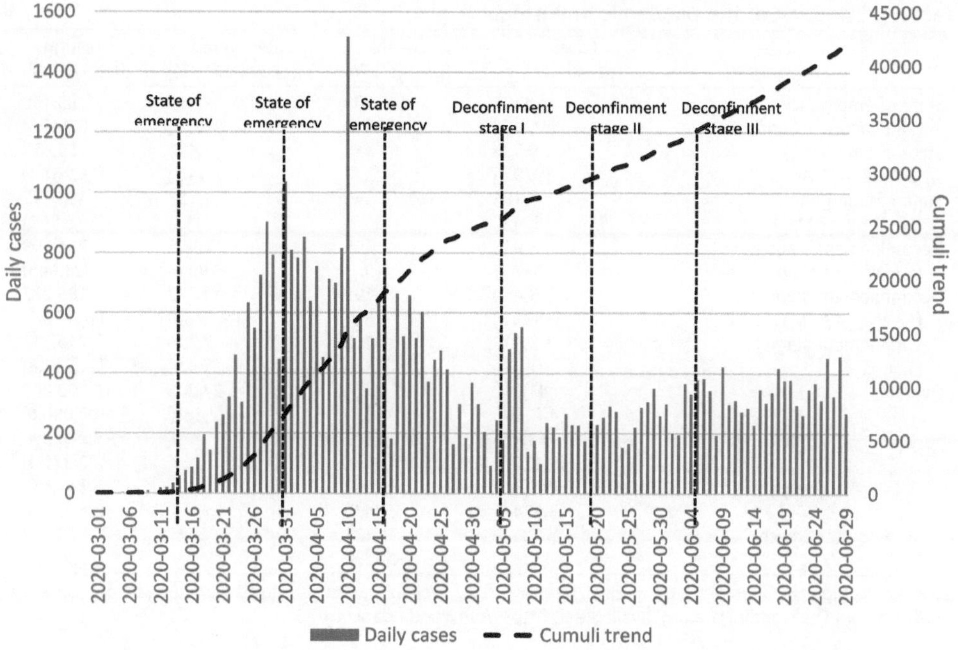

a - Daily evolution of Covid-19 cases and cumuli trend.in Portugal, March-June 2020

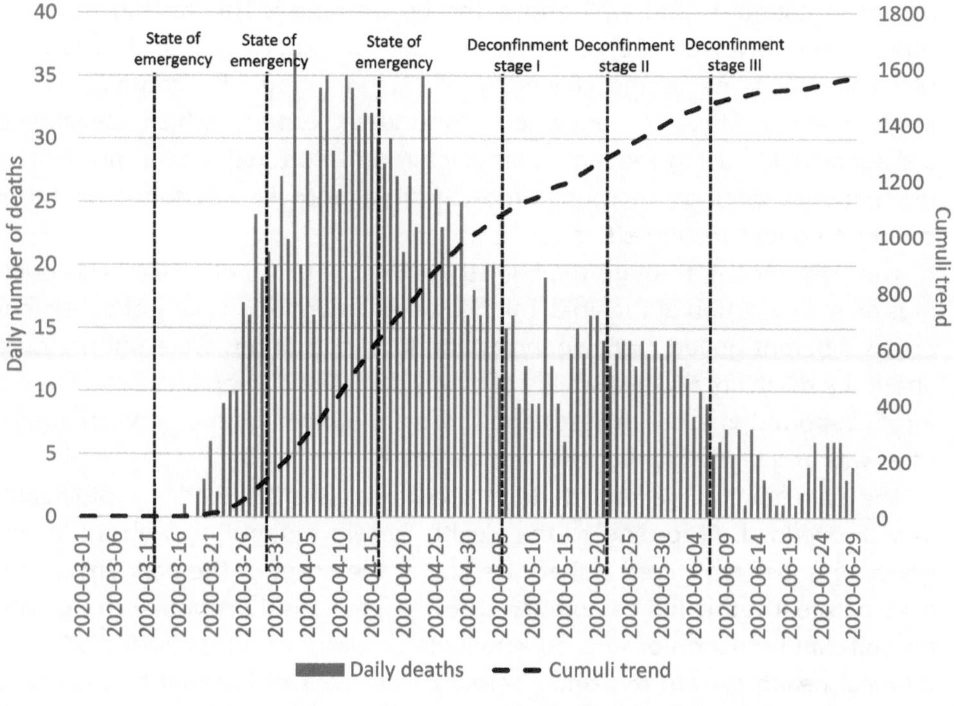

b - Daily evolution of deaths and cumuli trend.in Portugal, March-June 2020

Figure 1. (a) Daily evolution of Covid-19 cases and cumuli trend.in Portugal, March-June 2020. (b) Daily evolution of deaths and cumuli trend.in Portugal, March-June 2020.
Source: Portuguese Directorate-General of Health (DGH), available at https://covid19.min-saude.pt/.

Table 1. Evolution of the pandemic in Portugal.

	Cases [cases/1 M]	Deaths [deaths/1 M]	Recovered [recovered/1 M]	Testing [tested/1 M]
State of emergency (18 March – 2 April)	8392 [823]	208 [20.4]	65 [6,4]	85,108 [8,346.6]
State of emergency (3 April – 17 April)	9,988 [979.5]	448 [43.9]	451 [44.2]	155,613 [15,261.1]
State of emergency (18 April – 2 May)	6,168 [604.9]	366 [35.9]	1,152 [113]	196,912 [19,311.3]
Deconfinement stage I (4 May – 17 May)	3,846 [377.2]	195 [19.1]	2,965 [290.8]	214,599 [21,045]
Deconfinement stage II (17 May – 31 May)	3,464 [339.72]	192 [18.8]	14,773 [1,448.80]	185,277 [18,170.3]
Deconfinement stage III (1 June -)	9,412 [923]	158 [15.5]	7,796 [764.6]	216,311 [21,213.8]
Overall	41,912 [4,110.4]	1,568 [153.8]	27,205 [2,668]	1,102,066 [108,080.6]
Spain	248,770 [5,320.7]	28,343 [606.2]		3,290,388 [70,375.4]
Italy	240,310 [3,974.6]	34,738 [574.5]		5,341,837 [88,350.6]
Greece	3,376 [323.9]	191 [18.3]		308,392 [29,587.5]

Sources: Portuguese Directorate-General of Health (DGH), available at https://covid19.min-saude.pt/. Data on testing from OurWorldInData.org, available at https://ourworldindata.org/

the highest testing rates worldwide (significantly higher than other South European countries and well above the EU average[1]). This testing rate was due to the involvement of research centres, especially the Institute of Molecular Medicine at the University of Lisbon (under the coordination of Maria Manuel Mota, a renowned Portuguese expert) which developed a diagnostic kit, using reagents manufactured in Portugal – at a moment of international shortage of these products. The protocol was fundamental in bolstering public testing efforts.

The government, through the Ministry of Health (MH), held daily press briefings on the evolution of the epidemic. However, information was not consistent across different government agencies and local authorities were often critical about the reliability and availability of timely data. The discrepancy between the locally reported number of cases and those announced by the national authorities was frequently highlighted (Gomes 2020).

The main political message during the outbreak was the need to avoid health service overload. According to the Health System monitoring website, emergency episodes registered a sharp decline at the onset of the pandemic, with a 45 per cent reduction as compared to the previous 12 months; along with a significant reduction of surgical activity from March onwards (SNS 2020). The national health system remained below 65 per cent of hospital bed capacity throughout the first phase of the pandemic, with nine out of ten cases treated at home and just one per cent requiring intensive care (Demony, Gonçalves &

Waldersee 2020). The handling of the pandemic largely remained in the hands of the national health system, despite the private healthcare sector's reported availability to cooperate (Diário de Notícias 2021).

Few regions were as badly hit as the centre and northern regions during the early stages of the pandemic, particularly Oporto, Paços de Ferreira, Braga and Ovar. Urban areas with greater population density and proximity experienced higher contagion rates, whereas some regions (33 out of 278 municipalities in mainland Portugal) in the Alentejo or Centre Interior did not register any case. The latter stage of deconfinement was characterised by an upward trend in the number of cases reported in Lisbon.

Policy responses

'We are on': government management of the crises

This section examines Portuguese government management of the crises in three interrelated domains: organisation, communication, and policy responses. As for organisation, the Portuguese strategy was proactive and essentially centralised. Indeed, while assuming that the probability of a contagion in Europe would be unlikely (Direção-Geral de Saúde 2020), the Directorate General of Health (DGH) had activated a Task Force composed of health experts from different backgrounds (21 January) with the mission of gathering and analysing all epidemiological information.

With the first confirmed cases, several structures were either created or activated to ensure overall coordination across policy sectors and political hierarchies. The National Civil Protection Commission (Comissão Nacional de Proteção Civil – CNPC) was activated to function permanently, instead of its usual sporadic operation at the request of the Ministry of Internal Administration. CNPC is a coordinating body with the responsibility for implementing collaborating mechanisms between government bodies and services, ensuring operational coordination. The declaration of the state of emergency (18 March) and, later, the declaration of the state of calamity (3 May)[2] were followed by the creation of a Crisis Cabinet, a ministerial level crisis monitoring office coordinated by the Ministry of Internal Administration and comprised of eight ministers who defined measures to minimise the social and economic impact of the pandemic.[3] Beyond horizontal coordination, efforts were also devoted to ensuring coordination with other levels of governance – central and local government (regions and municipalities). This was reinforced by the assignment of a secretary of state to each of the five NUTS II[4] regions with the mission of coordinating all public bodies and services, aligning their action with the municipal authorities, and articulating their action with the main monitoring structure.

Portugal, despite its complex administrative structure, widespread across several public or semi-public institutions, displays a high degree of centralisation. The Covid-19 crisis reinforced this feature, as crisis management was centralised in the Government and the PM – as the chain of command of the health system response depicted in Figure 2 demonstrates.

As for the political communication dimension, it was assured by a daily press conference with the presence of the Director General of Health and the Minister of Health with updates on the epidemic itself and on the main policy measures. In this sense, the Minister of Health gained public relevance as she became the main political actor (alongside the PM), communicating the government's public health strategy. As for the Director General of Health, a government nominated health expert, she mainly addressed issues regarding the epidemiological situation and the technical grounding of policy measures. Communication was essential in implementing decisive measures which, to a large extent, followed recommendations from consultative bodies, such as the National Health Council (hereafter, the Council). Inputs from both independent consultative structures and task forces were, nonetheless, 'validated' and communicated by the DGH. The Ministry of Internal Administration came to the forefront whenever legal mechanisms such as the state of alert, calamity or emergency were activated. Additionally, the PM regularly appeared at and oversaw press conferences whenever specific policy packages were adopted.

Significant investment was dedicated to communication channels, with a dedicated website and a mobile application, social media presence and monitoring as well as the production and dissemination of specific information packages for different sectors. 'We are ON' ('Estamos ON') – the government dedicated webpage[5] – played with the polysemic meaning of the expression: online information and active involvement of government in terms of social and economic measures to tackle the crises.

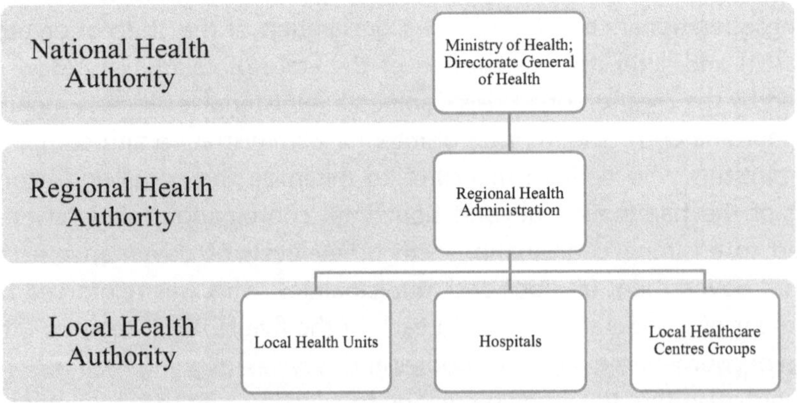

Figure 2. Centralised decision-making structure in Portuguese public health policy.

Portuguese policy responses were also proactive – largely owing to the severe lessons drawn from the experiences of other countries, such as Spain and Italy. Portugal took early action in the contention and mitigation stages of the epidemic, which contributed to the effective response. Schools were shut down in mid-March, amid a small controversy with the Council and from that point on, university rectors gradually decided on the closure of higher education institutions. Moreover, the declaration of the state of emergency (18 March) put the country on lockdown when the epidemiological scenario was far less complicated than in Spain or Italy,[6] when equivalent measures were taken. It is important to highlight that the lockdown in Portugal was classified as partial, consisting in the general duty of home confinement. Nonetheless, it allowed going out for several reasons beyond health or professional matters such as, for instance, family assistance or physical exercise.

Other timely and multi-sector policy measures were also largely proactive and responded to both the public health and the socio-economic crises. As depicted in Table 2, a considerable share of the policy measures was taken within the first weeks after the first confirmed cases – and before the declaration of state of emergency.

The government response in terms of the health system followed the World Health Organisation guidelines for a viral outbreak. Policy action during the contention phase focused mainly on information, strengthening the health system, increasing social distance, and limiting travelling, which was rapidly accomplished. Mask wearing became mandatory in May (Decree-law 20/2020, 1 May). With hospitals claiming to have exhausted their capacity, a Medical Helpline (*Linha de Apoio ao Médico*) was created to validate suspect cases.[7] Furthermore, 296 million euros were unlocked to increase the capacity of the health sector, and measures were defined to simplify the bureaucratic burden associated with hiring workers, even allowing the hiring of retired doctors. At this time there was already a concern with reducing the risk of transmission, as health authorities advanced swiftly with the identification and contact tracing of infected individuals and the isolation of sick individuals or those in quarantine.

As the mitigation phase began (23 March), social distancing measures were extended and the reduction of the risk of transmission was prioritised through the general duty of home confinement, the suspension of religious services and visits to care homes, hospitals or prisons. Moreover, all immigrants with pending cases before the Portuguese Immigration and Borders Service were granted temporary residency rights, including access to the NHS, also reducing the risk of transmission.

The Covid-19 crisis was not contained within policy boundaries. Travel restrictions and social distancing measures brought the economy almost to a halt in crucial sectors such as tourism and services, leading to a sudden reduction of household disposable income during the second quarter of 2020, which presented a growth rate of –4.3 in relation to the previous quarter (OECD

Table 2 Main policy measures, by date, sector and value

Measures	M€
13/03 STATE OF ALERT Public Health Measures	
Increase the capacity of the health sector	**296**
Border control with Spain through mutual agreement	
Flights to and from Italy suspended	
Prophylactic isolation of travellers entering the country	
COVID-19 support telephone line for consular emergencies (Portuguese abroad)	
Suspension of events >100 people	
Closure of educational establishments	
Access to commercial spaces restricted	
Exceptional regimes for purchase of supplies and services	
State of calamity in Ovar, implementation of sanitary cordon	
Comprehensive public awareness campaign on the epidemic	
Socio-economic Measures	
Deferral of payment of taxes and social contributions	
For working parents, justified absences with financial support	
Income support for sick/quarantined workers and families	
Income support for self-employed workers/dependent employees	
Credit lines to companies / operators fishing and aquaculture	2
Short-term credit line for agriculture	250
Catering / Restaurant industry	600
Industry	1.300
Tourism (including SMEs)	1.100
Increased ceilings for export credit insurance schemes for metallurgical, mould, metal and mechanical industries	100
Credit lines to companies most affected by epidemic	200
Credit line to support micro-companies in the tourism sector	60
Simplified lay-off mechanism for companies	
No distribution of profits under lay-off	
19/03 STATE OF EMERGENCY I Public Health Measures	
Specific programme for nursing homes testing; two new diagnostic centres (30/3)	
Suspension of flights from/to extra-EU	
Pardoning of prison sentences	
Partial Lockdown – duty of home confinement	
No events or gatherings >10 people	
Scientific and technological-based initiatives with immediate and effective implementation	
Mandatory telework	
Closure of non-essential businesses	
Reduction of public transport capacity	
Temperature control sensors in airports	
Suspension of religious ceremonies/services	
Suspension of visits to retirement homes, hospitals or prisons	
Civil requisition of goods or services to combat epidemic	
Socio-economic Measures	
Credit line for micro-enterprises in the tourism sector	
Credit line for social economy sector	
New SMS line to support victims of domestic violence	
Short-term export credit line for the agriculture sector	50
Reinforcement of credit lines to companies most affected by epidemic	200
Credit line to support the Fisheries and Aquaculture sector	20
Increased ceilings for export credit insurance schemes	
Special conditions for personal credits	
Extension of social protection benefits	
Suspension of termination of rental contracts, protecting tenants	
Financing of Covid-related R&D projects	4.5
Additional protection measures for the Fisheries and Aquaculture sector	4.7
Foreigners with pending applications to be treated as permanent residents – access to public services	

(*Continued*)

Table 2 (Continued).

30/04 STATE OF EMERGENCY II Public Health Measures	
Implementation of sanitary cordon in São Miguel island, Azores	
Implementation of sanitary cordon in Câmara de Lobos, Madeira	
Mobile application - COVID 19	
Domestic travel banned for Easter period	
Distance learning until end of school year	
Partial pardons for prisoners with sentences up to 2 years	
Reinforcement of the supply of ventilators and protective equipment in hospitals	
Reinforced measures to tackle domestic violence and mental health	
Restart of in-person classes (14/04) for high school exam-takers only	
Requirement to wear protective gear in public places	
Socio-economic Measures	
Deferral of payment of rents for tenants with income loss	
Simplified rules for availability of medical devices and protection gear on the market	
Maximum limit of 15% for profit on sale of protective equipment	
Financial support to municipalities	
Credit line for treasury support to companies affected by COVID	400
Emergency support financing to artists and cultural entities most affected	1
Moratoria on local authorities' contributions to the Municipal Fund	
18/04 STATE OF EMERGENCY III Public Health Measures	
Domestic travel banned for the 1 May weekend	
Simplified scheme of direct adjustment for the acquisition of equipment, goods and services – health sector	
TV-schooling for primary level education	
Mass population testing in retirement homes	
Reinforcement of labs testing capacity	
Socio-Economic Measures	
Reduced VAT on masks and disinfectant gel	
Waiving VAT and customs duties on protective equipment	
Financial support of humanitarian fire brigades	
Acquisition of media space for institutional advertising	1
Tax and social security contribution deferrals for companies and employees.	6.2 billion
Guaranteed credit lines for medium, small and micro enterprises in affected sectors, operated through the banking system	3.7 billion
Financial support for those temporarily furloughed by their employer	1 billion/ month
Support for start-up companies	25
Support programme to the associative movement for Portuguese emigrants	600
No distribution of dividends for companies under state support	
Public Health Measures	
Mandatory telework	
Mass testing plan for daycare centre workers.	
Immunity testing plan involving 17 hospitals nationwide by the National Health Institute	
Duty of home confinement	
Public transport at 2/3 capacity and passengers with masks	
Public services (some) reopen by appointment only	
Face mask mandatory in public spaces in contact with other people	
No gatherings > 10 people	
Compulsory confinement for sick /in quarantine	
Reopening of small commerce and specific services	
Temperature control allowed in workplace	
Socio-economic Measures	
Support to the entrepreneurship ecosystem	
Exceptional regime for insurance contracts	
Programme to support commerce / services (micro/small) (EU funds)	
Adapt Programme to relaunch micro and SMEs	
Financial support to wine sector	
Financial mechanism to support fishermen	
Financial support to artists and cultural entities	

(*Continued*)

Table 2 (Continued).

17/05 STATE OF CALAMITY II Public Health Measures	
Reopening of larger commerce and restaurants (1/2 capacity) Reopening of nurseries and specific years of secondary schools Reopening of cultural facilities	
1/06 STATE OF CALAMITY III Public Health Measures	
Religious ceremonies allowed (DGH rules) Start of the bathing season (DGH rules) Partial teleworking Reopening of shopping malls (except in Lisbon region) Reopening of pre-schools and daycare centres Reopening of cultural venues and gyms Extension of the flexibilisation of contracts in the SNS	
Socio-economic stability programme (PEES) (approved 6/06)	**15494,5 ME**
Workforce – reskilling and upskilling programmes	3287,9
Income support for affected workers, including self-employed and nonstandard workers	
Promotion of jobs and economic activity (among others, culture and tourism)	
Telework promotion – public administration and interior regions	
Strengthening of the Health System	1462,4
Universal access to Digital School	
Poverty – affordable housing; expansion of family social transfers	
Credit lines	9626,2
Moratorium on bank loan repayments	
Fiscal measures	
Capitalisation fund	
SME accelerator programme	
Promotion of new business sectors (among others, Covid-related, digital economy, blue economy, agriculture)	
Support local and regional finances	1118
Increase efficiency and capacity of public administration	
Increase efficiency of tax courts	
Shorten insolvency proceedings	
Land / sea borders remain closed, international flights suspended	
No events or gatherings > 20 people	
Partial teleworking	
Reopening of water parks, language schools and similar	
Lifting of restrictions in Lisbon region	
Extension of the flexibilisation of contracts in the SNS	

Sources: Declarations of the Council of Ministers, available at https://www.portugal.gov.pt/pt/gc22/governo/comunicados-do-conselho-de-ministros; Socio-Economic Stability Programme, available at https://pees.gov.pt/; Policy measures taken against the spread and impact of the coronavirus, available at https://www.nuoi.missaoportugal.mne.pt/images/20200518_coronavirus_national_policy_measures_revised_version_pt.pdf
Note: *All reopenings were subject to strict Directorate General for Health rules

2020b). Before the declaration of the state of emergency, political authorities implemented significant support packages directed at both individuals and companies, as presented in Table 2. The government announced measures, which included credit lines to businesses and other sectors most disrupted by the pandemic, such as the tourism sector, along with the deferral of certain fiscal obligations. At the individual level, income support measures were deployed targeting working parents, sick or quarantined workers, self-employed workers, and laid-off employees. As the crisis unfolded, the support measures to businesses became more targeted, acknowledging the fact that micro, small and medium enterprises faced greater challenges in coping with the sudden economic shock.

The decelaration of the pandemic led to a three-phase deconfinement period starting in May, subject to re-evaluation every two weeks, discussed in informal meetings with the main political actors and relevant experts. As stated elsewhere (Lodge & Boin 2020) this stage tends to be characterised by political decisions regarding which areas to open and under what conditions, leaving room to lobbying efforts – a pattern also evident in Portugal. The national representatives of the tourism and shopping centre sectors pressured public authorities, but with no immediate success (Larguesa 2020). Commerce, services, and cultural venues were gradually reopened, as well as some educational establishments (0–5 years old and specific secondary-school courses). While not originally envisaged in the initial deconfinement plan, gyms were also allowed to operate under strict safety rules, because of pressures from the sector.

In June 2020, government launched a short and medium-term recovery programme to reduce the socio-economic impact of the pandemic.[8] This programme addressed four main pillars (employment, social, enterprises, institutions), and was mostly funded by the new European instrument SURE (Support to mitigate Unemployment Risks in an Emergency). In line with other advanced economies, the fiscal stimulus package announced was considerably stronger than in the previous economic crisis (Moreira & Hick 2021).

The role of experts

The government grounded important decisions and communicative efforts on scientific guidelines, with the PM reassuring citizens that the 'political system would be humble and would support all decisions on scientific and technical advice' (Reis 2020). Indeed, different ministerial offices held regular meetings with sectorial experts (academics, reputed technicians, and others). This was a relevant strategy, given the general high level of citizens' confidence in scientists: in 2018, 34 per cent of Portuguese citizens reported high levels of trust in science, well above the EU average (25 per cent) (Gallup 2018). The role of experts and scientific reports was elevated to a central source of legitimisation of political decisions, bolstering politicians when risky and controversial decisions had to be taken (Innerarity 2013, p. 72). From early March, weekly (and later, biweekly) informal private meetings took place with representatives of all state authorities, party leaders, social partners and experts from the most relevant national health institutions, namely the Infarmed (the National Authority for Medicines and Health Products).

The government's scientific advice relied on two expert structures, both consultative. The first was the Covid-19 Task Force, activated at the end of January by the DGH, which was composed of health experts from different specialities. Its mission was to gather and analyse all available epidemiological information as well as to operationalise and implement the necessary measures for prevention and control of the infection in the community, through the policy guidance of the World Health Organisation and the European Centre for Disease Prevention and Control. This Task Force mirrored the growing prominence of scientific and technical experts in the policy process in a context of limited information while ensuring the coordination with European and world expert agencies.

The second structure was the National Health Council, a consultative structure (with representatives of the public, private and social sectors, including scientific and academic institutions), operating under the Minister of Health for the prevention and control of risks to public health. In the context of the pandemic, it provided input to the elaboration of the National Contingency Plan and in the grounding of the levels of alert and of the state of public calamity. Disagreements between the Council and the government were visible only regarding schools' closure in early March 2020. As in other matters, there was no indisputable foundation for this specific measure and the differences in positions within the Council became clear during the meeting on 11 March, which culminated with the recommendation not to close educational establishments at that point. Arguably, the different types of expertise that compose the Council led to a lack of consensus as the consequences of children's social distancing would have a broad impact on the lives of families and the economy, which ultimately prevailed in the Council's verdict. The government would, however, decide the opposite way, after securing the support of opposition parties and citing the recommendations of the European Centre for Disease Prevention and Control recommendations to support its decision.

Overall, while the diversification of expert knowledge resulted in some debate around issues such as school closures, the mandatory use of masks or the right moment to start deconfinement, it did not result in instances of deep tensions or open conflicts. In general, during confinement, debate was rather homogeneous, even on public media.

Throughout the first phase of the crisis, the Portuguese government continuously searched for expert legitimisation, be it from intramural experts, independent advisory bodies, or international organisations. Despite its decisions being grounded on scientific advice, it also secured popular legitimation by adopting feasible and acceptable measures, ensuring that other political players embarked on a common narrative. It would, hence, recognise that while scientific advice could 'alleviate the burden of political responsibility, science is still science and politics, politics' (Innerarity 2013, p. 76).

It was during the deconfinement stages that disputes with experts became more visible. In fact, health experts and representatives of the Portuguese Medical Association came forward stating that the rise in testing alone did not justify the increase in cases, thus contradicting government claims (RTP 2020).

This opened a breach in the common crisis-management narrative, which escalated into a broader political dispute. By the end of June, the political conflict over the pandemic was evident and the PM decided to suspend the meetings at which political actors and health experts had debated the pandemic's evolution and management since early March. As a commentator argued at the time, 'knowledge has been essential while concerns were mainly sanitary, it remained useful when they were mainly economic, but it has become an inconvenience now that concerns are now mainly political' (Neves 2020).

Impact of state structure: reigniting a perennial debate

It has been conventionally established that a country's structural organisation influences its responses in critical times. Portuguese local government is relatively fragile. The Portuguese national government holds local authorities on a tight leash, particularly concerning their financial means. This was amplified by the context of austerity in the wake of the Troika's intervention (Silva & Teles 2018). Since 2018, a renewed effort in transferring competences to municipalities was pursued. The process, however, was not implemented homogeneously, as only a handful of municipalities accepted the decentralisation package in terms of health management, for instance. Health services remain a sector with high levels of centralisation, despite the widespread opposite trend across European countries (Simões et al. 2017).

To a large extent, the centralised and unitary nature of the Portuguese state ensured rapid and coordinated action to contain the epidemic, particularly as it lies in the hands of the central government to declare a state of emergency or to apply sanitary cordons to municipalities. While the brunt of responsibility for the devising and implementation of the policy response fell on the shoulders of the central government and its health authorities, local municipalities played a significant role on the ground. Coordination with local government was enforced as a strategy to avoid disjointed responses to the crisis. On 2 March, the Costa government published a decree instructing local authorities and other public entities to elaborate contingency plans based on national and European recommendations.[9] Local municipalities quickly complied.

Local governments were responsible for assistance in the organisation of testing and social distancing actions, as well as for the well-being of specific groups such as the elderly and those with chronical or long-term illnesses. Additionally, when the sanitary situation warranted, municipal authorities had the power to request the central government to implement localised full lockdowns (sanitary cordons). Indeed, this was the situation in the Municipality of Ovar as the spread of the virus spiralled out of control, even before the declaration of the nationwide state of emergency. In contrast, in late March, other municipalities harshly criticised the DGH when a sanitary siege of Oporto was under consideration, questioning the scientific consistency and the reliability of data concerning the epidemiological situation in Oporto (Cabrita-Mendes 2020).

While local governments were provided with the opportunity to design localised measures – suggesting a greater degree of subnational responsibilities – they were also constrained, which generated pockets of resistance towards the government's plans. First, they were not granted the power to publicly provide information on the evolution of the pandemic. During the emergency period, the disclosure of the numbers of infected people became a prominent focus of conflict between the MH and a group of mayors, who accused the minister of imposing a gag on local government (RTP Notícias 2020). The incident was indicative of the underlying tensions that pervade Portugal's centralism. Second, some mayors claimed that centralisation inhibited rapid action. Indeed, the delays in distributing testing swabs and the overall logistics of distribution of personal protective equipment was a main point of conflict, with some mayors protesting about delays and the lack of clear guidelines (Observador 2020).

Beyond the sanitary front, local government played a role in mitigating the social and economic impacts of crisis. Many municipalities eased payments for tenants of public housing, and other public services such as water provision or public transportation. To face the heightened demand for local public services, restrictions on municipal debt spending were lifted (Visão 2020b).

The situation was very different in the Azores and Madeira autonomous regions. These territories enjoy a greater degree of fiscal, managerial, and political autonomy vis-à-vis municipalities, and have their own directly elected legislative assembly and regional government. Greater autonomy, in this case, generated more intense measures to curb the spread of the virus. Both regions put in place social and economic mitigation packages, which included credit lines to businesses, extensions on the payment of tax obligations, exemptions from payment of electricity and water consumption, etc. Both autonomous regions enacted mandatory prophylactic isolation of 14 days for anyone coming into the regions from the mainland, and Madeira closed its ports and marinas. Additionally, both autonomous regions pushed the central government to close the airports in the regions to commercial flights. This request was denied, triggering a minor political incident over the competencies of the autonomous regions, leading the Ministry of Internal Administration to declare that 'matters of external borders and circulation in the national space are the strict competence of the Government of the Republic' (Berenguer 2020).

While working within a relatively restrictive scenario, local governments were crucial in coping with the public health emergency and played a countercyclical role in terms of meeting the needs of local communities as the economic and social effects of the pandemic evolved. Both the central government and the National Association of Portuguese Municipalities (Associação Nacional de

Municípios Portugueses) claimed the need for a stronger liaison with subnational governments, along with increasing local investment to keep up with the rising demand for public services at the local level (Campeão das Províncias 2020).

Overall, then, the centralised (vertical) structures and instruments reinforced some control over local governments to minimise the potential risks of fragmented policy responses, while also allowing considerable room of manoeuvre and additional powers to subnational governments. Hence, the Portuguese case illustrates the positive association between centralisation and effectiveness in slowing down and containing the spread of the virus (Toshkov, Carroll & Yesilkagit 2021).

Such a combination in the management of the crisis is likely to reignite the perennial debate in Portugal concerning the level of (de)centralisation, not least given citizens' perception that local governments were crucial players in containing the spread of the virus. This perception was reinforced by national politicians dubbing some mayors as national 'heroes' (Carmo 2020).

The political response

Institutional dynamics

The Portuguese party system has proven remarkably stable in the aftermath of the political and economic crisis (Freire 2016; Lisi 2015). The country's leading parties are the PS, the PSD, the conservative CDS-PP (Centro Democrático Social–Partido Popular – Social Democratic Centre–Popular Party), which has also been part of government coalitions, the PCP and the BE (since 1999). Unlike its South European counterparts (Bosco & Verney 2016), the Portuguese party system has shown low levels of volatility and party system fragmentation, no significant changes in the patterns of competition and the alternation in government between the two mainstream parties. Until 2015, competition revolved around the two main parties (PS and PSD) and coalition formation typically took place at the right of the political spectrum. The lack of cooperation on the left – explained by both ideological and historical factors – was seen as a central and defining characteristic of the country's party system (Jalali 2007; Jalali, Moniz & Silva 2020). The unprecedented cooperation of 2015–2019 among left-wing parties 'strengthened the perception that the party system was ripe for a reconfiguration' (Jalali, Moniz & Silva 2020). This was particularly noticeable with the emergence of two new parties on the right, CH (Chega – Enough) and IL (Iniciativa Liberal – Liberal Initiative), which each managed to win a single seat in the 2019 elections, thus providing a significant platform for these new challengers.

Portugal faced a remarkable context regarding the institutional dynamics around the government's handling of the crisis. As this section seeks to demonstrate, the climate of cross-party collaboration, strongly underpinned by the President of the Republic's plea for political stability, was a key factor in understanding the evolution of the first phase of the pandemic.

Nevertheless, there were pockets of criticism. At a very early stage, the health crisis was politicised by the right-wing parties in opposition, the CDS-PP and the CH. While the former's main contention was targeted at the contradictory recommendations issued by health authorities, the latter envisioned the eruption of the pandemic as an opportunity to bring its securitarian politics to the foreground, by proposing a constitutional reform allowing for the coercive internment of citizens infected with the virus (Renascença 2020). These offensives were quickly deflected by prime minister Costa, who reinstated full confidence in the health authorities. The failure of this initial attempt to politicise the crisis set the mood for the period of emergency that followed, which was characterised by a general tone of agreement and confidence in the government's handling of the sanitary crisis.

The PM repeatedly urged his former partners on the left to make a 'collective effort' and feel a 'sense of responsibility' (Expresso 2020b) while also highlighting the role of the official opposition in establishing national unity in the face of the pandemic crisis. The role of the PSD was fundamental in rooting the government's narrative. By urging the party's militants to 'demonstrate union and solidarity with the government' and claiming that opposing government measures during a pandemic would be 'unpatriotic' (Sá 2020), party leader Rui Rio reinforced the 'common enemy narrative', leading to greater support for the government. Rio's conciliatory tone also stressed that the 'PM's fortunes would be everyone's fortunes', thus strongly contributing to citizens setting aside potential partisan biases that could emerge and influencing how the public perceives leaders (Baker & Oneal 2001). Rio's leadership was distinctly marked by this guarantee of collaboration with the executive, leaving open the possibility for a government supported by the PSD in the future (Fernandes 2020). This tactic of non-confrontation, which lasted throughout the state of alert and the state of emergency, proved critical in ensuring the necessary political stability for the government's successful handling of the pandemic crisis.

Any analysis of the institutional dynamics must encompass the role of the President of the Republic, who played a key role in guaranteeing stability and public consensus, collaborating closely with Costa. As Portugal is a semi-presidential regime, the political leadership rests with the government. The President, however, holds the 'power to persuade, a power that is reinforced by a president's popularity' (Fernandes & Jalali 2017, p. 129). Since Marcelo Rebelo de Sousa took office, in 2016, he successfully managed his popularity levels (Fernandes & Jalali 2017), a strategy that yielded him enough public support to substantially influence both the PM and the opposition leaders regarding the pandemic crisis management. In fact, as the sanitary situation worsened, the President took the initiative and called for a state of emergency to be put in effect in mid-March.

The state of emergency's main objective was to intensify social distancing measures and to restrict citizens' right of mobility, if necessary. The activation of this expedient was a pivotal moment in the history of the Portuguese democracy, as it was the first time in over 40 years that a state of emergency had been declared. Its truly exceptional nature led both the president and the prime minister to highlight that the state of emergency would not be 'an interruption of democracy' but rather 'democracy trying to prevent an irreparable interruption in people's lives' (Botelho 2020).

The state of emergency was initially supported by the parties on the right, while on the left the initiative received a cautious reception – a position shared by the PM himself. For Costa, the President's initiative was unwarranted at the time, but he pledged to support it if the request was formalised, thus avoiding political tensions with the Presidency. Both the radical left parties, the PCP and the BE, judged this option to be hasty considering that there was still room for tighter virus containing procedures, under the country's civil protection laws. Both parties were uncomfortable with the idea of restraining civil rights and of restrictions on strikes in healthcare and goods distribution. While the BE accepted the state of exception, the PCP assumed a tougher position, arguing that the temporary suspension of rights was unnecessary and potentially dangerous (Ferreira 2020).

The concrete measures of the state of emergency decree were announced and approved by a wide majority in Parliament on 18 March. Only the PCP and the minor neoliberal party, IL, abstained. The state of emergency would be renewed twice during the pandemic's first phase. As the situation developed, the PCP's position hardened, with the party voting against the third renewal (see Table 3).

While the sanitary situation provided a general cross-party consensus, the emerging social and economic crises became the focal point of party politics, as the country moved from the state of emergency to a less severe state of calamity. The former partners of the Contraption government, the

Table 3. Parties' voting behaviour, by state of emergency.

	In favour	Against	Abstention
1st State of Emergency (18 March 2020)	BE; CDS-PP; CH; PAN; PS; PSD		IL; JKM; PCP; PEV
2nd State of Emergency (2 April 2020)	BE; CDS-PP; PAN; PS; PSD	IL	CH; JKM; PCP; PEV
3rd State of Emergency (16 April 2020)	BE; CDS-PP; PAN; PS; PSD	IL; JKM; PCP	CH; PEV

Source: website of the Assembly of the Republic: https://www.parlamento.pt/Paginas/estado-emergencia.aspx
Note: Joacine Katar Moreira (JKM) – non-attached Member of Parliament.

PCP and the BE, assumed a more critical position, calling out the government for what they claimed to be the insufficient protection for dismissed and laid-off workers. Both parties pushed for the outlawing of dismissals and the prohibition of the distribution of dividends, insisted on the civil requisition of private health providers, and called for additional social support measures for those affected by the crisis. While the left's proposals were targeted at workers, the PSD defended the simplification of the lay-off and credit lines for struggling business (PSD 2020), stressing the need to increase testing capacity and the acquisition of ventilators. For its part, the CDS-PP pressed for the hastening of the state's liability payments to pump liquidity into the economy. Indeed, three months after the start of the crisis on national territory, well into the deconfinement stage, political support from opposition parties strongly decreased and the President of the Republic emerged as the government's last stronghold.

A final note on the institutional dynamics must be devoted to the role of the European Union. The Portuguese government and the Minister of Finance and President of the Eurogroup (Mário Centeno), along with another nine Finance Ministers of the hardest hit member-states, sought to pave the way for a renewed debate on issuing Eurobonds (coronabonds). While this attempt faced considerable reservations from other European member states, it stimulated a debate on the role of EU solidarity in face of a crisis. In Portugal, it opened a debate on the role of the EU in proving aid, with Costa seizing the opportunity to politicise the issue in his favour.

United around a common narrative: societal dynamics

The first phase of the pandemic was clearly marked by high levels of uncertainty – both regarding the potential duration of the confinement, the government measures to flatten the epidemic curve and its negative effects on the economy. As demonstrated elsewhere, within contexts of political anxiety, citizens tend to turn to political actors 'who can provide information and advocate policies that will protect them from threats' (Albertson & Gadarian 2015, p. 73).

At the same time, crises 'represent the hour of the executive', arising as opportunities to demonstrate leadership both in terms of framing the debate (meaning-making) and of critical decision-making (Boin & Hart 2012). Both the government and the PM – along with another crucial political actor, the President of the Republic – became highly visible in the public arena and in control of the public narrative of the crisis. As previously demonstrated, communication sought to be scientifically framed, as a strategy to 'reduce public and political uncertainty and inspire confidence in the crisis leader' (Boin, Ekengren & Rhinard 2017, p.79).

While citizens turned to political elites, the supply side also ensured the effectiveness of the policies adopted, particularly regarding the social distancing measures designed to control the epidemic peak so as to not to overwhelm the healthcare system. The government and the opposition, supported by the President of the Republic, enforced a common narrative to help citizens reshape their individual behaviour, searching for a common (national) goal. This narrative was central not only in generating higher levels of government support, but also in ensuring the successful implementation of social distancing rules.

To a large extent, the pandemic brought the country together around the goal of defeating the virus, resonating a 'rally-round-the-flag' effect. As Mueller (1970) posited in his seminal article, the rally effect occurs in the face of a 'specific, dramatic and sharply focused' event, perceived as a threat. This boosts incumbents' support, with citizens side-lining their partisan biases. The rally is reinforced by the absence of standard forms of opposition and emerges due to 'information environment changes because opposition leaders fall silent or support the president during a crisis and a portion of the public follows those elite partisan cues' (Murray 2017, p. 1). The media also contributed to this rally effect, particularly during the initial stages of the crisis, as government became the main source of information (Baum 2002). Overall, the combination of government narrative and the absence of elite criticism, either from the media or the opposition, generated the 'tendency of the public to "index" their opinions to the tenor of elite debate to which they are exposed' (Groeling & Baum 2008, p. 1066).

Indeed, the Portuguese handling of the first stage of the pandemic depicted the 'rally-round-the-flag' effect clearly. The PM's satisfaction ratings rose significantly, as depicted in Figure 3. In the early stages of his response to the coronavirus pandemic, Costa's approval rating soared, reaching a highpoint not too long after the declaration of national emergency. As Portugal underwent the first stages of deconfinement, these ratings improved to 75.3 per cent – an increase of nearly 34 per centage points from the 41.4 per cent registered in early October just after the general elections. Likewise, the approval ratings of the government also reached an unprecedented level by mid-April, after the second extension of the emergency period (Expresso 2020b).

Nine out of ten Portuguese citizens supported the state of emergency – a level that did not decrease as it was renewed twice. An overwhelming majority (92 per cent) considered the restrictions on personal freedoms justified by the scale and severity of the pandemic (Intercampus 2020a). Moreover, citizens would by-and-large agree with the government's often-repeated argument in favour of lockdowns, claiming it would postpone the epidemic wave, reducing the strain on the health system.

Rallies, however, have been demonstrated to be ephemeral. In fact, the first polls after the end of the state of emergency depicted a decline in government support. Deconfinement stages, starting in early May, were beset with political

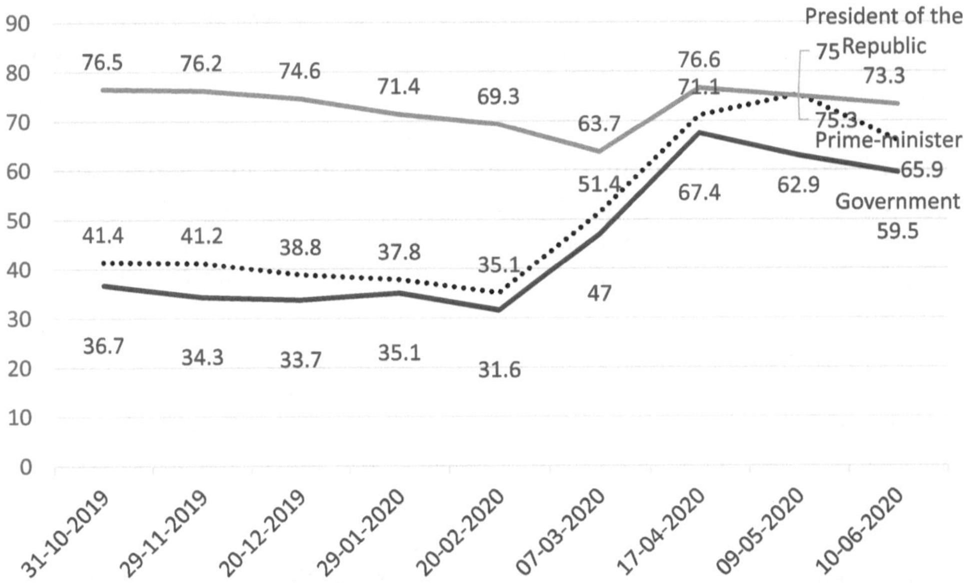

Figure 3. Performance evaluation of the government, the Prime Minister and the President of the Republic during the first phase of the pandemic in Portugal.
Sources: The Portuguese Regulatory Authority for the Media (ERC).
Note: percentages report to percentages of respondents who evaluate the performance as positive and very positive.

crisis. Declining levels of government support were conditioned by a political crisis that emerged due to the May First rally, which was authorised despite strict social distancing measures. Indeed, when the third state of emergency was enacted (18 April), participation in the official celebrations of the Workers' Day was legally authorised. This decision was criticised by a vast majority of citizens and the opposition parties, particularly since during the same weekend, the government banned travel between municipalities and, only a week earlier, the 25 April commemorations of the overthrow of the dictatorship in 1974 had been held amidst severe restrictions.

The decline in support may also be explained by citizens' perception that the deconfinement phase was premature – 57.6 per cent declared they opposed the opening of schools (Intercampu 2020b) – along with a greater political and public scrutiny of how the response to Covid-19 was handled.

Conclusions

During the first phase, the Portuguese case was acclaimed as a miracle, a reflection of the appraisal that the country had acted fast and adopted stringent measures. This article argues that politics matter in dealing with the pandemic. Specifically, three arguments are presented. First, it is argued that the pandemic hit Portugal at a time of political stability, exceptional in the context of Southern

Europe. The Socialist government was buoyed by good economic results and citizens' confidence in national political institutions. Second, it is argued that the consensus among the main political actors on matters of public health and social distancing reinforced the common narrative that was crucial in reshaping citizens' individual behaviour. Citizens' support for government measures and the consensus regarding the government's positive performance also framed citizens' positive attitudes towards the measures adopted to flatten the curve. Hence, lower levels of political polarisation around the government's handling of the crisis and a climate of cross-party collaboration, crucially underpinned by the President's actions, are key factors in understanding the Portuguese case. The third argument pertains to the organisational level, particularly the centralisation of power and decision-making that enabled a cohesive policy response. The two autonomous regions with a higher degree of fiscal, managerial, and political autonomy did not jeopardise this cohesive policy response, particularly given their pleas for tighter measures to deal with the pandemic.

With the onset of the pandemic crisis, Portugal witnessed a rallying effect around the country's leadership. This was translated into a unified message that enabled the government to enact stringent confinement measures quickly. The Portuguese case illustrates how citizens increasingly endorsed their national leaders as the Covid-19 pandemic worsened. Politicians, especially the official opposition, called a coronavirus truce, which was reflected in an absence of criticism in the media.

What happened in the first phase of the pandemic?

The rampant growth in cases during the deconfinement stages suggest that the miracle was a short-lived mirage. From September 2020 onwards, infection rates started to rise, and a new state of emergency was approved in parliament, with the support of the main opposition party. However, four parties – the PCP, the PEV (Partido Ecologista 'Os Verdes' – Portuguese Green Party), the CH and the IL – voted against it, suggesting increasing partisan opposition. This was accompanied by a tiered regional system of confinement, a strategy pursued by the government to avoid the unpopular economic burden of a new lockdown, despite public disagreement with health experts, who called for tighter and more restrictive measures. In January 2021, Portugal quickly raced to the top of the world infection and death rate rankings. After the relaxing of restrictions over Christmas – a measure strongly criticised by parties and experts and for which the PM took responsibility – and given the virulence of a new British variant of the virus, Costa re-imposed a nationwide lockdown on 13 January and tightened measures a week later by closing schools and imposing stricter frontier controls. With the health system on the verge of collapse, Portugal asked for European assistance, namely from Austria and Germany.

This phase of the pandemic also exposed tensions between parties. Even if parties were willing to support government strategies to contain the virus, they became increasingly critical over the issue of balancing social spending and fiscal prudence. This became particularly visible after the voting of the 2021 state budget proposed by Costa. Indeed, in November 2020, for the first time since the 2015 Contraption, the BE voted against a budget proposed by Costa, and 82 budget amendments were passed against the government's will. While there were no widespread anti-lockdown protests (as occurred in the Netherlands, Belgium, and Austria) or relevant anti-mask movements, citizens became increasingly frustrated with the government's management of the pandemic. Also, the high expectations regarding the vaccination programme (that began in late December) led citizens to drop their guard.

With regard to the future, the different phases of the pandemic have exposed the country's social inequalities, with the virus disproportionately affecting the most fragile groups, particularly those living in socioeconomically vulnerable municipalities. These economic and social effects are likely to fuel populist narratives, considering that the spectre of the eurozone crisis-era austerity is still fresh in the memory of Portuguese citizens. Likewise, the pandemic and the importance of the national health system may ignite polarisation around the role of state structures. This is certainly a new avenue for research, concerning the potential effects of the pandemic in terms of the party system and government interaction with the President of the Republic, with the Portuguese case emerging as a particularly interesting one given its capacity in thwarting the rise of populist forces.

Notes

1. Data from OurWorldInData.org, available at https://ourworldindata.org/
2. In Portugal, while the declaration of the 'state of emergency' is a prerogative of the President, its operationalisation is the responsibility of the government and it must be approved in parliament by a simple majority. It may involve the limitation of certain citizens' rights and freedoms and the reinforcement of civil administrative authorities. This constitutional expedient lasts for 15 days and can be renewed if necessary. As for the 'state of calamity', it is enacted by the government through a Council of Ministers Resolution according to the Legal Framework of Civil protection.
3. See Order 3545/2020, 21 March 2020; and the Order n. ° 5373-A/2020, 8 May 2020.
4. Nomenclature of Territorial Units for Statistics: North; Centre; Lisbon Metropolitan Area; Alentejo; Algarve.
5. https://covid19estamoson.gov.pt/
6. Spain took similar measures three days before Portugal, with 209 cases per million people; and 2.9 reported deaths per million. Italy had over 151 cases per million and 7.6 deaths per million. Lockdown was established in Portugal with only 44 cases per million and 1 death.
7. Order 3186-B/2020, 6 March.

8. Socio-Economic Stability Programme (PEES/SESP).
9. Order 2836-A/2020, 2 March 2020.

Acknowledgments

This research was supported by the Research Project "Changing European Elections: The impact of Eurozone bailouts on European Parliament election campaigns", funded by the National Foundation for Science and Technology (PTDC/IVC-CPO/3481/2014). It was also supported by the Research Project "DECIDE – Decentralized Territorial Governance: coordination, capacity and accountability of governance arrangements in complex regional settings", funded by the National Foundation for Science and Technology (PTDC/CPO-CPO/32502/2017); and by the Operational Programme 780 "Competitiveness and Internationalization" (FEDER) (POCI-01-0145-FEDER-032502).

Disclosure statement

No potential conflict of interest was reported by the author(s).

ORCID

Patrícia Silva http://orcid.org/0000-0002-7044-2723
Edna Costa http://orcid.org/0000-0003-2341-6482
João Moniz http://orcid.org/0000-0002-5523-6817

References

Albertson, B. & Gadarian, S. (2015) *Anxious Politics – Democratic Citizenship in a Threatening World*, Cambridge University Press, Cambridge.

Aximage (2020) 'O conhecimento do novo Coronavírus e a perceção das suas consequências', Aximage, available online at: http://www.erc.pt/download/YToyOntzOjg6ImZpY2hlaXJvIjtzOjQxOiJtZWRpYS9zb25kYWdlbnMvb2JqZWN0b19vZmZsaW5lLzg4OC42LnBkZiI7czo2OiJ0aXR1bG8iO3M6MTE6ImNvcm9uYXZpcnVzIjt9/coronavirus

Baer, W., Dias, D. & Duarte, J. (2013) 'The economy of Portugal and the European Union: from high growth prospects to the debt crisis', *The Quarterly Review of Economics and Finance*, vol. 53, no. 4, pp. 345–352.

Baker, W. & Oneal, J. (2001) 'Patriotism or opinion leadership? The nature and origins of the "rally 'round the flag" effect', *Journal of Conflict Resolution*, vol. 45, no. 5, pp. 661–687.

Bastos, J. (2020) 'Costa diz que não falta nada, mas nos hospitais diz-se que falta o básico', *Expresso*, 23 March, available online at: https://expresso.pt/coronavirus/2020-03-23-Costa-diz-que-nao-falta-nada-mas-nos-hospitais-diz-se-que-falta-o-basico

Baum, M. (2002) 'The constituent foundations of the rally-round-the-flag phenomenon', *International Studies Quarterly*, vol. 46, no. 2, pp. 263–298.

Berenguer, M. (2020) 'Madeira e Açores querem fechar já os aeroportos. Governo diz que não', *Público*, 15 March, available online at: https://www.publico.pt/2020/03/15/sociedade/noticia/madeira-acores-querem-fechar-ja-aeroportos-governo-nao-1907859

Boin, A. & Hart, P. (2012) 'Aligning executive action in times of adversity: the politics of crisis co-ordination', in *Executive Politics in Times of Crisis*, eds M. Lodge & K. Wegrich, Palgrave Macmillan, New York, pp. 179–196.

Boin, A., Hart, P., Stern, E. & Sundelius, B. (2017) 'Meaning making: constructing a crisis narrative', in *The Politics of Crisis Management: Public Leadership under Pressure* (2nd ed.), eds A. Boin, P. Hart, E. Stern & B. Sundelius, Cambridge University Press, Cambridge, pp. 78–101.

Bosco, A. & Verney, S. (2016) 'From electoral epidemic to government epidemic: the next level of the crisis in Southern Europe', *South European Society & Politics*, vol. 21, no. 4, pp. 383–406.

Botelho, L. (2020) 'Costa e Marcelo a uma só voz: "Não é uma interrupção da democracia"', *Público*, 18 March, available online at: https://www.publico.pt/2020/03/18/politica/noticia/costa-marcelo-so-voz-nao-interrupcao-democracia-1908431

Cabrita-Mendes, A. (2020) 'Câmara do Porto rejeita cerco sanitário do Porto e critica declarações de Graça Freitas', *Jornal Económico*, 30 March, available online at: https://jornaleconomico.sapo.pt/noticias/camara-do-porto-rejeita-cerca-sanitaria-no-porto-e-critica-declaracoes-de-graca-freitas-568353

Campeão das Províncias (2020) 'Primeiro-ministro reuniu hoje com Associação de Municípios em Coimbra', 22 May, available online at: https://www.campeaoprovincias.pt/noticia/primeiro-ministro-reuniu-hoje-com-associacao-de-municipios-em-coimbra

Campos, A. & Carvalho, P. (2020) 'Muitas camas e sem doentes: grande parte dos hospitais de campanha ficaram vazios', *Público*, 15 May, available online at: https://www.publico.pt/2020/05/15/sociedade/noticia/camas-doentes-parte-hospitais-campanha-ficaram-vazios-1916606

Carmo, C. (2020) '"Portugueses não esquecerão". Marcelo deixa rasgados elogios a Rio e diz que Malheiro foi um "herói"', *TSF*, 22 May, available online at: https://www.tsf.pt/portugal/politica/marcelo-elogia-rio-pela-atuacao-exemplar-como-lider-da-oposicao-12227230.html

Demony, C., Gonçalves, S. & Waldersee, V. (2020) 'Portugal relaxes coronavirus lockdown with 'sector-by-sector' plan', *Reuters*, 30 April, available online at: https://www.reuters.com/article/us-health-coronavirus-portugal/portugal-relaxes-coronavirus-lockdown-with-sector-by-sector-plan-idUSKBN22C36R

Diário de Notícias (2021) 'Hospitais privados com 894 camas afetas ao SNS e 230 doentes covid', 27 January, available online at: https://www.dn.pt/sociedade/hospitais-privados-com-894-camas-afetas-ao-sns-e-230-doentes-covid-13284180.html

Direção-Geral de Saúde (2020) 'Atualização – Surto de pneumonia por novo Coronavírus (2019-nCoV) na China', available online at: https://www.dgs.pt/a-direccao-geral-da-saude/comunicados-e-despachos-do-director-geral/atualizacao-de-24012020-surto-de-pneumonia-por-novo-coronavirus-2019-ncov-na-china-pdf.aspx

Eurostat (2020a) 'Government deficit/surplus, debt and associated data', available online at: http://appsso.eurostat.ec.europa.eu/nui/submitViewTableAction.do

Eurostat (2020b) 'Total unemployment rate', available online at: https://ec.europa.eu/eurostat/databrowser/view/tps00203/default/table?lang=en

Expresso (2020b) 'Covid-19. Marcelo e Governo capitalizam popularidade com gestão da pandemia, aponta sondagem', 4 April, available online at: https://expresso.pt/coronavirus/2020-05-04-Covid-19.-Marcelo-e-Governo-capitalizam-popularidade-com-gestao-da-pandemia-aponta-sondagem

Fernandes, J. & Jalali, C. (2017) 'A resurgent presidency? Portuguese semi-presidentialism and the 2016 elections', *South European Society & Politics*, vol. 22, no. 1, pp. 121–138.

Fernandes, M. (2020) '"O Governo que vier terá sempre de ser de salvação nacional", quando economia estiver em primeiro lugar', *Observador*, 29 March, available online at: https://observador.pt/2020/03/29/o-governo-que-vier-tera-sempre-de-ser-de-salvacao-nacional-quando-economia-estiver-em-primeiro-lugar/

Ferreira, J. (2020) 'A resposta à pandemia para lá do estado de emergência', *Público*, 19 March, available online at: https://www.publico.pt/2020/03/19/politica/opiniao/resposta-pandemia-estado-emergencia-1908433

Freire, A. (2016) 'The condition of Portuguese democracy during the Troika's intervention, 2011–15', *Portuguese Journal of Social Science*, vol. 15, no. 2, pp. 173–193.

Gallup (2018) 'Wellcome global monitor: how does the world feel about science and health?', *Gallup*, available online at: https://wellcome.ac.uk/sites/default/files/wellcome-global-monitor-2018.pdf

Gomes, M. (2020) 'Os dados "macro" da DGS continuam distantes dos dados "micro" dos autarcas', *Público*, 15 April, available online at: https://www.publico.pt/2020/04/15/politica/noticia/dados-macro-dgs-nao-coincidem-dados-micro-autarcas-1912017

Groeling, T. & Baum, M. (2008) 'Crossing the water's edge: elite rhetoric, media coverage, and the rally-round-the-flag phenomenon', *The Journal of Politics*, vol. 70, no. 4, pp. 1065–1085.

Innerarity, D. (2013) *The Democracy of Knowledge*, Bloomsbury, London.

Intercampus (2020b) 'Sondagem Intercampus: 9 de maio', Intercampus.

Intercampus (2020a) 'Sondagem Intercampus: 8 de abril', Intercampus.

Jalali, C. (2007) *Partidos E Democracia Em Portugal: 1974-2005: Da Revolução Ao Bipartidarismo*, Imprensa de Ciências Sociais, Lisbon.

Jalali, C. (2011) 'The president is not a passenger: Portugal's evolving semi-presidentialism', in *Semi-Presidentialism and Democracy*, eds R. Elgie, S. Moestrup & W. Yu-Shan, Palgrave Macmillan, London, pp. 156–173.

Jalali, C., Moniz, J. & Silva, P. (2020) 'In the shadow of the 'government of the left': the 2019 legislative elections in Portugal', *South European Society & Politics*, vol. 25, no. 2, pp. 229–255.

Joël, M. E., Dufour-Kippelen, S. & Samitca, S. (2010) 'The long-term care system for the elderly in Portugal', *European Network of Economic Policy Research Institutes*, available online at: http://www.ancien-longtermcare.eu/sites/default/files/ENEPRI%20_ANCIEN_%20RR%20No%2084%20Portugal.pdf

Larguesa, A. (2020) 'Donos dos shoppings pressionam Governo para reabrir na zona de Lisboa', *Jornal de Negócios*, 4 June, available online at: https://www.jornaldenegocios.pt/empresas/comercio/detalhe/donos-dos-shoppings-pressionam-governo-para-reabrir-na-zona-de-lisboa

Lisi, M. (2015) *Party Change, Recent Democracies, and Portugal: Comparative Perspectives*, Rowman & Littlefield, Lanham.

Lodge, M. & Boin, A. (2020) 'Great easing? Leaders face a tragic dilemma but they should not hide behind the backs of expert', available online at: https://blogs.lse.ac.uk/covid19/2020/05/14/leaders-face-a-tragic-dilemma-economic-collapse-or-mass-causalities/

Ministério da Saúde (2019) *Relatório Do Grupo Trabalho Serviços De Urgência*, Ministério da Saúde, Lisbon.

Moreira, A. & Hick, R. (2021) 'COVID-19, the Great Recession and social policy: is this time different?', *Social Policy & Administration*, vol. 55, no. 2, pp 261–279.

Moreira, A., Léon, M., Coda Moscarola, F. & Roumpakis, A. (2021). 'In the eye of the storm ... again ! Social policy responses to COVID-19 in Southern Europe', *Social Policy & Administration*, vol. 55, no. 2, pp. 339–357.

Moury, C., de Giorgi, E. & Barros, P. (2020). 'How to combine public spending with fiscal rigour? 'Austerity by stealth in post-bailout Portugal (2015-2019)', *South European Society & Politics*, vol. 25, no. 2, pp. 151–178.

Mueller, J. E. (1970) 'Presidential popularity from Truman to Johnson', *American Political Science Review*, vol. 64, no.1, pp. 18–34.

Murray, S. (2017) 'The 'rally-round-the-flag' phenomenon and the diversionary use of force', *Oxford Research Encyclopedia of Politics*, June 2017, pp. 1–18.

Neves, M. P. (2020) 'O fim das reuniões do Infarmed', *Público*, 11 July, available online in https://www.publico.pt/2020/07/11/opiniao/opiniao/fim-reunioes-infarmed-1923768

Observador (2020) '"O Ministério da Saúde deixou o nosso stock de zaragatoas chegar a zero", revela o Presidente da Câmara de Aveiro', 6 April, available online at: https://observador.pt/programas/resposta-pronta/o-ministerio-da-saude-deixou-o-nosso-stock-chegar-ao-zero-revela-jose-ribau-esteves/

OECD (2020b) 'Quarterly National Accounts', OECD Statistics Directorate.

Oliveira, M. M. (2019) 'Governo gasta quase 1.000 milhões de euros para pagar dívidas dos hospitais em 2019, *Eco*, 12 December, available online at: https://eco.sapo.pt/2019/12/12/governo-gasta-quase-1-000-milhoes-de-euros-para-pagar-dividas-dos-hospitais-em-2019/

Pereirinha, J. A. & Murteira, M. C. (2016) 'The Portuguese welfare system in a time of crisis and fiscal austerity', in *Challenges to European Welfare Systems*, eds K. Schubert, P. De Villota & J. Kuhlmann, Springer, New York, pp. 587–613.

Pereirinha, J. A. & Murteira, M. C. (2019) 'The Portuguese welfare system: a late European welfare system under permanent stress' in *Routledge Handbook of European Welfare Systems*, eds S. Blum, J. Kuhlmann & K. Schubert, Routledge: London, pp. 424–444.

PSD (2020) 'Rui Rio apresenta propostas para minorar os efeitos da crise na vida das empresas e das famílias', available online at: https://www.psd.pt/rui-rio-apresenta-propostas-para-minorar-os-efeitos-da-crise-na-vida-das-empresas-e-das-familias/

Reis, C. (2020) 'Fechar escolas só com aval das autoridades de saúde. Governo decide hoje', Diário de Notícias, 12 March, available online at: https://www.dn.pt/edicao-do-dia/12-mar-2020/fechar-escolas-so-com-autorizacao-das-autoridades-de-saude-diz-conselho-nacional-de-saude-publica-11916530.html

Renascença (2020) 'Revisão constitucional. Chega abre processo esta quarta-feira para permitir internamento compulsivo', 4 March, available online at: https://rr.sapo.pt/2020/03/04/politica/revisao-constitucional-chega-abre-processo-esta-quarta-feira-para-permitir-internamento-compulsivo/noticia/184117/

Rhodes, A., Ferdinande, P., Flaatten, H., Guidet, B., Metnitz, P. G. & Moreno, R. P. (2012) 'The variability of critical care bed numbers in Europe', *Intensive Care Medicine*, vol. 38, no. 10, pp. 1647–1653.

RTP (2020) 'Reunião com Infarmed. Explicações não convencem partidos', 24 June, available online at: https://www.rtp.pt/noticias/politica/reuniao-com-infarmed-explicacoes-nao-convencem-partidos_v1239755

RTP Notícias (2020) 'Covid-19. Autarcas indignados com impossibilidade de terem informação diária dos concelhos', available at: https://www.rtp.pt/noticias/pais/covid-19-autarcas-indignados-com-impossibilidade-de-terem-informacao-diaria-dos-concelhos_a1220024

Sá, P. (2020) 'Rio escreve aos militantes. "Não é patriótico atacar agora o governo"', *Diário de Notícias*, 15 April, available online at: https://www.dn.pt/poder/rio-escreve-aos-militantes-nao-e-patriotico-atacar-agora-o-governo-12071813.html

Santana, R., Sousa, J. S., Soares, P., Lopes, S., Boto, P. & Rocha, J. V. (2020) 'The demand for hospital emergency services: trends during the first month of COVID-19 response', *Portuguese Journal of Public Health*, vol. 38, no. 1, pp. 30–36.

Silva, P. & Teles, F. (2018) 'The biggest loser? Local public services under austerity measures in Portugal' in *Local Public Services in Times of Austerity across Mediterranean Europe*, eds A. Lippi & T. Tsekos, Palgrave Macmillan, New York, pp. 73–94.

Simões, A. J., Augusto, G. F., Fronteira, I. & Hernández-Quevedo, C. (2017) 'Portugal: health system review', *Health Systems in Transition*, vol. 19, no. 2, pp. 1–184.

SNS (2020) 'Serviços de Urgência', available online at: https://www.sns.gov.pt/monitorizacao-do-sns/servicos-de-urgencia/

Statista (2020) 'Coronavirus (COVID-19) death rate in countries with confirmed deaths and over 1,000 reported cases as of June 19, 2020, by country', available at: https://www.statista.com/statistics/1105914/coronavirus-death-rates-worldwide/

Toshkov, D., Carroll, B. & Yesilkagit, K. (2021) 'Government capacity, societal trust or party preferences: what accounts for the variety of national policy responses to the COVID-19 pandemic in Europe?', *Journal of European Public Policy*, pp. 1–20.

Visão (2020a) 'Covid-19: infeções afetam 246 lares, menos de 10% do universo nacional – governo', 14 June, available online at: https://visao.sapo.pt/visaosaude/2020-06-14-covid-19-infecoes-afetam-246-lares-menos-de-10-do-universo-nacional-governo/

Visão (2020b) 'Covid-19: PR promulga regime excecional de endividamento para as autarquias', 3 April, available online at: https://visao.sapo.pt/atualidade/politica/2020-04-03-covid-19-pr-promulga-regime-excecional-de-endividamento-para-as-autarquias

OPEN ACCESS

Regaining Trust: Evidence-Informed Policymaking during the First Phase of the Covid-19 Crisis in Greece

Stella Ladi, Angelos Angelou and Dimitra Panagiotatou

ABSTRACT

Analysing the handling of the pandemic's first phase in Greece, the article attempts to explain the reasons for its relative success. It suggests four main reasons: First, the predominance of evidence-informed policymaking led by strong and decisive leadership. Second, a timely and firm crisis response, driven by the prior experience of other European countries with the pandemic. Third, the public sector's digital turn and a tight scheme of intra-government coordination. Fourth, a transparent and effective communication strategy signalling that public health was a priority, which subsequently led to high citizen compliance with the restrictive measures. The second phase of the pandemic is also discussed to nuance this claim and show that the long duration of the crisis brought new challenges to its management. The article provides insights into how countries with limited resources and weak administrative capacity can effectively manage such crises.

It is widely acknowledged that Greece was successful in managing the first phase of the Covid-19 crisis. Between the identification of the first index case on 26 February 2020 and the lifting of the lockdown measures in late June 2020, the number of deaths in the country remained low and the spread of the virus was limited. Such an outcome was greeted as a positive surprise by both politicians and commentators (Hatzigeorgiou & Raj 2020). Indeed, one would expect Greece to be amongst the most severely hit countries, similar to Italy and Spain. A popular tourist destination, including for visitors from countries that were severely affected by the virus (although the latter started spreading in late February, a month with low tourist inflows), the country is also densely populated with most of the population living in two urban centres, Athens and Thessaloniki. Besides, physical contact and close interpersonal relationships are well-embedded in the Greek culture. Subsequently, one would expect these conditions to favour the quick transmission of the virus.

In addition, Greece was thought to lack the institutions and the capacity that would allow it to effectively manage the spread of the pandemic. The country is known for its dysfunctional public sector in which partisan ties have often guided its policymaking decisions, whereas experts' input is rarely followed in implementing evidence-informed public policies. Moreover, the Economic Adjustment Programmes accompanying the international bailouts of the last decade had led to the serious deterioration of the public health sector. Despite all the above, during the period examined here (with a cut-off point of 1 July 2020), the Greek government managed to keep the spread of the virus under control and eventually to reopen its borders to outside visitors.

The analysis below aims to discuss how Greece managed to achieve such an outcome during the first phase of the pandemic. The article is organised as follows: First, the country background is discussed. The next section maps the first phase of the Covid-19 pandemic in Greece, giving an overview of the adopted measures. This is followed by a presentation of the government's early response to the pandemic and an analysis of its initial success. The following section offers a first assessment of the political and societal reaction to the government's crisis-management policies. Finally, some theoretical and empirical conclusions are offered, and a brief assessment is made of the changes that occurred during the second phase of the pandemic.

State structure and health system in Greece before Covid-19

The Greek public administration has often been blamed for inefficiency, slow procedures, lack of technological innovation and clientelistic practices. Scholars have identified certain features that make its performance wanting: it is heavily centralised and politicised, while its bureaucratic culture is unwelcoming to change (Spanou & Sotiropoulos 2011, p. 733) and deeply rooted in legal formalism, hierarchy, and centralisation (Featherstone 2015). Although the latter feature proved key for the efficient cooperation between the central and regional governments, on the eve of the pandemic it seemed as it would set up the Greek state for disaster. At the same time, while the eurozone crisis and the implementation of three Economic Adjustment Programmes (EAPs) (2010, 2012 and 2015) improved some aspects of Greece's public administration, they imposed austerity measures which translated into a cost-cutting exercise across the board, affecting the delivery of public services (Ladi 2020).

Furthermore, the country is traditionally characterised by a policymaking style which is closer to the incremental and garbage-can models rather than rational policymaking (Ladi 2013). Policymaking does not follow a predictable sequence of actions, and decisions are normally the result of political and electoral calculations as well as of last-minute fixing solutions that lack strategic planning. Greece has also been characterised as a party democracy in which stakeholders gain power and influence via their relationships with political parties (Pappas 1998; Ladi 2020, p. 449), while party officials and political advisors are central in the shaping and implementing of public policies (Spanou 2008). This feature has undermined the capacity of the public administration in the past as the career progression of public servants ended up being tied to their political links rather than performance standards (Sotiropoulos 2007; Anastasatou, Nitsi & Katsikas 2018).

In addition to its public administration challenges, Greece also faced problems with regards to its healthcare system. The Greek national health system (Εθνικό Σύστημα Υγείας) was inaugurated in 1983 and is a highly centralised system similarly to most administrative structures in the country. Since its inception it has failed to provide comprehensive healthcare coverage, leaving a big part of primary care to private-sector providers. Until recently, it also seemed to be pervaded by clientelism, with certain occupation-based insurance funds maintaining privileged access to it (Petmesidou 2019, pp. 20–23).

The three EAPs that were implemented between 2010–18 introduced a mixture of measures involving both cost-cutting actions to reduce public sector spending, but also reforms aiming to rectify the above inefficiencies and inequalities (Economou et al. 2017; Angelaki 2016). Other reforms involved the unification of the health insurance funds and the introduction of EOPPY (Εθνικός Οργανισμός Παροχής Υπηρεσιών Υγείας – the National Health Services Organization) aiming to equalise the provision of healthcare among the population. It is also worth noting that, with respect to the division of labour between the central government and regional authorities, the health system remained largely centralised, despite certain provisions included in the EAPs pushing towards decentralisation (Petmesidou 2019, p. 28).

The Covid-19 emergency found Greece with a health system still absorbing these reforms. Health expenditure was about 8 per cent of GDP at the beginning of the pandemic, below the EU average of 9.9 per cent (Eurostat 2020). Moreover, the country's hospital infrastructure was in decaying condition, while physical and human resources were unevenly distributed, with Athens and Thessaloniki enjoying most services. Adding to that, the primary health care system is still not fully developed, causing problems with access and coordination (Economou et al. 2017). Finally, shortages of personnel were also very much prevalent at the onset of the pandemic. The sole positive figure was the number of physicians and in particular specialists which remained above the EU average (Eurostat 2020).

With respect to epidemiological monitoring, although a basic infrastructure was present before the Covid-19 pandemic, the field's services were not prioritised and remained understaffed. The handling and monitoring of infectious diseases lie with the Directorate of Public Health in the Ministry of Health at the central level with services offered at the regional and local levels. The National Public Health Council (ESYDY – Εθνικό Συμβούλιο Δημόσιας Υγείας) is responsible for the coordination of public health organisations with a duty to control communicable diseases (Economou et al. 2017). An Influenza Pandemic Action

Plan was in place since 2005 and it had undergone substantial revisions in 2009 in light of the influenza A (H1N1) pandemic (Economou et al. 2020). Despite the above division of labour and the responsibilities that it entailed, the first National Action Plan for Public Health (2008–12), which was developed by ESYDY, was never implemented (Economou et al. 2017) and a new National Action Plan was only legislated in March 2020 as a response to the evolving situation (Greek Law 4675/2020).

Mapping the first phase of Covid-19 in Greece

Despite the limited capacity of the Greek state in terms of public administration, healthcare infrastructure and pandemic preparedness, the spread of the virus was far more limited in Greece compared to the EU average (even accounting for under-reporting being in place). The first index case was confirmed on 26 February 2020 and consequent positive cases that were reported in late February and early March involved people who had travelled to areas with high infection rates and their contacts. The first Covid-19-related death in Greece was reported on 12 March 2020. The number of Covid-19 tests that were conducted in the country as well as the number of confirmed cases, deaths and recovered cases per million people are illustrated in Table 1.

It should be noted that Greece, similarly to many other countries, faced criticism vis-a-vis the relatively low number of tests it conducted. Indeed, during the first phase, testing was limited to citizens returning from abroad, patients with severe symptoms, and healthcare personnel who developed symptoms. At the same time, a very strict track and trace system, followed by compulsory self-quarantine, was put into place early on (Economou et al. 2020). This strategy proved to be effective for managing the pandemic's first phase while it also optimised the utilisation of state resources. The dynamics of the propagation of the pandemic are schematically presented in Figure 1.

General lockdown rules

As Covid-19 had devastating effects in neighbouring Italy, the Greek government established a preventive strategy very early. All carnival festivities were cancelled as early as 27 February 2020. Cases continued rising, and in response

Table 1. Confirmed cases, deaths, tests and recovered cases (total and per million people) during the first phase of the Covid-19 pandemic in Greece.

	Total	Per 1 m pop.
Confirmed cases	3,302	317
Deaths	190	18.2
Tests	285,989	27,440
Recovered	1,374	

Source: Worldometer (2020); Our World in Data (2020); Proto Thema (2020) – all as of 23 June 2020

(a)

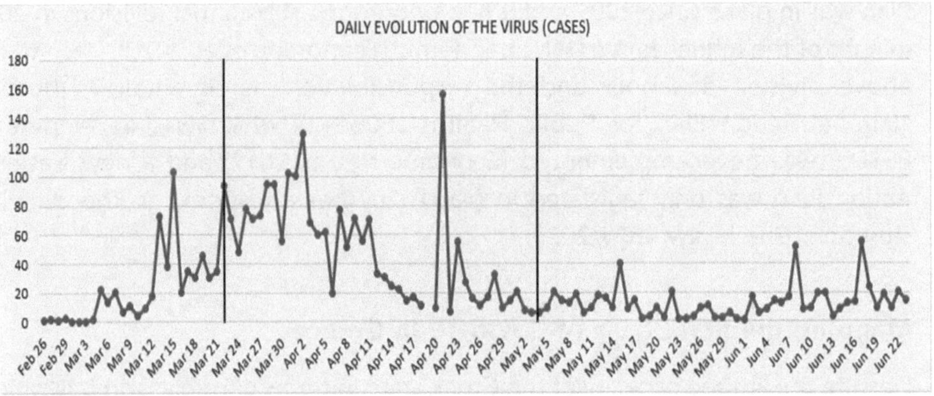

(b)

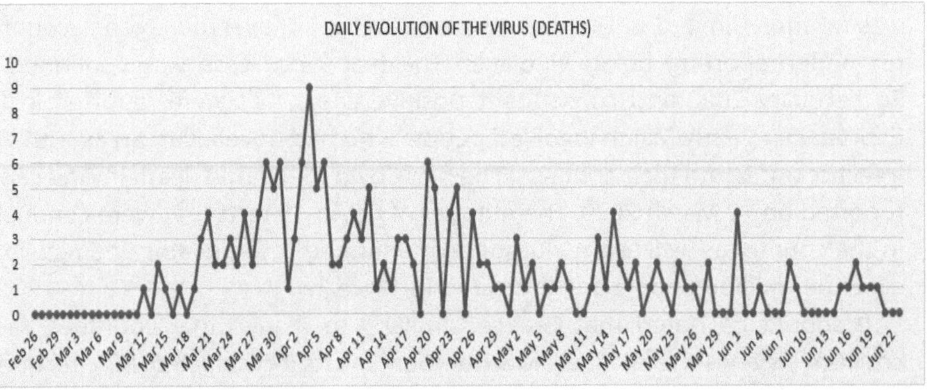

Figure 1. (a) Daily evolution of the virus and the cumuli trend during the first phase of the Covid-19 pandemic in Greece: Cases. (b) Daily evolution of the virus and the cumuli trend during the first phase of the Covid-19 pandemic in Greece: Deaths.
Source: Adapted from Greek Government (2020d) as of 23 June 2020.
Note: The vertical lines depict when the lockdown (22 March) and the easing of restrictive measures (4 May) started.

all conferences and big events of more than 1,000 people were cancelled at the beginning of March. Subsequently, it was announced that sports events were going to be held behind closed doors. In addition, all school trips were cancelled since many of the first cases were linked to travelling. On 10 March, more universal measures were enacted, starting with the closure of all educational establishments. In the next couple of days, the closure of courthouses, theatres, cinemas, gyms, playgrounds, clubs, shopping centres, cafes, restaurants, bars, museums, and archaeological sites was announced. Hotels followed and marinas, recreational parks and organised beaches were also shut. On 20 March, a decision was made to shield the islands by restricting travelling only to permanent residents and supply trucks. By then, public gatherings were restricted to ten people with the imposition of a fine of 1,000 euros in case of violation.

A total lockdown was announced on 22 March which entailed a ban on all non-essential travel and movement, with prescribed exemptions such as going to the pharmacy or visiting a medical doctor, helping people in need, and exercising in open space. People had to fill in a form or send a text message to a specified number when exiting their home, while they always had to carry ID. A fine of 150 euros for potential violations was imposed. Commuting to and from work was permitted only with a signed document from the employer or from the person herself in case of freelancers. At instances, such as during the Easter holidays when people traditionally visit family and friends and travel to the countryside, even stricter measures and fines were put in place (Economou et al. 2020). A detailed timeline of the restrictive measures adopted by the Greek government is quoted in Table 2.

Vulnerable groups: nursing homes and migrant camps

The timely closure and the suspension of visiting hours to nursing homes and open care centres proved to be catalytic in protecting the most vulnerable population and limiting the spread of the virus. By 25 March a total prohibition on visits from relatives to retirement and nursing homes was implemented. Moreover, the National Organisation of Public Health (EODY – Εθνικός Οργανισμός Δημόσιας Υγείας) conducted extensive tests in nursing homes and care units across the country. Such a proactive and preventive strategy was of particular importance during the first phase of the pandemic as in many European countries a major source of contagion occurred within such facilities (Ta Nea 2020a). Instead in Greece, as of 1 July 2020, none of the Covid-19-related deaths was linked to any of the country's 200 nursing homes. Adding to that, confirmed cases were only registered in one such facility, in mid-April (Skai 2020). The percentage rate of confirmed cases and deaths by age is illustrated in Figure 2.

Measures were also put in place to secure migrant camps by restricting movement and banning external visitors. It should be noted that the government was criticised for conducting very little testing within refugee camps as well as for 'health restrictions eroding the rights of migrants' (Carassava 2020). Nevertheless, very few cases were reported within refugee camps, with the mainland ones facing the highest rates of infection (Kousi, Mitsi & Simos 2021; Kondilis et al. 2020; International Office of Migration in Greece 2020). This is mainly attributed to the fact that entry and exit was restricted while most camps are situated in isolated areas, thus making it easier to impose an effective lockdown (Godin 2020). In addition, the timely intervention of specialised medical teams facilitated the implementation of locally imposed measures of prevention and control (InfoMigrants 2020).

Table 2. Timeline of Covid-19 restrictive measures during the first phase of the Covid-19 pandemic in Greece.

DATE	MEASURE
February 27	Cancellation of all carnival festivities
March 9	Cancellation of big events of more than 1,000 people, sports events and school trips; suspension of all flights to and from northern Italy
March 10	Closure of all educational establishments
March 12	Closure of all lawcourts, theatres, cinemas, clubs, gyms and playgrounds
March 13	Closure of all museums, archaeological sites, sports facilities, shopping centres, cafes, bars and restaurants – except for supermarkets, pharmacies and food stores offering take-away or delivery
March 14	Suspension of all flights to and from Italy; closure of all organised beaches and ski resorts
March 16	Suspension of all services in areas of religious worship of any religion or dogma; closure of retail shops; closure of borders with and suspension of all flights to and from Albania and North Macedonia; suspension of all flights to and from Spain; prohibition on all cruise ships and sailboats docking in Greek ports; imposition of 14-day home quarantine on those entering the country
March 18	Imposition of special restrictions on migrant camps and facilities in regard to movement and visitors; ban on public gatherings of more than ten people and imposition of a 1,000 euros fine on violators; closure of external borders – in common with EU member-states – to non-EU nationals
March 21	Restriction on travel to the islands – except for permanent residents and supply trucks
March 22	Closure of all hotels – except three each in Athens and Thessaloniki and one per regional unit; closure of all parks, recreation areas and marinas
March 23	Imposition of total lockdown and restriction on all non-essential movement throughout the country – imposition of a 150 euros fine on violators; suspension of all flights to and from the UK and Turkey
March 28	Suspension of all flights to and from Germany and the Netherlands
April 4	Extension of lockdown until 27 April
April 23	Extension of lockdown until 4 May

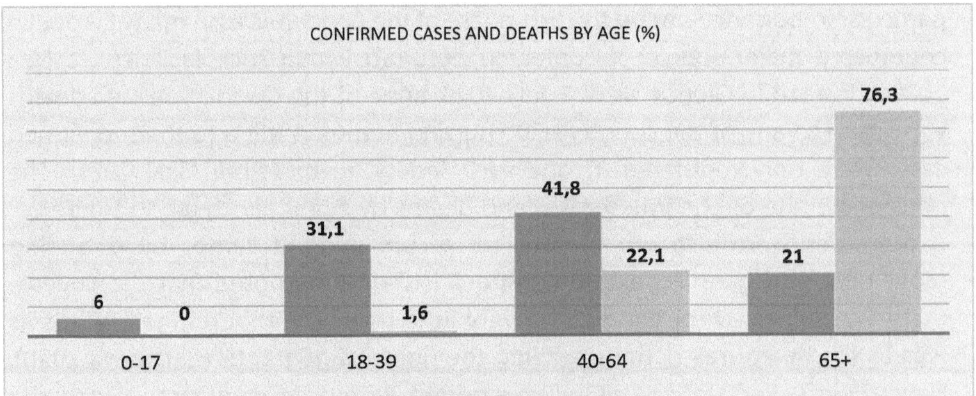

Figure 2. Confirmed cases and deaths by age during the first phase of the Covid-19 pandemic in Greece. Source: Adapted from Greek Government (2020d) as of 23 June 2020.

The response of the healthcare system

Although the health system in Greece presented a mixed image at the beginning of the pandemic, it managed to cope well during the first phase. This was mainly attributed to the low number of Covid-19 patients. Subsequently, there was a quick mobilisation of health services and treatment was universal and free including for the most vulnerable. Thirteen Covid-19 reference hospitals were designated and four were dedicated only to Covid-19 patients (Economou et al. 2020).

One of the key concerns from the beginning of the crisis was the country's low capacity in terms of hospital beds and critical care beds. Yet, with little prior preparation, 3,307 beds for the hospitalisation of Covid-19 cases were secured by the end of March, while by mid-April this number equalled 4,007 hospital beds. Of these beds 3,610 were available to host Covid-19 patients, while the remaining ones were occupied at the time. With respect to ICU beds, Greece faced the beginning of the pandemic with only 565 (about six critical care beds per 100,000 people); yet, by mid-April they had increased to 1,000; 350 of which were designated for Covid-19 patients with 256 being free at the time (Covid-19 Health System Response Monitor 2020).

In addition, during this short period of time some important investment was made in the national health system with the recruitment of 5,094 staff (610 doctors, 2,042 nurses and 2,082 health personnel) (Kikilias 2020). While most of the new personnel had short-term contracts, recruitment surpassed the initial planning of 2,000 additional hires (Covid-19 Health System Response Monitor 2020). The national health system also reinforced regional hospitals and health units (Economou et al. 2020) as well as Primary Health Care Services, with five health centres in Attica being fully dedicated to Covid-19 patients, a number that could increase depending on demand in different regions.

Overall, the Ministry of Health's budget was boosted with 160.5 million euros with the promise that extra resources would be provided as the situation developed. It is estimated that on top of that, around 100 million euros were channelled to the Ministry of Health through cash or in-kind donations (e.g. medical consumables, ICU beds, respirators etc.). Another 79.7 million euros was granted by the European Regional Development Fund (Economou et al. 2020).

The economic measures

The outbreak of Covid-19 and the subsequent lockdown brought a new economic crisis with immediate as well as long-term effects. Like other European governments, the Greek government put in place measures for the easing of the short-term effects. These included measures aiming at supporting business (for instance, a four-month suspension of tax and social security contributions for businesses and enterprises affected by Covid-19) as well as measures targeted to protect jobs and to avoid a surge of unemployment (Greek Government 2020c). For instance, a law was passed to allow arrangements for part-time employment with a job retention clause and schemes for income subsidies were put into place. Table 3 presents a list of targeted actions for special categories of businesses and citizens that were passed during the first phase.

Table 3. Main economic measures and government spending during the first phase of the Covid-19 pandemic in Greece.

MEASURES	GOVERNMENT SPENDING (in euros)
Support for the Greek NHS including for the provision of medical equipment, ICU, pharmaceuticals as well as the recruitment of health sector staff	273 million
Facilitation of parents with children below 15 years old working in the private and public sector through a special leave scheme funded by 25 per cent by the Greek state following the closure of educational establishments	45 million (until mid-June)
Payment of a special allowance of 800 euros (for the period between mid-March and end April) and 533 euros (May) to self-employed, freelancers and owners of small firms with up to five employees affected by the pandemic on the basis of specific NACE codes*	0.9 billion (until mid-June)
Payment of a special allowance of 800 euros (for the period between mid-March and end April) and 533 euros (May) to employees of firms affected by the pandemic whose labour contacts have been suspended on the basis of specific NACE codes	2.7 billion (until mid-June)
Payment of a special allowance of 800 euros (for the period between mid-March and end April) and 533 euros (May) to employers with up to 20 employees affected by the pandemic on the basis of specific NACE codes	73 million
Payment of a special Easter bonus to a total of 113,000 public servants working in hospitals, the National Emergency Aid Centre, the National Organisation of Public Health and Civil Protection	62 million
Partial payment of Easter bonus to private sector employees whose labour contracts have been suspended	187 million
Provision of direct aid -instead of training vouchers as initially planned- of 600 euros to individuals in six scientific sectors (economists/accountants, engineers, lawyers/notaries, doctors, teachers and researchers)	108 million
Extension of payment of regular unemployment benefit for employees, long-term unemployment benefit and unemployment benefit for freelancers and self-employed workers for two months	232 million
Payment of unemployment benefit of 400 euros to 155,000 beneficiaries who became long-term unemployed from April 2019	6 million
Coverage of social security contributions of the self-employed affected by the pandemic and of employees working in firms affected by the pandemic whose labour contracts have been suspended on the basis of specific NACE codes for the period between mid-March and late May	1.3 billion
Coverage of interest payments on loans of businesses affected by the pandemic for three months (April, May, June) on the conditions that their loans are performing and that they sustain the same number of employees	800 million
Suspension of VAT and other tax obligations' payments for businesses and self-employed affected by the pandemic for four months on the basis of specific NACE codes	-
Reduction by 40 per cent in commercial rent paid by firms affected by the pandemic as well as in primary and student residence rent for employees of firms affected by the pandemic for three months (March, April and May) on the basis of specific NACE codes	-
Suspension of tax payment obligations for property owners who receive reduced rent	-

Source: Greek Government (2020a; 2020b); European Commission (2020a); European Commission (2020b)
Note: *NACE stands for 'Nomenclature of Economic Activities' or the statistical classification of economic activities in the European Union.

Easing of the first lockdown

In Greece, the opening-up after the pandemic's first phase started on 4 May 2020 and was gradual. It began with the lifting of mobility restrictions and the opening of small shops and businesses, and it successively included the opening of high schools, the rest of the retail sector, archaeological sites, schools, and churches. From June onwards, year-round hotels and camping sites reopened along with museums and gyms. Strict protocols and rules concerning safe distances were put in place, while venues and public transport functioned with limited capacity. Finally, the use of face masks in closed spaces became mandatory by Ministerial Decision on 8 August, while their use in public spaces never raised intense reactions among the population.

As Greece exited the first phase, it also increased its testing capacity (from 700–800 tests per day at the beginning of the pandemic to 5,500 tests in June) (Economou et al. 2020). However, the surveillance of the opening up phase proved to be more challenging since citizens and businesses suffered from lockdown fatigue. Some local lockdowns were imposed, mainly in the north of Greece where there was a rise in the number of cases (Covid 19 Observatory 2020b).

Overall, the easing of the lockdown and the gradual re-opening of the country was driven by the improved picture vis-a-vis the spread of the pandemic. It came at the right time for the tourist season, signalling that saving the economy and allowing for some tourist flows was a priority for the government at that point (Mitsotakis 2020b). A timeline featuring the easing of the lockdown measures after the first phase is provided in Table 4.

The policy response

In this section it is argued that the main factors contributing to Greece's success in managing the first phase of the pandemic were the government's choice to follow an evidence-informed style of policymaking, the proactive nature of the measures, the public sector's digital turn, tight intra-government coordination and, finally, a clear communication strategy.

Table 4. Timeline of the easing of lockdown measures during the first phase of the Covid-19 pandemic in Greece.

DATE	MEASURE
May 4	First stage of easing restrictions: lifting of lockdown and reopening of some stores (hairdressers, bookstores, sports equipment stores, electrical appliance stores)
May 11	Second stage of easing restrictions: reopening of remaining retail shops and high schools -for senior grade students only
May 17	Lifting of measures regarding participation in Divine Liturgies and other religious services
May 18	Third stage of easing restrictions: lifting of restrictions on movement across the country (mainland, Crete and Evia); reopening of high schools (all other grades of secondary education) and foreign language centres; reopening of archaeological sites, zoos, shopping malls and aesthetic/ dietary institutes
May 25	Reopening of cafes and restaurants with outdoor seating; lifting of restrictions on movement to the islands
June 1	Reopening of nursery schools, kindergartens, primary schools, year-long hotels, camping sites, open-air cinemas and public swimming pools
June 6	Reopening of indoor restaurants, cafes and other facilities
June 8	Reopening of dancing schools, bars and clubs
June 15	Reopening of seasonal hotels, museums, sport facilities, recreational parks and wellness centres
July 1	Reopening of regional airports to international flights – except for direct flights from the UK and Sweden until 15 July

Evidence-informed policymaking and proactive measures

As crises entail scarce information about their nature and implications, policy-makers have to diverge from their usual political deliberations and seek advice on the technical aspects of the emerging problem; yet, following evidence-informed policies during crises is not an obvious path and indeed constitutes a political choice. This was very much the case for the Greek government during the first phase of the Covid-19 crisis. The government had to decide on the optimal measures for handling the pandemic by considering a multiplicity of variables including the severity and the contagiousness of the virus, health sector capacity, treatment costs, and the economic, social, and psychological implications of the different containment strategies. Yet, as crisis-management decisions remain political and entail redistributive consequences, the government faced the dilemma of relying on the advice of public health experts or adjusting its policy response according to other aims such as economic growth (Boswell 2009, p. 6).

From these two options, it chose to place a committee of independent health experts at the centre of its crisis-response. Observing the predominance of evidence-informed policymaking in Greece is quite a change from the usual modus operandi, as past efforts to apply some type of evidence-informed policymaking to imminent problems have usually fallen through (see, for instance, Tinios 2013; Trantidis 2016 on the reform of the pension system).

However, this time experts appeared to guide the decision-making process independently of the political calculus and their political affiliations, marking a clear break from the previous pattern. At the beginning of February, a National Experts Committee on Public Health (Επιτροπή εμπειρογνωμόνων και ειδικών λοιμωξιολόγων για το νέο κορονοϊό) was put in place on the suggestion of the Minister of Health and with the agreement of the Prime Minister (PM). Subsequently, Professor of Pathology and Infectious Disease, Sotiris Tsiodras, became the spokesperson of the Ministry of Health for Covid-19. The committee was placed at the forefront of the crisis-management effort. It provided advice and guided government policy with respect to the severity and the contagiousness of the virus, its potential implications for different sections of the population, the optimal measures for the treatment of those infected and the gradual deconfinement of the general population.

The committee tended to reflect the mainstream views of the international medical community and to transmit the general guidelines as recommended by the relevant international bodies. In this sense, it operated as the official contact-point between international expert bodies and the Greek state. In particular, it was in direct contact with the World Health Organisation (WHO) and the European Centre for Disease Prevention and Control (ECDPC) to receive the latest updates. By doing so, the committee ignored views that were cited by certain international experts, suggesting that the contagiousness of the virus was exaggerated and that its effects were not as grave as initially thought (e.g. Ioannidis 2020).

It is important to note that the committee's approach during the first phase of the pandemic was generally uncontested by the government. In particular, the de facto head of the crisis management effort, i.e. the head of the General Secretariat of Civil Protection and Crisis Management, Nikos Chardalias, developed a smooth and close cooperation with the head of the experts' committee. At the same time, PM Kyriakos Mitsotakis remained engaged during the whole period while exhibiting constant support for the work of the committee.

The composition of the committee reveals that the government chose to prioritise medical scientific advice as the latter was articulated by the predominant experts in the field. The committee was composed of around 30 health scientists, including medical doctors and epidemiologists, practitioners, and academics. The influence of health scientists and experts is also indicated by the fact that a potential alternative body of experts, the National Public Health Council (ESYDY) already mentioned above, being comprised of public servants and health scientists with diverse backgrounds, appeared less involved with the actual management of the crisis. This was the case even though ESYDY's mandate included the handling of such health crises (Greek Ministry of Health 2016).

The experts' committee, and by extension the Greek government, appeared to derive certain lessons from the short but intense Covid-19 outbreak in other countries, engaging in effective intra-crisis learning (Moynihan 2009). As Italy faced an earlier outbreak in February, with a dramatic rise of cases, they drew lessons from this incident and assumed that an equally 'loose' approach might lead to the same devastating results. Consequently, they opted for a more conservative approach and imposed a lockdown shortly after the first case was confirmed.

In addition, the government appeared to place the economic impact of the lockdown or its potential electoral backlash below public health considerations. This was reflected in the limited role played by the Ministry of Finance and the government's economic advisors during the first phase of the pandemic; their actions were mainly focused on suggesting measures that would remedy the contraction caused by the restrictive measures (Greek Ministry of Finance 2020). Only after the first phase was successfully handled did economists take a more active role in the decision-making process. In late May 2020 the government established the Covid-19 Observatory (Παρατηρητήριο για τον Covid-19) under the head of the Council of Economic Advisers.

Public sector response: the digital turn and intra-government coordination

Another element that facilitated the management of the crisis and enabled citizen compliance was a sudden turn of the Greek state towards e-services. The Mitsotakis government had announced after its election in July 2019 that e-governance was a priority, but this was not the first time that a Greek government had voiced such a commitment (Ta Nea 2019). To the surprise of all, a new comprehensive portal (gov.gr) was launched on 26 March, offering services such as on-line prescriptions and other e-services for which citizens would traditionally have had to queue up and congregate. Universities and schools started offering classes online. In addition, several helplines were put into place at a lightning speed (Greek Government 2020c). The role of the Ministry of Digital Governance during this period was central. A few of the new e-services that were delivered during the first three months of the pandemic were already under preparation but were then speeded up due to the unfolding crisis (Pierrakakis 2020).

The timely and efficient coordination between the central government and regional/local governments was also crucial in terms of successful crisis-management. Indeed, this was a major challenge as effective whole-of-government coordination was a recurring problem for the Greek state during crises. The government addressed this by gathering all responsibilities related to the pandemic under a single authority, the General Secretariat of Civil Protection and Crisis Management, whose head was promoted to Deputy Minister on 15 March 2020. The central government remained the key actor in the decision-making process, which meant no evident contradictions between the instructions issued by the different levels of government.

This was the case even though local authorities had substantial responsibilities vis-à-vis the management of the pandemic. Notably, they were responsible for the provision and maintenance of measures for the protection of public health, e.g. health checks of shops and businesses. Moreover, they were responsible for informing citizens about public health issues; about the implementation of public health programmes planned by the Ministry of Health or other ministries; and about the publication of local health provisions and measures for public health (European Committee of the Regions n.d.).

Nevertheless, the government chose to mitigate coordination costs and to take the lead with respect to pandemic management. The centralised structure of the Greek state, translated in this context to the General Secretariat of Civil Protection and Crisis Management taking the lead and delegating tasks to regional and local level authorities, contributed significantly to building consensus between different levels of government and managing the crisis more effectively. However, the emergence of local spikes and the need to occasionally impose local lockdowns suggest that some further delegation of authority to the local level might have produced more effective measures during the pandemic's later phases.

A successful communication strategy

An important element of successful crisis-management during the first phase was a clear communication strategy. There was a succinct and steady message coming from the government and the PM himself, that this was an emergency, and that the priority was to save human lives. The government clearly signalled that the economy was the next most important issue to deal with (Mitsotakis 2020a). The press conference held every evening at 6pm was led by Professor Tsiodras and became immediately very popular. He was followed by the recently appointed Deputy Minister of Civil Protection and Crisis Management, who announced new measures. A clear link between evidence and policy was established and fake news were discussed on almost a daily basis. This struggle against fake news was also backed up by the mainstream media.

A personal style of communication, which was often emotional, was used by all officials involved, including the PM who appeared live on TV five times between March and May 2020. At the same time, the daily briefings were based on transparency; efforts were made to present all existing evidence and to clearly signal the known-unknowns. To further reinforce this sense of transparency, journalists were encouraged to pose questions to attain a more thorough overview of the government's containment strategy. In addition to the daily briefings, the parliament also remained open and active with all sessions being publicly broadcast.

Overall, the appointment of Tsiodras as the government spokesperson and the adoption of such a communication strategy is in line with the expectations in the literature. This approach is occasionally employed by governments during crises in order to lend credibility and authority to the adopted policies, i.e. to reinforce public support for the government's problem-solving capacity (Boswell 2009, p. 7). It also aims to lead citizens to comply with the government's crisis-related measures as the former are expected to perceive the latter as the most efficacious and reliable solutions. In effect, by appointing a respected scientist to lead the effort both operationally and in terms of communication and by adopting a transparent modus operandi, the Greek government clearly signalled that its crisis-management policies predominantly served the goal of public health. Moreover, the government's choice to limit the role of politicians during this period should also be attributed to the above rationale. In particular, only the PM and the Deputy Minister of Civil Protection and Crisis Management had a prominent role while other relevant officials, including the Minister of Health, appeared to be less involved.

The government's approach also benefited from a generally favourable treatment by most media outlets. The content of restrictive measures did not appear as a contentious topic in the major Greek media (Chatzopoulou & Exadaktylos 2021). On the other hand, the public discourse in Greece seemed to be far more polarised with respect to the government's and the EU's response to the pandemic. In addition, this sense of polarisation seemed to spread with respect to the actions of other societal actors, including political parties, local authorities and the church. Such a level of contestation became even more pronounced during the pandemic's later phases.

All in all, the government's initial communication strategy bore fruits as most Greeks followed the restrictive measures, at least during the first phase of the pandemic. According to an opinion poll, 90.3 per cent of the respondents fully complied with the imposed health measures on personal hygiene while another 78.6 per cent complied with social distancing measures (HIT 2020, April). In this sense, it can be argued that having experts and scientists proposing these measures was of paramount importance, since people perceived them as impartial and backed by solid scientific evidence (Chrysopoulos 2020).

Societal and institutional dynamics

Public opinion and public trust

The predominance of expert advice during the first phase of the pandemic in Greece was not only positively associated with the government's crisis-management performance but also brought about another indirect and quite significant effect. According to initial surveys, the general public reacted positively to the government's evidence-informed response and levels of trust in the government and public institutions increased (Prorata 2020, April). Hence, 65 per cent of Greeks believed that the government was on top of the Covid-19 health crisis with only 15.5 per cent expressing the opposite viewpoint while 59.5 per cent fully trusted information issued by the Ministry of Health and the government (HIT 2020, April). This was indeed a break from the previous pattern of scepticism as the prolonged economic crisis and subsequent austerity measures had negatively affected citizens' trust in the government and public institutions (Drakos, Kallandranis & Karidis 2016).

What, therefore, seems to have happened in Greece during the first phase of the pandemic is that the decision of the government to invoke and largely base its policy strategy on expert advice helped the former not only to legitimise the adopted policies but also to increase citizens' compliance with them. According to more recent surveys, 75.3 per cent of the respondents posit that the use of experts' input generally leads to better policy decisions with only 3.9 per cent expressing the opposite viewpoint (YouGov 2021, March). Yet, trust in the government seems to have dropped, although only slightly, as the duration of the pandemic was prolonged (Dianeosis 2021, March).

The initial increase in public trust during the first phase of the pandemic also influenced the public's voting intentions, with an increasing gap between the governing ND (Νέα Δημοκρατία – New Democracy) and the official opposition SYRIZA (Συνασπισμός Ριζοσπαστικής Αριστεράς – Coalition of the Radical Left) as well as a significant personal lead of PM Mitsotakis (with 48 per cent) over

SYRIZA's leader Alexis Tsipras (26 per cent) in terms of citizens' trust (e.g. Metron Analysis 2020, April; Alco 2020, June). This trend did not change much over this period as illustrated in Figure 3.

Political dynamics

The pandemic's early phase constitutes a break from the usual pattern of political discourse in Greece. Scholars have characterised the Greek political system as being particularly polarised, perpetuating a culture of deep political divisions

(a)

(b)

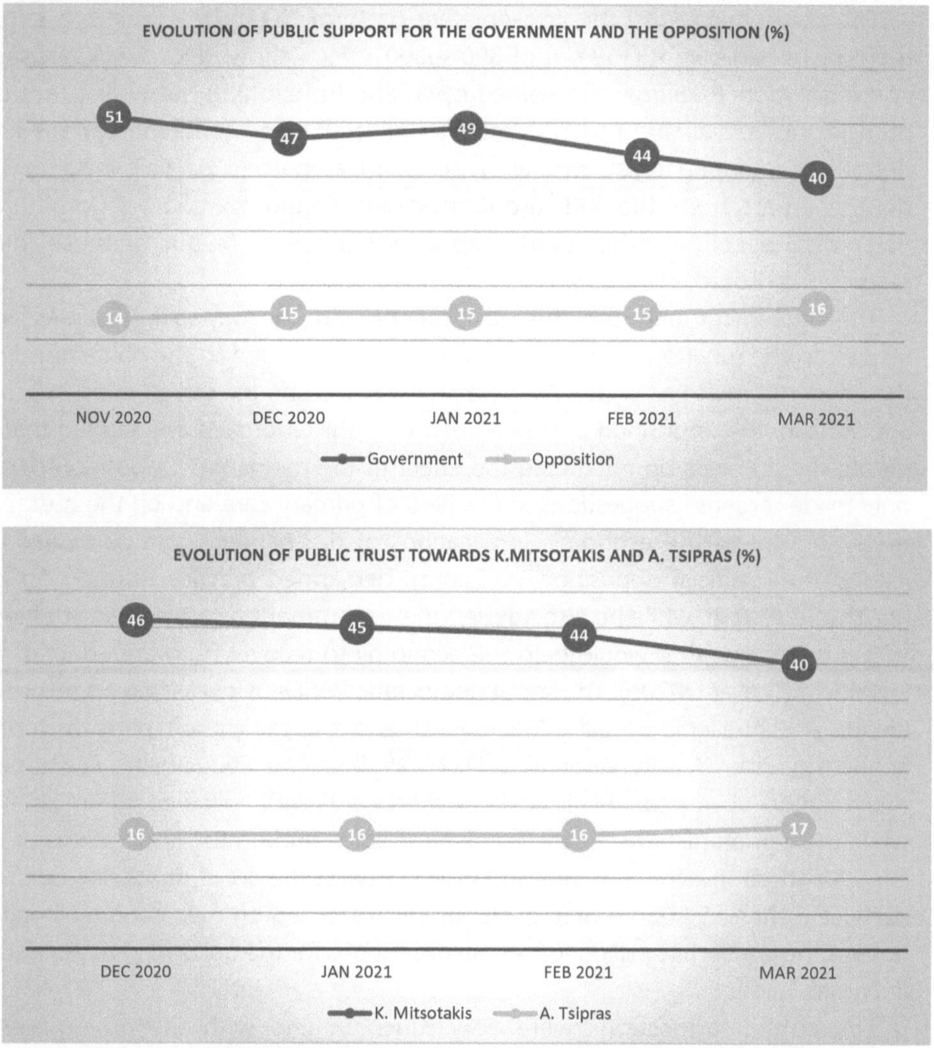

Figure 3. (a) Evolution of public support for the government and the opposition from November 2020 to March 2021 in Greece. (b) Evolution of public trust in the prime minister (K. Mitsotakis) and official opposition leader (A. Tsipras), November 2020-March 2021.
Source: Adapted from Metron Analysis (2021).

(Diamandouros 1994; Trantidis 2016, p. 31). The latter have changed in nature over time, with cleavages varying from left to right and from pro to anti-European, yet the element of polarisation has remained intact with opposing political forces depicting each other as 'enemies'. Following the country's prolonged financial crisis, Greece faced the Covid-19 crisis with its society and political system being deeply polarised once more (Andreadis & Stavrakakis 2019). As the Covid-19 crisis emerged, the relevant literature suggested two distinct alternatives vis-a-vis this phenomenon: either polarisation would recede for the sake of crisis management (a 'rally-around-the-flag' effect), or it would amplify the existing divisions leading to further polarisation (Chatzopoulou & Exadaktylos 2021, p. 4). Yet, the picture was a tad more nuanced during the pandemic's first phase.

The pandemic found the conservative party of ND in power with a strong majority in parliament (158 out of 300 seats), which allowed for quick decisions and legislation. Parliament remained open and functioning but with a reduced number of MPs allowed to be present (up to 25) and parliamentarians kept debating essential legislation with all political parties participating in the debate. Apart from the KKE (Κομμουνιστικό Κόμμα Ελλάδος – Communist Party of Greece), all other parties appeared to be in favour of these initial restrictions (Bourdaras 2020).

The agreement between the government and the opposition parties with respect to the functioning of the parliament also extended to the containment of the pandemic in its first phase. As the crisis escalated and the government imposed a lockdown, the opposition parties agreed with this approach and argued that all efforts should focus on mitigating the effect of the pandemic. Opposition parties only made targeted suggestions in the field of primary care and on the measures taken to address the economic implications of the pandemic. In particular, the leader of the official opposition, A. Tsipras, demanded practical support for the healthcare system, while he also advised the government to provide an additional stimulus package that would help the economy to recover from the effect of the lockdown (Ta Nea 2020b). The social democratic PASOK (Πανελλήνιο Σοσιαλιστικό Κίνημα – Panhellenic Socialist Movement), and the radical left party of former finance minister Yannis Varoufakis, DiEM 25 (Μέτωπο Ευρωπαϊκής Ρεαλιστικής Ανυπακοής – European Realistic Disobedience Front), followed a similar line, while the communist KKE focused on labour rights and on the implications of the crisis for those in economic precariousness. Finally, the small right-wing populist party EL (Ελληνική Λύση – Greek Solution) also focused on the economic implications of the crisis while calling for certain exceptions for the upcoming Easter period (Ioannou 2020).

The above suggestions were very much in line with the government's priorities and proposals, yet the administration had also to consider the existing budget constraints and hence limit the extent of its proposals to less generous measures. Nevertheless, none of the parliamentary parties contested the government's strategy of an extensive and strict lockdown.

Moreover, they all made an effort to halt potential fake news and not to give any support to alternative policies that were based on dubious scientific claims. In this sense, the Covid-19 pandemic served to lower tensions between parties, as it did in the society.

Yet, this conciliatory tone did not last long. Once the focus of the political debate moved to the handling of the pandemic's economic implications around mid-April, political tensions rose. As the government brought additional financial measures, SYRIZA and PASOK accused it of not disclosing whether these would be funded by the country's credit line or the ordinary budget (Tsatsouli 2020). A few days later, the government came under criticism again with respect to the handling of financial assistance. In particular, the government decided to allocate financial aid to certain groups of self-employed professionals on the condition that they would follow online training programmes. The latter appeared to be designed in a haphazard manner, leading opposition parties to question both the way the financial aid would be distributed but also the content thereof. Given the outcry, the government soon decided to change course and distribute the handout without the training-related precondition (Giokas 2020).

Another topic of political contestation had to do with how the government treated private healthcare providers during the early phase of the crisis. In particular, the opposition criticised the government for doubling the compensation that private clinics would receive whenever treating Covid-19 patients. SYRIZA insisted that the government should enrol private clinics and compensate them uniformly. The opposition parties equally levelled criticism with respect to the low level of testing and the high pricing of diagnostic tests in private clinics. They suggested that the government was over-compensating the latter, while also offering very little free testing.

By June and as the restrictive measures had been eased, political tensions escalated even further. The opposition's criticism was articulated along two lines. First, SYRIZA argued that the economic effects of the pandemic were further exacerbated by the government's previous economic failures. The second line of criticism revolved around the management of the communication campaign on Covid-19. All opposition parties accused the government of deciding in a non-transparent manner which media outlets would undertake this campaign and receive the subsequent funding (ANT1 2020). The media campaign played in favour of the government's prevention strategy as it allowed the propagation of a coherent message that emphasised scientific evidence and gave clear sanitary guidelines to citizens.

Conclusions

This article identified the elements that can explain the successful management of the first phase of the Covid-19 crisis in Greece. The government chose to inform and guide its policies by following closely the suggestions of the relevant experts' committee. By placing a committee of health experts at the forefront of the effort, the government followed a conservative but effective and proactive lockdown strategy, which resulted in limiting the dispersion of the virus. In addition, the public sector, via centralisation and tight coordination, managed to respond effectively by adopting new tools, like the digitalisation of public services. Finally, the government planned a clear communication campaign, based on the above scientific advice. This contributed to high citizen compliance during the first phase of the pandemic. In addition to citizens, the opposition also backed the government's response at least during the containment phase. The low number of deaths and the increase in public trust towards the government suggest that this approach can be labelled as a successful case of virus containment.

Although this rosy picture did not last for very long, it is worth analysing, since it proves that the Greek institutions, political system, and society have the ability to adapt and confront such an emergency. In particular, the article shows that previously overlooked features of policymaking, like the employment of experts, digital tools, and targeted raise-awareness campaigns can bring exponential benefits to the political system and the public. Indeed, some of the policy innovations introduced during this first phase are still in use. A useful exercise would be to identify lessons learned from the eurozone crisis and explore the resilience built into the political and social fabric of Greece. Subsequently, it may be possible to gauge whether the resilience gained during the previous crisis enabled a better management of the Covid-19 pandemic. In addition, further research can be conducted on whether evidence-informed policymaking can lead to higher compliance and to increased levels of trust towards governments.

All in all, the above insights suggest that even countries with low administrative capacity and tight budget constraints can manage major health incidents by employing the advice of experts, acting quickly, and creating an effective and convincing communication strategy. They subsequently speak to how expert knowledge can affect a state's crisis-management effort and under what conditions evidence-informed policies can augment problem-solving capacity during crises.

The Greek response to the second phase of the pandemic: a brief assessment

As the country successfully exited the first phase, an 'Intervention Mechanism' (Μηχανισμός Παρέμβασης), chaired by the PM and with the participation of the key actors of the first phase, was put into place. This body was composed of some health experts but mainly of close economic and political advisors to the

PM. Following advice from the Covid 19 Observatory, the 'Intervention Mechanism' was responsible for reinstating lockdown measures (Covid 19 Observatory 2020a). This Mechanism aspired to transpose the evidence-informed style of policymaking to the summer months in an effort to take timely decisions with respect to the pandemic's second phase (Mitsotakis 2020c). Nevertheless, as discussed below, it proved less effective than the earlier system of crisis management.

The second phase of the pandemic unravelled from October 2020 onwards. The marginally manageable, yet consistent, pressure on the national health system and the gradual increase in the number of cases, including in the refugee population after the burning of the Moria camp in September, resulted in Greece climbing up the list of countries ranked according to deaths per millions.

While the Greek strategy during the first phase proved successful, it seems that it lacked resilience overtime. The lack of warning country cases, along with the low number of deaths and infections that were recorded during the first phase, allowed the Greek government to postpone restrictions until the second phase was in full swing. The latter choice should also be attributed to the government's newfound focus on the economy. Indeed, economic concerns became much more salient, and economists took a more active role when it came to decisions on confinement (Haldoupis 2020). Given that the tourist industry represents a sizeable revenue stream for the Greek economy, the government tried to keep the country open for as long as possible during the summer/ fall period.

Moving to evidence-informed policies, the long duration of the crisis revealed the limited capacity of the government to shape a resilient and flexible strategy for the medium and long-term. With the emergence of the second phase, the government soon adopted a strict lockdown, following the advice of its experts' committee. In addition, Greece developed great testing capacity compared to the first phase. Yet, as the crisis dragged on, confinement fatigue also increased, leading to lower compliance. This was one of the reasons that the initial strategy proved less effective during the second phase. The experts' committee remained mainly of a medical nature, not involving scientists from disciplines that could offer solutions to compliance and fatigue problems (e.g. behavioural scientists and social psychologists). Indeed, Greece was one of the few countries employing an expert committee solely constituted of medical experts (Ladi, Panagiotatou & Angelou 2021). Having little experience of working closely with experts and convinced by its initially successful strategy, the government did not seem to grasp the benefits of receiving multidisciplinary input that would contribute towards a comprehensive and resilient crisis-management policy. Such lack of multidisciplinary expertise ended up making medical advice less efficient.

Moreover, problems appeared with respect to the communication strategy. While the initial message was based on unanimous expert advice as expressed by Professor Tsiodras, during the second phase the members of the experts' committee would go public, almost daily, expressing their individual views and underlining disagreements within the committee and, occasionally, with the government. The implications of this phenomenon were exacerbated by changes in the televised press conferences. After May 2020 press conferences were held two or three times per week and after a while on an as-needed basis. From autumn 2020 onwards, they were held by a variety of actors, most notably the Minister of Health, other high-ranking government officials, and different members of the experts' committee. Finally, the government's public messaging in favour of restraint and prudence was further undermined by some officials participating in large unofficial gatherings or seeking special exceptions (Smith 2021).

In addition to the above challenges, the government also faced a more polarised political landscape. The opposition parties openly criticised the government's strict lockdown strategy as inefficient. They also vocally objected to the government's choice to legislate on issues that required extensive deliberation (e.g. education reform, labour law) during an emergency period that left little room for such consultations. The increased polarisation together with the lockdown fatigue led to a proliferation of protests that further fed the spread of the virus. Finally, the government's economic capacity to support those most affected gradually decreased, leading to intense political contestation vis-à-vis the post-pandemic recovery.

The prolongation of the crisis also led to the contestation of the government's emergency policymaking approach. At the beginning of the crisis, the government legislated based on a sense of urgency to save lives. This mode of rule worked well as uncertainty was high, and the public had little knowledge about Covid-19. Yet, as the crisis continued, this modus operandi was contested. Societal and political actors sought to re-politicise the debate and questioned the decision-making process (whether policies really reflected experts' advice) and the content of the policies (whether a strict lockdown was the optimal policy). In this sense, the initial form of policymaking, i.e. of closely linking expert input with legislation and executive implementation, had to be adjusted to include elements of public deliberation. In this more nuanced process, the Greek state proved less effective compared to the pandemic's first phase.

Disclosure statement

No potential conflict of interest was reported by the author(s).

ORCID

Stella Ladi http://orcid.org/0000-0002-3021-3352

References

Alco (2020) 'Voting intention opinion poll conducted on behalf of Open Channel' in '*Δημοσκοπήσεις: Κυριαρχία Μητσοτάκη – Μεγάλο ποσοστό πρώην ψηφοφόρων του ΣΥΡΙΖΑ στη ΝΔ*' [Opinion polls: Predominance of Mitsotakis – Large section of former SYRIZA's voters to support New Democracy], ed. P. Thema, 10 June, available online at: https://www.protothema.gr/politics/article/1015169/dimoskopiseis-kuriarhia-mitsotaki-megalo-pososto-proin-psifoforon-tou-suriza-sti-nd/

Anastasatou, M., Nitsi, E. I. & Katsikas, D. C. (2018) 'Η μεταρρύθμιση του ενιαίου μισθολογίου στο Δημόσιο' [The reform of the common wage-grid for the public sector], in *Διαρθρωτικές Μεταρρυθμίσεις στην Ελλάδα κατά τη Διάρκεια της Κρίσης, 2010–2014* [Structural Reforms in Greece during the Crisis (2010–2014)], ed. D. Katsikas, Bank of Greece, Athens, pp. 47–80.

Andreadis, I. & Stavrakakis, Y. (2019) 'Dynamics of polarization in the Greek case', *The Annals of the American Academy of Political and Social Science*, vol. 681, no. 1, pp. 157–172.

Angelaki, M. (2016) 'Policy continuity and change in Greek social policy in the aftermath of the sovereign debt crisis', *Social Policy and Administration*, vol. 50, no. 2, pp. 262–277.

ANT1 (2020) 'Μητσοτάκης - Τσίπρας: Κόντρα στην Βουλή για κορονοϊό και οικονομία' [Mitsotakis - Tsipras: fight in parliament over the coronavirus and the economy], 12 June, available online at: https://www.ant1news.gr/eidiseis/article/571184/mitsotakis-tsipras-kontra-stin-boyli-gia-koronoio-kai-oikonomia

Boswell, C. (2009) *The Political Uses of Expert Knowledge Immigration Policy and Social Research*, Cambridge University Press, Cambridge.

Bourdaras, G. (2020) 'Εκτακτα μέτρα λόγω κορωνοϊού και στο Κοινοβούλιο' [Emergency measures due to the coronavirus also in the Greek Parliament], *Kathimerini*, 12 March, available online at: https://www.kathimerini.gr/1068726/article/epikairothta/politikh/ektakta-metra-logw-korwnoioy-kai-sto-koinovoylio

Carassava, A. (2020) 'Greece extends lockdown on more than 120,000 migrants, refugees', *Voa News*, 21 June, available online at: https://www.voanews.com/covid-19-pandemic/greece-extends-lockdown-more-120000-migrants-refugees

Chatzopoulou, S. & Exadaktylos, T. (2021) 'Whose opinion is it? Public debates and repertoires of action in Greece during the first Covid-19 lockdown period', *Javnost - The Public*, vol. 28, no. 2, pp. 185–201.doi:10.1080/13183222.2021.1919381

Chrysopoulos, P. (2020) 'Six ways Greece has successfully flattened the coronavirus curve', *Greek Reporter*, 22 April, available online at: https://greece.greekreporter.com/2020/04/22/six-ways-greece-has-successfully-flattened-the-coronavirus-curve/

Covid 19 Observatory (2020a) '1η Έκθεση Κυβερνητικής Επιτροπής' [1st Governmental Committee Report], 29 May, available online at: https://covid19.gov.gr/1i-ekthesi-paratiritiriou-kyvernitikis-epitropis/

Covid 19 Observatory (2020b) '5η Έκθεση Κυβερνητικής Επιτροπής' [5th Governmental Committee Report], 19 June, available online at: https://covid19.gov.gr/5i-ekthesi-kyvernitikis-epitropis/

Covid-19 Health System Response Monitor (2020) 'Policy responses from Greece', available online at: https://www.covid19healthsystem.org/countries/greece/livinghit.aspx?Section=2.1%20Physical%20infrastructure&Type=Section

Diamandouros, N. (1994), *Cultural Dualism and Political Change in Post-authoritarian Greece*, Instituto Juan, Madrid.

Dianeosis (2021) 'Πανελλαδική έρευνα κοινής γνώμης για την πανδημία του κορωνοϊού – 5ο κύμα' [Panhellenic public opinion survey on the Covid-19 pandemic – 5th wave], March, available online at: https://www.dianeosis.org/wp-content/uploads/2021/03/pandemic_questionnaire_wave_5-1.pdf

Drakos, K., Kallandranis, C. & Karidis, S. (2016) 'Determinants of trust in institutions: survey-based evidence from the European Union', *Regent's Working Papers in Business & Management*, Working paper 1607, available online at: https://www.regents.ac.uk/sites/default/files/2018-11/rwpbm1607-drakos-k-kallandranis-c-karidis-s.pdf

Economou, C., Kaitelidou, D., Karanikolos, M. & Maresso, A. (2017) 'Greece: health system review', *Health Systems in Transition*, vol. 19, no. 5, pp. 1–166.

Economou, C., Kaitelidou, D., Konstantakopoulou, O. & Vildiridi, L. (2020) 'Policy responses for Greece', *Covid 19 Health System Response Monitor*, 5 June, available online at: https://www.covid19healthsystem.org/countries/greece/livinghit.aspx?Section=1.1%20Health%20communication&Type=Section

European Commission. (2020a) 'Policy measures taken against the spread and impact of the coronavirus', 14 April, available online at: https://ec.europa.eu/info/sites/info/files/policy_measures_taken_against_the_spread_and_impact_of_the_coronavirus_14042020.pdf

European Commission. (2020b) 'Policy measures taken against the spread and impact of the coronavirus', 25 June, available online at: https://ec.europa.eu/info/files/policy-measures-against-spread-coronavirus_en

European Committee of the Regions. (n.d.) 'Division of powers: Greece–public health', available online at: https://portal.cor.europa.eu/divisionpowers/Pages/Greece-Public-health.aspx

Eurostat. (2020) 'Healthcare expenditure statistics', available online at: https://ec.europa.eu/eurostat/statistics-explained/index.php/Healthcare_expenditure_statistics

Featherstone, K. (2015) 'External conditionality and the debt crisis: the 'Troika' and public administration reform in Greece', *Journal of European Public Policy*, vol. 22, no. 3, pp. 295–314.

Giokas, A. (2020) 'Υπόθεση «σκοιλ ελικικου»: Το παρασκήνιο πίσω από το φιάσκο της τηλεκατάρτισης' [The Skoil elikou case: the background of the remote learning fiasco], *Ta Nea*, 26 April, available online at: https://www.ethnos.gr/politiki/102098_ypothesi-skoil-elikikoy-paraskinio-piso-apo-fiasko-tis-tilekatartisis

Godin, M. (2020) 'COVID-19 outbreaks are now emerging in refugee camps. Why did it take so long for the virus to reach them?', *Time*, 9 October, available online at: https://time.com/5893135/covid-19-refugee-camps/

Greek Government (2020a) 'Covid-19 portal: economy & labour', available online at: https://covid19.gov.gr/category/oikonomia-ergasia/

Greek Government (2020b) 'Covid-19 portal: taxation', available online at: https://covid19.gov.gr/katavoli-tou-60-tou-misthomatos/

Greek Government (2020c) 'Covid-19 portal', available online at: https://covid19.gov.gr/

Greek Government (2020d) 'Covid-19 live analytics', available online at: https://covid19.gov.gr/covid19-live-analytics/

Greek Law 4675/2020, available online at: https://www.e-nomothesia.gr/kat-ygeia/nomos-4675-2020-phek-54a-11-3-2020.html

Greek Ministry of Finance (2020) 'Τοποθέτηση του Υπουργού Οικονομικών κ. Χρήστου Σταϊκούρα για το Κυβερνητικό Σχέδιο Επανεκκίνησης της Ελληνικής Οικονομίας' [Statement by the Minister of Finance, Mr. Christos Staikouras, on the government's plan to restart the economy], 20 May, available online at: https://sbe.org.gr/newsletters/covid/covid_38/2.pdf

Greek Ministry of Health (2016) 'Άρθρο 24 – Εθνικό Συμβούλιο Δημόσιας Υγείας' [Article 24 - National Council of Public Health], 13 May, available online at: http://www.opengov.gr/yyka/?p=1693

Haldoupis, N. (2020) 'Ώρες αγωνίας για την πανδημία: Το σενάριο ύφεσης το 2021' [Anxiety over the pandemic: The recession scenario for 2021], *Business Daily*, 25 October, available online at: https://www.businessdaily.gr/oikonomia/28909_ores-agonias-gia-tin-pandimia-senario-yfesis-2021

Hatzigeorgiou, M. N. & Raj, M. (2020) 'Why is Greece an outlier in EU's Covid-19 response?', *EU Observer*, 19 May, available online at: https://euobserver.com/opinion/148397

HIT (2020) 'Online survey conducted by the Institute of Communication and Literacy in Health and the Media (hit.org.gr) in collaboration with the healthpharma.gr portal', 23-28 April, available online at: https://www.in.gr/wp-content/uploads/2020/05/eyuer1588602317474.pdf

InfoMigrants (2020) 'Greece: first cases of coronavirus among migrants on Lesbos', 13 May, available online at: https://www.infomigrants.net/en/post/24707/greece-first-cases-of-coronavirus-among-migrants-on-Lesbos

International Office of Migration in Greece (2020) 'IOM raises concern over increasing Covid-19 cases recorded in Greece mainland refugee and migrant camp', 2 April, available online at: https://greece.iom.int/en/news/iom-raises-concern-over-increasing-covid-19-cases-recorded-greece-mainland-refugee-and-migrant

Ioannidis, J. (2020) 'The infection fatality rate of COVID-19 inferred from seroprevalence data', Pre-print version, *medRxiv*, available online at: https://www.medrxiv.org/content/10.1101/2020.05.13.20101253v3

Ioannou, H. (2020) 'Συναίνεση σε άδεια έδρανα για την κρίση του κορονοϊού' [Consensus in front of empty seats on the front of Covid-19], *Efsyn*, 3 April, available online at: https://www.efsyn.gr/politiki/boyli/237774_synainesi-se-adeia-edrana-gia-tin-krisi-toy-koronoioy

Kikilias, V. (2020) Speech in the Greek parliament, 12 June, available online at: https://www.moh.gov.gr/articles/ministry/grafeio-typoy/press-releases/7276-apanthsh-ypoyrgoy-ygeias-basilh-kikilia-sthn-epikairh-eperwthsh-80-boyleytwn-toy-SYRIZA-me-thema-ta-problhmata-sth-diaxeirish-ths-pandhmias-kai-oi-proteraiothtes-gia-thn-epomenh-mera-sto-e-s-y

Kondilis, E., Puchner, K., Veizis, A., Papatheodorou, C. & Benos, A. (2020) 'Covid-19 and refugees, asylum seekers, and migrants in Greece', *BMJ (Clinical Research Ed.)*, vol. 369, available online at: https://www.bmj.com/content/369/bmj.m2168

Kousi, T., Mitsi, L.-C. & Simos, J. (2021) 'The early stage of Covid-19 outbreak in Greece: a review of the national response and the socioeconomic impact', *International Journal of Environmental Research and Public Health*, vol. 18, p. 322.

Ladi, S. (2013) 'Evidence-based policymaking in Greece', in *Greece's Horizons: Reflecting on the Country's Assets and Capabilities*, eds P. Sklias & N. Tzifakis, Springer, Heidelberg, pp. 71–78.

Ladi, S. (2020) 'Government policy-making' in *The Oxford Handbook of Modern Greek Politics*, eds. K. Featherstone & D. Sotiropoulos, Oxford University Press, Oxford, pp. 441–456.

Ladi, S., Panagiotatou, D. & Angelou, A. (2021) Database created as part of the project 'A global mapping of the use of expertise and evidence-informed policies in the management of the Covid-19 pandemic', funded by Research England Quality-related Research Strategic Priorities Fund, Queen Mary University of London, available online at: https://www.qmul.ac.uk/gpi/projects/covid-map/

Metron Analysis (2020) 'Voting intention opinion poll conducted on behalf of Mega Channel' in Kanellis, V. (2020) 'Δημοσκόπηση: Τεράστια διαφορά ΝΔ από ΣΥΡΙΖΑ – Τι λένε οι πολίτες για τον κορονοϊό' [Opinion poll: huge gap between New Democracy and SYRIZA – what citizens think of Covid-19], *Ta Nea*, 30 April, available online at: https://www.tanea.gr/2020/04/30/politics/dimoskopisi-terastia-diafora-nd-apo-SYRIZA-ti-lene-oi-polites-gia-ton-koronaio/

Metron Analysis (2021) 'Metron forum 2.0' conducted on behalf of Mega Channel, March, available online at: https://www.candiadoc.gr/wp-content/uploads/2021/03/dimoskopisi.pdf

Mitsotakis, K. (2020a) 'Διάγγελμα του Πρωθυπουργού Κ. Μητσοτάκη της 17ης Μαρτίου 2020 για τον κορονοϊό' [Address of the Prime Minister K. Mitsotakis of 17 March 2020 on Covid-19], available online at: https://www.youtube.com/watch?v=GzcAXE2Ofx4

Mitsotakis, K. (2020b) 'Διάγγελμα Κυριάκου Μητσοτάκη για την εργασία, τον τουρισμό & την οικονομία 20/ 05/2020' [Address of K. Mitsotakis for labour, tourism and the economy, 20 May 2020], available online at: https://www.youtube.com/watch?v=bl1jc3ZsLnQ

Mitsotakis, K. (2020c) 'Ενημερωτικό σημείωμα για την τηλεδιάσκεψη υπό τον Κυριάκο Μητσοτάκη, για τον κορονοϊό και την εισαγωγική τοποθέτηση του Πρωθυπουργού' [Information note on the teleconference related to the Covid-19 measures and introductory remarks by the Prime Minister], available online at: https://primeminister.gr/2020/08/05/24531

Moynihan, D. (2009) 'From intercrisis to intracrisis learning', *Journal of Contingencies and Crisis Management*, vol. 17, no. 3, pp. 189–198.

Our World in Data (2020) 'Coronavirus pandemic: daily updated research and data', 22 June, available online at: https://ourworldindata.org/

Pappas, T. (1998) *Making Party Democracy in Greece*, Palgrave Macmillan, Hampshire and London.

Petmesidou, M. (2019) 'Challenges to healthcare reform in crisis-hit Greece', e-cadernos *CES*, vol. 31, pp. 19–42.

Pierrakakis, K. in Papageorgaki, C. (2020) 'Μια διαδικτυακή συζήτηση για τον ψηφιακό μετασχηματισμό του κράτους' [An online discussion on the digital transformation of the state], *Dianeosis*, 3 June, available online at: https://www.dianeosis.org/2020/05/pempto_dianeosis_live/

Prorata (2020) 'Η Ελλάδα στην εποχή του κορονοϊού: Η τρίτη έρευνα' [Greece in the era of coronavirus: The third survey], 26 April, available online at: https://prorata.gr/2020/04/26/i-ellada-stin-epoxi-koronoiou-i-triti-ereyna/

Proto Thema (2020) 'Covid-19 live updates', 23 June, available online at: https://longform.protothema.gr/koronoios/

Skai (2020) 'Ξεκινούν έλεγχοι του ΕΟΔΥ σε όλα τα γηροκομεία της Αττικής' [EODY starts conducting random testing across Attica's nursing homes], 13 April, available online at: https://www.skai.gr/news/greece/koronoios-ksekinoun-elegxoi-tou-eody-se-ola-ta-girokomeia-tis-attikis

Smith, H. (2021) 'Greek PM criticised for lunch that breached Covid restrictions', *The Guardian*, 7 February, available online at: https://www.theguardian.com/world/2021/feb/07/greek-prime-minister-criticised-for-lunch-with-up-to-40-people

Sotiropoulos, D. (2007) *Κράτος και Μεταρρύθμιση στη Σύγχρονη Νότια Ευρώπη* [State and Reform in Contemporary Southern Europe], Ekdoseis Potamos, Athens.

Spanou, C. (2008) 'State reform in Greece: responding to old and new challenges', *International Journal of Public Sector Management*, vol. 21, no. 2, pp. 150–173.

Spanou, C. & Sotiropoulos, D. (2011) 'The Odyssey of administrative reforms in Greece, 1981-2009: a tale of two reform paths', *Public Administration*, vol. 89, no. 3, pp. 723–737.

Ta Nea (2019) 'Κυριάκος Πιερρακάκης: Ο κεντροαριστερός και έμπιστος του πρωθυπουργού στο υπουργείο Επικρατείας και Ψηφιακής Διακυβέρνησης' [Kiriakos Pierrakakis: The man of the centre-left and trusted by the Prime Minister in the Ministry of State and Digital Government], 8 July, available online at: https://www.tanea.gr/2019/07/08/politics/kyriakos-pierrakakis-o-kentroaristeros-kai-empistos-tou-prothypourgou-sto-ypourgeio-epikrateias-kai-psifiakis-diakyvernisis/

Ta Nea (2020a) 'Κορονοϊός: Η παγκόσμια τραγωδία με τους θανάτους σε γηροκομεία' [Coronavirus: the global tragedy of deaths in retirement homes], 22 April, available online at: https://www.tanea.gr/2020/04/22/world/koronaios-i-pagkosmia-tragodia-me-tous-thanatous-se-girokomeia/

Ta Nea (2020b) 'Μητσοτάκης και Τσίπρας έβαλαν σε καραντίνα τις μετωπικές αντιπαραθέσεις' [Mitsotakis and Tsipras put in quarantine their dramatic exchanges], 2 April, available online at: https://www.tanea.gr/2020/04/02/politics/parliament/mitsotakis-kai-tsipras-evalan-se-karantina-tis-metopikes-antiparatheseis/

Tinios, P. (2013) 'The pension merry-go-round: the end of a cycle?', in *From Stagnation to Forced Adjustment: Reforms in Greece, 1974-2010*, eds S. Kalyvas, G. Pagoulatos & H. Tsoukas, C. Hurst & Co. (Publishers) Ltd., London, pp. 117–133.

Trantidis, A. (2016) *Clientelism and Economic Policy: Greece and the Crisis*, Routledge, London.

Tsatsouli, A. (2020) 'Σε «μονομαχία» στη Βουλή καλεί ο Τσίπρας τον Μητσοτάκη για το «μαξιλάρι» των 37 δις. Ευρώ' [Tsipras invites Mitsotakis on a parliamentary showdown on the use of the 37 billion credit line], *in.gr*, 16 April, available online at: https://www.in.gr/2020/04/16/politics/vouli/se-monomaxia-sti-vouli-kalei-o-tsipras-ton-mitsotaki-gia-maksilari-ton-37-dis-eyro/

Worldometer (2020) 'Covid-19 Coronavirus Pandemic', 23 June, available online at: https://www.worldometers.info/coronavirus/?utm_campaign=homeAdvegas1?

YouGov (2021) Public opinion survey commissioned to YouGov as part of the project 'A global mapping of the use of expertise and evidence-informed policies in the management of the Covid-19 pandemic', funded by Research England Quality-related Research Strategic Priorities Fund, (Queen Mary University of London Team Leader: Dr Stella Ladi).

Surviving the Covid-19 Pandemic under Right-wing Populist Rule: Turkey in the First Phase

Özge Kemahlıoğlu and Oya Yeğen

ABSTRACT

Turkey survived the first phase of the Covid-19 pandemic relatively successfully. Compared to some other populist governments, the AKP did not deny the seriousness of the crisis or the importance of medical expertise. The demographics of the population helped, but precautionary measures and the healthcare reform implemented earlier also contributed to this relative success. As a right-wing populist party, the AKP implemented healthcare and economic policies that appealed simultaneously to business and low-income groups. Populist rhetoric blaming the opposition and exclusion from policy-making of unfavourable sectors including opposition-run municipalities deepened the existing polarisation. The crisis response also revealed how the personalised and centralised nature of the executive in the new presidential system can lead to inconsistencies and arbitrariness.

We analyse the first phase of the pandemic in Turkey (10 January – 30 June 2020) to shed light on the political and socio-economic factors that shaped the government's response. The incumbent AKP (Adalet ve Kalkınma Partisi – Justice and Development Party) holds a populist stance that takes advantage of international conflicts and blames international enemies and domestic elites in response to the country's economic and political problems (Elçi 2019). As a right-wing populist government, it faces the challenge of responding to the demands of business and simultaneously appealing to low-income groups (Öniş & Kutlay 2020). Our analysis shows that these populist characteristics were also noticeable in the government's response to the pandemic. The leaders' rhetoric included frequent comparisons with the 'West' and accusations against the opposition as the enemy. The healthcare and economic policies appealed to the low-income sectors through measures such as coverage of medical expenses, a ban on layoffs, cash support for unpaid leave, and short-term work allowance, but they also served business interests, and restrictions were carefully crafted to maintain economic activity. The response mostly relied on deficit financing, posing questions about its sustainability.

Unlike some other populist governments, however, the Turkish government did not deny the seriousness of the pandemic. The government consulted experts and started taking preventive measures. In other right-wing populist governments, such as Brazil and the US, the presidents' rhetoric underestimated the crisis, and the policy responses were relatively slow and limited in some areas. While the Turkish government was careful to maintain economic production, restrictions were imposed to prevent the health system from collapsing. For example, Turkey started imposing limited lockdowns in March and extended contract tracing in April, whereas Brazil introduced its first stay-home restrictions in May, and the US implemented only limited contact tracing (Hale et al. 2021).

Our analysis starts with an overview of the pandemic's evolution and Turkey's preparedness for the crisis. A detailed discussion of the central government's healthcare and economic policies follows with emphasis on how the AKP's healthcare reform and recent switch to executive presidential system affected its response. The next section focuses on the sub-national response, highlighting the conflicts with the central government. The polarised nature of the government-opposition dynamics is discussed next. The right-wing populist elements in the healthcare and economic policies are also underlined. This is followed by a section on the media, public opinion, and civil society.[1] We conclude with an overview of the political response, emphasising the personalised and exclusionary nature of the policy-making process that led to inconsistencies and arbitrariness in the policy implementation and further polarisation. We suggest that these problems with the populist government's policymaking and the short-term focus of the measures pose a challenge for the sustainability of the response to the prolonged crisis.

Crisis preparedness in 'New Turkey'

The political-economic landscape of Turkey has been transformed under AKP in the context of neoliberal restructuring (Öniş 2009). Its economic and social position has been conceptualised as social neoliberalism (Dorlach 2015) or neoliberal populism (Özdemir 2020). In the post-2011 era, the governing party under the leadership of Recep Tayyip Erdoğan has gradually weakened civil liberties, eroded checks and balances, and centralised power in a process of backsliding. This became institutionalised after the 2018 presidential elections which installed the executive presidential system, adopted via a referendum conducted under a state of emergency (Esen & Gumuscu 2020). The new system concentrated all the executive powers in one person. The responsibilities previously exercised by the prime minister and the council of ministers were transferred to the president and the parliament's legislative authority was trimmed. These changes, its supporters claimed, would rationalise decision-making and provide efficient governance. The public health crisis over Covid-19 presented a litmus test for these claims.

Instituted in the 2000s, the healthcare reform process has been the most comprehensive of AKP's reform projects (Dorlach 2015; Yilmaz 2017). The reforms unified the fragmented public health insurance schemes, including the non-contributory health insurance programme (Green Cards) for low-income groups, under the newly established SGK (*Sosyal Güvenlik Kurumu* – Social Security Institution). As a result, Turkey achieved universal health insurance coverage where monetary contributions are compulsory except for the low-income sector. Dubbed the 'Turkish Model', the hybrid healthcare system adopted an egalitarian approach that has gone along with 'passive privatisation', where the SGK partly reimburses for services provided in private sector hospitals including intensive care treatment (Yılmaz 2017, p. 231; Agartan 2012). New private hospitals opened across the country and the bed capacity increased. Most notably, between 2011 and 2018, intensive care beds increased by 82 per cent and reached 38,098 in 2018 (Ministry of Health 2018). When Covid-19 arrived, Turkey had 40 ICU (intensive care unit) beds per 100,000 population (Ministry of Health 2020a).

Turkey's healthcare system is oriented towards hospital-based services. As of 2010, primary care doctors are no longer civil servants but contracted independent professionals. Rather than providing service to a specified geographical area (Akman et al. 2017), a family doctor on average is responsible for more than 3,000 patients. The absence of a referral system allows patients to skip primary care services, resulting in a disjointed system where frequent consultations occur at the second and third tier institutions and physicians experience an increased workload. As Table 1 shows, Turkey's healthcare spending per capita is less than one-third of the OECD average and, at 4.2 per cent of GDP, much less than the EU average.

The construction of city hospitals under the public-private partnership (PPP) model allowed Turkish construction companies and foreign investors to build gigantic complexes on public land and then lease them to the Ministry of Health (MoH) for 25 years. The size and location of these hospitals and the financing of these projects by foreign currency loans had been the target of much criticism (Pala 2018). The PPP investment model allowed the private sector to benefit from public rent and for the AKP to build its loyal business class and attract foreign direct investment. With the construction of these huge complexes in suburban areas, small hospitals in city centres were closed down and hence, bed capacity has not increased substantially. Operational since 2017, at the onset of the Covid-19 pandemic, Turkey had ten such hospitals with an average capacity of 1,417 beds (Transparency International Turkey 2020).

The experience of earthquakes in 1999 led Turkey to reform its management and coordination structure. It took steps to align with EU public health *acquis*, specifically with regard to the early warning and response systems (EWRS) for communicable diseases. Previously, Turkey had faced difficulties in addressing the avian influenza crisis (Corbacioglu, Celik & Saran 2016).[2] With lessons

Table 1. Healthcare indicators in Turkey compared to OECD/EU averages.

TURKEY AND OECD AVERAGE COMPARED†					
	Health expenditure as a share of GDP (2018)	Health expenditure per capita $ (2018)	Practicing doctors per 1,000 population (2017)	Practicing nurses per 1,000 population (2017)	Hospital beds per 1,000 population (2017)
OECD average	8.8	3,994	3.5	8.8	4.7
Turkey	4.2	1,227	1.9	2.1	2.8

TURKEY AND EU AVERAGE COMPARED††					
	Health expenditure as a share of GDP (2017)	Health expenditure per capita € (2017)	Practicing doctors per 1,000 population (2016)	Practising nurses per 1,000 population (2016)	Hospital beds per 1,000 population (2016)
EU average	9.6	2,773	3.6	8.4	5.1
Turkey	4.2	824	1.8	1.9	2.8

Source: †OECD Health at a Glance 2019, ††Health at a Glance: Europe 2018
Note: The data for Turkey include doctors, as well as educators, managers and researchers working in the health sector.

learned from the 2009 influenza pandemic and the recommendations of the World Health Organisation (WHO), in 2019 it revised the action plan (Pandemic Influenza National Preparedness Plan) (Ministry of Health 2019). According to a WHO Europe assessment in 2010, Turkey overall met the International Health Regulations (IHR) requirements, and its health system's surge capacity was well developed. However, as Table 1 shows, the capacity of the healthcare service in terms of doctors, nurses and hospital beds is significantly less than the OECD and EU averages.

Turkey hosts the largest refugee population worldwide. According to official data that excludes irregular migrants, by April 2020, Turkey had more than 3.5 million Syrians under temporary protection with only 63,518 staying in camps (Karakaş 2020). Refugees who are registered with temporary protection status have access to healthcare services provided by SGK's general health insurance scheme. Together with community health centres and family health centres that continued to serve Syrians, newly established migrant health centres address the refugees' needs. Integration of Syrian health workers with WHO-supported projects (Yılmaz 2019) and establishment of new migrant health centres, with funds from the EU but under the supervision of the Ministry of Health, contributed to Turkey's capacity.

All public health institutions were brought under the Turkish Public Health Institute (Türkiye Kamu Hastaneleri Kurumu TPHI) overseeing primary healthcare services, public health measures, communicable diseases and the early warning and response system (Ekmekci 2016, 885). In compliance with EU legislation that is in line with IHR 2005, Turkey had identified TPHI as the institution responsible for the epidemic surveillance of communicable diseases. A central goal of the reform programme was to diffuse the centralised power of the Ministry of Health and reorganise its role in the healthcare system. However, after Turkey adopted the presidential system, partial reversals occurred (Emergency Decree Law 694, 25 August 2017). Responsibilities that were previously assigned to subsidiary institutions were transferred back to Ministry of Health (Hoxha 2020). The TPHI was reorganised as a General Directorate of Public Health (Kamu Hastaneleri Genel Müdürlüğü, GDPH) under the direct control of the ministry.

As Turkey entered the Covid-19 crisis, its health sector had increased its ICU capacity and had certain advantages such as a young health workforce.[3] In May 2019, it had instituted an updated plan for a possible influenza pandemic. However, a major vulnerability of Turkey was the state of its economy. The declining economic performance in the late AKP era had become more daunting, especially after the summer 2018 currency crisis. External debt, high unemployment, and inflation rates had all improved since the 2018 market shock and following a short contraction in 2019, the situation had stabilised.[4] However, this could only be achieved by expanding cheap credit and public spending ahead of the 2019 municipal elections. Overall, the declining foreign reserves, the dollar-denominated debt in both the public and private sectors and the dependence on foreign financing have meant that when the pandemic hit, the country had limited tools to address the economic fall back.

Arrival and evolution of the Covid-19 pandemic

The spread of Covid-19 caught Turkey at a time when the country was occupied with other crises, including an economic one discussed in the previous section. Internationally Turkey was closely involved in the Libyan conflict. In February 2020, fighting in Idlib, Syria, intensified and the country was shocked by the news of an airstrike that, according to official accounts, killed 33 soldiers. Following the government's response to call Europe into action, thousands of refugees then went to the Bulgarian and Greek borders and attempted to enter EU territory.

Amid all these crises, Turkey reported its first case on 10 March 2020 and its first coronavirus death on 17 March. The number of cases jumped significantly in a short time, suggesting that the virus had arrived earlier (Figure 1). In less

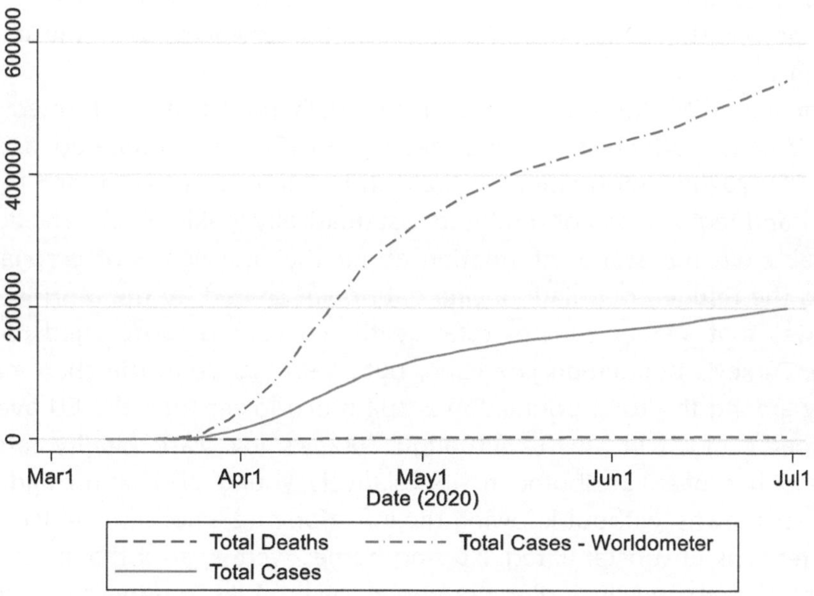

Figure 1. Cumulative trend in cases and deaths in the first phase of the Covid-19 pandemic in Turkey (1 March-30 June 2020).

Source: Ministry of Health, https://covid19.saglik.gov.tr/EN-69532/general-coronavirus-table.html; Worldometers, https://www.worldometers.info/coronavirus/

Note: After the announcement by the Ministry of Health that their data reported number of 'patients' rather than cases in July 2020, Worldometers updated its data using the figures shared in November. Here, we report both the official figures and Worldometers' predicted figures.

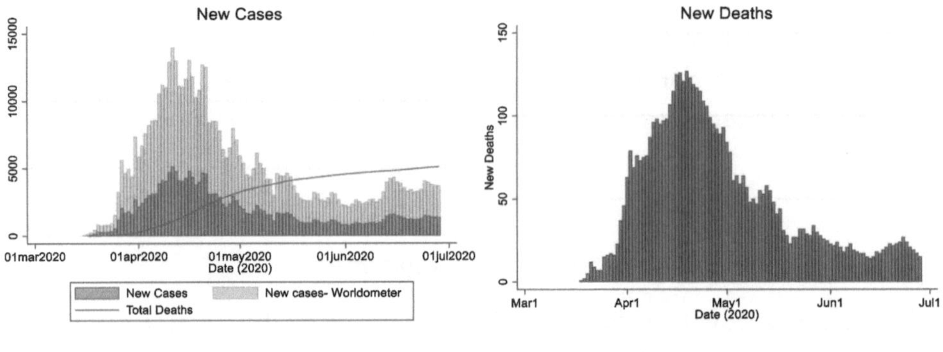

Figure 2. Evolution of cases and deaths in the first phase of the Covid-19 pandemic in Turkey (1 March-30 June 2020).

Source: Ministry of Health https://covid19.saglik.gov.tr/EN-69532/general-coronavirus-table.html; Worldometers, https://www.worldometers.info/coronavirus/

than a month, Turkey was among the top ten countries with the highest number of cases. The number of deaths increased from mid-March till mid-April and as Figure 2 shows, reached its peak at 127 deaths on 19 April. In comparison to other countries with similar high case numbers, Turkey's case-fatality rate remained low (at 2.6 per cent as of 30 June 2020). Reports of excess mortality as well as anecdotal evidence of false negatives identified by CT scans and clinical symptoms raised doubts about under-reporting.[5] As discussed in detail later, the Ministry of Health acknowledged the problems with the data in Autumn 2020.

Data shared by the MoH included only daily/total tests performed; new cases, deaths, patients recovered; patients in ICU, and intubated patients (HASUDER 2020b). Information on the distribution of cases according to age, gender and region was not disclosed systematically (Cakir 2020).[6] The authorities also did not share information about the prevalence of coronavirus among the refugee population. One data point shared by the MoH in early June was that 93 per cent of total deaths concerned those aged 65 and above. Turkey's population is ageing, but at 9.1 per cent, the share of the elderly among the total population is still much lower than the EU average (19.2 per cent) (TÜİK 2020). Although Turkey's low case fatality rate for Covid-19 has been attributed to its relatively young population and age-based lockdowns, without knowing the infection rate among the elderly, any claim remains unsubstantiated. Nursing homes were spared thanks to early preventive measures, including comprehensive guides, routine daily screenings and coordinated safeguards such as staff shifts. According to piecemeal information shared by the Ministry of Family, Labour and Social Services, deaths in nursing homes accounted for 4 per cent of all coronavirus-related

Table 2. Number of Covid-19 cases and deaths in Turkey (1 March-30 June 2020).

Total cases	199,906/ 543,753†	Total cases/ 1 Million	2,370/6,447†
Total deaths	5,131	Total deaths/ 1 Million	61
Total tests	3,381,650	Total tests/ 1 Million	40,097

Source: MoH, https://covid19.saglik.gov.tr/EN-69532/general-coronavirus-table.html; †Worldometers, https://www.worldometers.info/coronavirus/

deaths. Because the family remains as the main caregiver, the elderly that live in nursing homes make up a mere 0.4 per cent of the country's old population (Akkan & Canbazer 2020).

A mobile app (*Hayat Eve Sığar*) developed by the MoH[7] to contact trace and monitor positive cases collected a wide range of data, raising issues of privacy. Yet, the insights gained from the density maps were very limited. For example, Zonguldak, a mining city where respiratory diseases are common, was placed under partial lockdowns. However, the authorities shared no regular data on cases and deaths for the province. At the beginning of the outbreak, Turkey had insufficient test kits, and testing was only initially conducted in the capital city. Gradually the Ministry of Health authorised more testing labs, which brought the total number to 137 by the end of June. As such, the testing criteria gradually expanded and Turkey ramped up its testing capacity, with over 3 million tests conducted by 30 June (Table 2). With the summer tourist season approaching, as Figure 3 shows, the country eased the lockdown measures and transitioned to a 'controlled social life' phase in June.

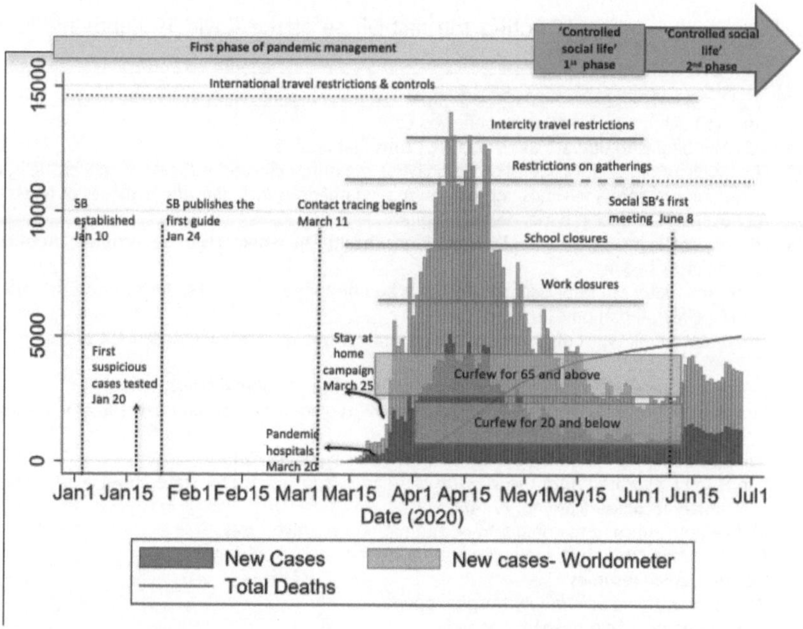

Figure 3. Restrictions and health measures in the first phase of the Covid-19 pandemic in Turkey (1 March-30 June 2020).

Source: Official sources include ministerial circulars, presidential decisions and decrees; Covid 19 Health System Response Monitor, WHO.

Pandemic in times of economic despair

Health crisis

After the virus was reported by the WHO, Turkey began implementing some proactive measures, such as using thermal cameras at airports, suspending flights and closing land borders (Table 3). The first proactive measure was the establishment of the Scientific Board (Bilim Kurulu – SB) composed of medical experts. Following the identification of the first case on 10 March, as illustrated by Table 4, Turkey introduced some distancing measures and gradually interrupted parts of social life by closing down schools, restaurants, entertainment activities, non-essential shops; postponing international and national events; and suspending religious services, NGO activities and sports events. By 27 March, two weeks after the announcement of Turkey's patient zero, international flights had been suspended and intercity travel was restricted. Some of the restrictions, such as the closure of shopping malls and the suspension of sports events, came only after the public demanded stricter measures.

Fahrettin Koca, the Minister of Health, was the most visible leader of Turkey's pandemic management. His daily TV briefings attracted much attention and despite criticism of the lack of demographical and geographical data, Koca seemed to have gained the trust and appreciation of the public. The fact that President Erdoğan was not the most visible figure in the government's policy response was surprising. Even before the adoption of the presidential system,

Table 3. Main health measures during the first phase of the Covid-19 pandemic in Turkey (1 March-30 June 2020).

HEALTH MEASURES	
March 11	Contact tracing begins for new confirmed cases
March 14	ALO 184 begins to operate as coronavirus consultation line
March 18	First Ministry of Interior circular on coronavirus measures: closure of theatres, concert halls, cafes, restaurants, sports facilities and ban on mass gatherings including the activities of NGOs
March 20	All hospitals are declared 'pandemic hospitals'
March 23	Ministry of Health announces 32,000 additional healthcare workers is to be recruited; production of ventilators began
April 3	Masks mandatory in public spaces, April 6 a ban on the sale of masks, decision to distribute free masks; May 4 ban on sale lifted.
April 4	Treatment for all types of providers placed under SGK coverage, reimbursement prices are increased
April 9	Emergency service coverage of SGK extended to communicable disease
April 13	Presidential Decision extending coverage to all; PPE, diagnostic tests and necessary medicines to be provided free of charge (No. 2399)
April 17	Raise penalties for violence against health workers (Law no. 7243)
April 17	Funds to be allocated from the Ministry of Treasury and Finance for state university's medical and dentistry faculties. (Law no. 7244)
April 18	Mobile app launched to contact trace and monitor positive cases
May 15	Covid-19 mandatory hygiene guidelines for businesses are published
May 20	Health tourism resumes
May 21	Başakşehir Çam ve Sakura City hospital opened
May 29	Sancaktepe new field hospital opened
May 31	Yeşilköy (former Atatürk Airport) field hospital opens & Hadımköy (renovated) opens
June 17	Masks made mandatory for Istanbul, Ankara and other cities

Source: Authors' compilation from official sources including parliamentary bills, ministerial circulars, presidential decisions and decrees; Covid 19 Health System Response Monitor, WHO.

Table 4. Turkey: Thematic timeline of restrictions and health measures during the first phase of the Covid-19 pandemic in Turkey.

1. International travel restrictions &controls		**2. Intercity travel restrictions**	
January 22	Thermal camera control with China	March 27	Intercity travel restricted
February 4	Thermal camera control expanded	*April 3*	Entrance ban for 31 cities
Feb 3	Flights to China suspended	*April 2*	Domestic flights suspended
Feb 23	Borders with Iran closed	*June 1*	Intercity travel & domestic flights resume
Feb 29	Flight to Italy, South Korea, Iraq suspended		
March 18	All lands borders closed		
March 27	All international flights suspended		
June 1	International flights resume		
3. School closures		**4. Workplace closures**	
March 16	Schools and universities are closed	*March 23*	Civil servants to work from home or in shifts
March 23	Distance learning for K-12 via state tv and online platform & online learning in universities	*March 25*	Stay at home campaign launched
June 1	Daycare centres open	*June 1*	Civil servants begin work, administrative leave is possible for 60 and above
5. Restrictions on gatherings		**6. curfews**	
March 16-22	Non-essential shops close (shopping centres open on May 11, rest by June 1)	April 11-12 (31 provinces)	
March 21	Hairdressers and barbers close (open on May 11)	April 18-19 (31 provinces)	
March 16- 22	Restaurants, cafes, parks, gardens, museums, pools, gyms close (open on June 1)	April 23-26 (11 provinces)	
March 16	Religious services suspended (relaxed on May 29 & open on June 24)	May 1-3 (31 provinces)	
March 16	Theatres, cinema, venues, bars and wedding salons (open on June 15 & Wedding halls June 15)	May 9-10 (24 provinces)	
March 16	NGOs activities suspended	May 16-19 (15 provinces)	
March 19	Sporting events suspended (football season resumes on June 12)	May 23-26 (81 provinces)	
March 19	All international and national organizations and activities suspended	May 30-31 (15 provinces)	
March 13-22	Legal proceedings suspended (resume on June 15)	(cancelled) June 6-7 (15 provinces)	
April 5	Parliament suspends work (opens on June 2)	June 20, 27, 28 (81 provinces daytime lockdown)	
7. Age-specific stay at home orders		**8. Advisory boards**	
For 65 and older between 22 March and 9 June, 2020 (relaxation from May 10 onwards)		*Jan. 10*	Scientific Board (SB) established by Ministry of Health
For 20 and younger between 4 April and 9 June, 2020 (relaxation from May 13 onwards)		*Jan. 22*	SB carries out risk assessment
		Jan. 24	SB published its first COVID-19 guide
		April 4	Social Sciences Board is established
9. Isolation & quarantine		**10. Other Preventive measures**	
Jan 20	First suspicious case tested	*March 24* public transportation restricted to 50% capacity (ends on June 1)	
March 9	14-day self-isolation for all traveling from abroad		
March 15	Returning pilgrims in 14-day quarantine	*March 26* working in 14-day shifts in nursing homes (ends on June 1)	
March 27	First localized quarantine for villages in Rize		
June 11	Mandatory 14-day quarantine ends for Turkish citizens returning from abroad	*June 17*, wearing of masks made mandatory in Istanbul, Ankara and some other cities	

Source: Authors' compilation from official sources including parliamentary bills, ministerial circulars, presidential decisions and decrees; Covid 19 Health System Response Monitor, WHO.

Turkish politics were personalised around Erdoğan's leadership, leading scholars to call this phenomenon the 'Erdoğanisation of Turkish politics' (Selçuk, Hekimci & Erpul 2019). In response to Covid-19, although President Erdoğan remained the decisive decision-maker, announcing important decisions after cabinet meetings, measures were also announced by different ministries possibly to avoid backlash to the president. In some instances, this caused confusion and revealed the absence of coordination between the actors in the weakly institutionalised cabinet. For example, the first weekend lockdown was announced on 10 April by Süleyman Soylu, the Interior Minister, two hours before it would take effect, and sparked panic buying. The debacle could have been avoided if the Health Minister had communicated it in his press conference that day, or if Erdoğan had announced it a few days before in his national address.

Hasty decision-making followed by policy reversals was another element of the government's management of the crisis (Bakir 2020). Examples include the declaration of curfews for people younger than 20 and older than 65 and then allowing exemptions for those employed, as well as changing the mask distribution policy. The government initially banned the sale of masks and took the responsibility to distribute them for free, but after changing the mask distribution method several times, it lifted the ban. With parliament closed for 45 days and the opposition marginalised, it was the public's reaction which influenced the policy reversals. Another public backtracking was over the decision to cancel the weekend curfew in the first week of June, when Erdoğan tweeted that he 'as president' decided to cancel it a few hours after the Interior Minister had issued the decision via a circular. The case illustrates Erdoğan's proclivity throughout the crisis to let his ministers announce and implement policies that would not necessarily be popular with the public as well as his position as the ultimate decision-maker who can easily deflect blame if a decision turns out to be unpopular.

A striking feature of the government's crisis management was its legal reliance on administrative acts based on the 1930 Public Health Law and the 1949 Provincial Administration Law. This is worth exploring, not only because the former is an old piece of legislation enacted under the 1924 Constitution, but also because the current constitution clearly allows for the declaration of a state of emergency in case of an 'outbreak of dangerous epidemic diseases' (Art. 119). Although Turkey has never declared a state of emergency for any other reason outside of a national security threat, it has regularly invoked emergency powers, most recently instituting them for 18 months after the failed coup attempt in 2016. Either because of this recent experience of emergency rule or because of economic considerations, the government chose not to declare a state of emergency for Covid-19. Instead, it restricted fundamental rights and freedoms mostly through ministerial circulars and executive decisions, in violation of the constitution that requires limitations to be enacted by formal law. Localised quarantines for buildings, districts and towns as well as curfews specific to particular provinces and age groups were issued with no clear statutory basis. While the use of localised quarantines, decided by provincial and district-level public health councils, allowed the government to be more flexible and to respond based on the particular conditions of that area, restrictions were also abused to ban marches and protests.[8]

With respect to substantive measures, Turkey's containment approach included age-specific stay-at-home orders for those below the age of 20 and above 65. Around 6,000 medical field teams carried out rigorous contact-tracing. Cases were monitored by primary care health workers via HSYS (Public Health Management System) – an electronic registration system. Such measures were credited with maintaining the healthcare system without experiencing overcapacity. A presidential decision (No. 2399) decreed that PPE, diagnostic tests and necessary medicines would be provided free of charge, regardless of individuals' health coverage and even to those who had not paid their premiums. The MoH's treatment algorithms, administered throughout the health sector, included most controversially early and broad use of hydroxychloroquine which was provided to patients free of charge.

The MoH had previously declared all hospitals, including those in the private sector, as 'pandemic hospitals'. To ensure that private hospitals would be reimbursed by state insurance, the pandemic was recognised as an emergency. In order to appease the private hospitals' financial concerns about covering the pandemic patients' intensive care treatment, the SGK reimbursements were doubled. Overall, the health crisis remained under control in the first phase of the pandemic.

Economic crisis

Before the Covid-19 crisis hit, Turkey had aggressively developed expansionary fiscal policies. With respect to substantive economic measures in response to the first phase of the pandemic, the government's performance was limited. The stimulus package (Economic Stability Shield – Ekonomik İstikrar Kalkanı), at 100 billion lira (14 billion euros), amounted to 2 per cent of GDP. With the exception of a modest increase in retirement pensions and of a social aid programme for families (2 billion lira in total, 1,000 lira per household), it mostly directed relief for the business sector through tax, premium and debt postponements (Table 5). In order to control the unemployment rate surge and to constrain the societal impact, the government barred layoffs for three months, and instituted a short-term working allowance for workers employed in sectors impacted by the pandemic. For employees placed on unpaid leave, it provided a cash wage support that was less than half the minimum wage.[9]

Table 5. Main economic measures during the first phase of the Covid-19 pandemic in Turkey (1 March-30 June 2020).

ECONOMIC MEASURES	
March 17	Central Bank cuts policy rates
March 18	Stimulus package (Economic Stability Shield) announced- **100 billion lira (14billion €)** Tax, debt and premium deferrals, expansion of Credit Guarantee Fund, increase in minimum retirement pension, postponement of social security premiums, cash aid for households in need, allowance for unpaid leave and short-work allowance system
March 26	Omnibus bill enters into force (Law no 7226) – monthly wage support to employers, measures to prevent evictions from workplaces, postpones taxes for the tourism sector, increases funds to be transferred to credit guarantee institutions, suspends legal time proceedings among other changes.
March 30	National Solidarity Fund launched
April 17	Omnibus bill enters into force (Law no. 7244): ban on layoffs for 3 months, short-term work allowance rules revised, cash wage support to workers who are entitled to unpaid leave; Turkish Wealth Fund acquires new rights to buy stakes of companies in distress among other changes.
April 22	Central Bank cuts policy rates
May 7	Banking Regulation and Supervision Agency issues a new regulation to impose fines for 'manipulation and misleading transactions'
May 7	Banking Regulation and Supervision Agency imposes exchange transaction ban with lira for three foreign banks – ends the ban three days later.
May 11	Turkish Wealth Fund injects capital into three state owned banks
May 19	30 per cent tax on imports for hundreds of products
May 20	Swap deal with Qatar
May 24	Banking Regulation and Supervision Agency raises taxes in currency swap transactions
June 1	Public Banks launch new loan campaigns for vacations, house purchase and other consumer spending
June 26	Omnibus bill enters into force (Law no. 7247): up to 5 per cent increase to domestic sovereign bond limits
June 30	Short-work allowance system extended for one month

Source: Authors' compilation from official sources; Policy Responses to Covid-19, (IMF 2020).

Although the reserves were low and continued to decline as Turkey tried to control the depreciation of the lira, which hit its lowest level against the dollar on 7 May, IMF loans had been ruled out. Instead, Turkey pursued other measures such as liquidity injection, credit expansion via public banks, interest rate cuts by the Central Bank, tax increases on currency and gold transactions, and a swap deal with Qatar. The Turkish Sovereign Fund, led by the president and his son-in-law, the Minister of Treasury and Finance Berat Albayrak, received the authority to buy the stakes of companies experiencing distress and to inject cash into state banks. In June, the fund acquired a controlling stake in Turkey's leading mobile operator, Turkcell. In order to protect its native manufacturing industry and find additional funds for the treasury, the Turkish government via presidential decision introduced a 30 per cent tax on thousands of imports, contradicting its neoliberal model. The emphasis on the need to be 'self-sufficient' was also reflected in the government-organised campaign that sought donations from the public to distribute to households under the Ministry of Family and Social Services' social aid programme (Social Protection Shield - Sosyal Koruma Kalkanı).[10] By June 2020, more than 1.5 million households had received a cash aid. Economic limitations did not prevent the government from carrying out its pandemic diplomacy and making medical aid shipments to select countries as a signal of its 'success' (Güngör 2021).

The role of experts in populist decision-making

Following the WHO's report on 5 January 2020 that there were cases of pneumonia of unknown cause, an operation centre was formed under the General Directorate of Public Health. Immediately after, on 10 January, the Ministry of Health established the Scientific Board [SB]. On 24 January, this advisory board, comprised of academics from different branches of medicine, carried out is first risk assessment and issued its first guideline for medical personnel. The early and comprehensive guides that were regularly updated, played an important role in keeping the healthcare workers informed and allowed the MoH to follow a coordinated response (Sakarya & Uzunköprü 2020). Similarly, the national treatment algorithms, initially based on China's experience, were revised with the feedback from the field and were communicated through the MoH's website to ensure that the health sector followed a standard approach.

Fahrettin Koca, the Minister of Health, is a medical doctor but also the founder of a private hospital and a former member of OHSAD, an interest group for private healthcare providers. He emphasised that the Covid-19 crisis was 'a healthcare-related problem, about which science and scientists will have the final say' (Ministry of Health 2020b). Whether an evidence-based decision-making was operationalised or not was the object of much speculation in the media, but Koca regularly convened meetings with the group and held a press conference afterwards. Yet, the public was not informed about SB's specific recommendations, and there was no transparency with regard to the indicators used by the board (HASUDER 2020b). With the country transitioning to the normalisation process, another advisory body composed of experts from the disciplines of sociology, religious sociology, statistics, psychology and communication was formed, reportedly to evaluate the pandemic's psychological and socio-economic impact. It held its first meeting in early June. However, it is not clear how the recommendations of the two advisory bodies were reconciled.

In the early weeks of the outbreak, the media formed the main source of information, causing an infodemic (Sakarya & Uzunköprü 2020). Based on survey data (HASUDER 2020a), the Association of Public Health Professionals informed the public that as the virus spread, conspiracy theories and alternative medicines received less public interest and scientific information became the main point of reference. The SB members took on the public information role by appearing on TV channels and giving interviews to print media. With the transition to 'normalisation', further questions arose as to whether the political authorities were relying on expert opinion when adopting and easing restrictions. Statements by members of the SB indicated that like the rest of the public, they also did not have access to full epidemiological data, and that a smaller group within the Ministry of Health was carrying out the evaluations (HASUDER 2020c). Another concern for academics arose with the MoH decision to establish a commission under its supervision to evaluate Covid-19 related scientific research proposals. Mandatory permission required from this commission posed an additional challenge to the independence of scientific research (Bilim Akademisi 2020).

Within the broader context of anti-elite rhetoric around the healthcare reform of the early 2000s, Erdoğan had repeatedly criticised doctors and portrayed them as 'self-interested professionals' (Agartan & Kuhlmann 2019). Critics have attributed increased violence against healthcare workers in the AKP period to this demeaning rhetoric, the redefinition of patients as consumers and the increased workload of doctors (CHP 2019). The Covid-19 crisis prompted the AKP government to adjust its rhetoric and pass a long overdue bill to protect healthcare workers against violence (Law no. 7243). Erdoğan personally announced that two of the newly opened field hospitals and a recently renovated city hospital would be named after renowned doctors who passed away as a result of Covid-19.[11]

As discussed later, the exclusion of medical associations led to major criticisms from the associations themselves and political opposition. The authorities also opened investigations against some officials of provincial medical chambers in Southeast Anatolia for reporting cases and deaths in their own cities (HRW 2020). The opposition-held Istanbul and Izmir municipalities formed their own advisory scientific boards, which were instrumental in shaping public opinion on additional measures for their cities.

Local cooperation or competition?

Turkey's tradition of centralised state structure shaped the local level handling of the crisis. The Turkish state has two types of administration at the subnational level: on the one hand, the decentralised structures of the central government administration at provincial/district level and on the other, municipalities at three levels: metropolitan city, district, and town. At the district level, the mayors and members of the legislative body are directly elected. The metropolitan municipality council is composed of indirectly elected members. After AKP came to power in 2002, similar to the dynamics of the healthcare reform, there was an attempt at decentralisation as part of the party's reformist agenda. Implemented in the first five years of AKP's rule, the reforms involved the devolution of services and improvements in administrative autonomy, but fiscal autonomy is still limited (Tan 2020). Political independence is even more restricted. The central government has the power to replace the elected mayor with an appointed officer (*kayyum*) and this authority has been used on numerous occasions since 2016.

In response to the Covid-19 crisis, two main institutions were employed to achieve local level policy coordination. The previously discussed 1930 Public Health Law establishes a permanent Public Health Council (*Umumi Hıfzıssıhha*

Meclisi) led by the governor (*vali*) at the provincial level and by the district-governor (*kaymakam*) at district level. These councils bring together representatives of the central government at the sub-national level, the municipality, and important actors in the healthcare sector, such as large public hospitals, doctors and pharmacists. The councils are responsible for the implementation of central government policies and also for complementing them with necessary measures to respond to the specific needs of the locality. On 28 March 2020, President Erdoğan announced the formation of Provincial Pandemic Councils (*İl Pandemi Kurulu*) under the leadership of the governors and with the responsibility to oversee policies and to take additional measures for the province if need arose. The Pandemic Influenza National Preparedness Plan formed the basis for these councils, whose membership was broader than the permanent Public Health Councils. However, it remained unclear how the responsibilities of the two institutions differed and how they were expected to coordinate their responses.

Although these bodies, especially the Health Councils, strive to bring together the central government and municipalities, coordination was hard to achieve when the opposition controlled the local governments. The three largest cities, including Istanbul where the Covid-19 virus was most widespread, are governed by the official opposition, CHP (*Cumhuriyet Halk Partisi* – Republican People's Party). In these cases, relations between the central and local governments included difficulties in cooperation, competition to claim credit, and even obstruction of local projects.

Over the last two decades, municipal healthcare assistance has been growing and has been important electorally for the local incumbents (Kemahlıoğlu & Özdemir 2018). Yet, the municipalities mostly provide supportive or preventive services. Therefore, with a few exceptions, the municipal healthcare facilities were not expected to be directly involved with the Covid-19 treatment. In the initial stages of the crisis, the mayors of the metropolitan municipalities in Istanbul and Adana attempted to play an active role by identifying locations for temporary field hospitals or even building one, but these responsibilities were quickly taken over by the central government.

The municipalities then turned towards assisting citizens during the lockdown periods and providing aid, especially as the economic crisis intensified in the later stages. When the first complete lockdown came – as a late evening announcement on 10 April – the mayors of the three largest cities responded with statements on how the municipalities would meet the basic needs of citizens. This was also one of the moments in which the lack of communication and coordination between the central government and municipalities became apparent. Ekrem İmamoğlu, the mayor of Istanbul, complained that the municipalities had not been informed about the lockdown in advance. The first response of Ankara's mayor, Mansur Yavaş, was more conciliatory, stating that the municipality was working with the governor to meet the citizens' needs and urging them not to panic. During the lockdown, CHP reported that the police tried to prevent the Istanbul municipality from distributing bread. Shortly after, the municipality communicated with the governor's office, and the municipalities' operations were able to continue. The provincial governor, in turn, utilised his own organisation [Vefa Sosyal Destek – Faithful Social Aid[12]] to distribute bread and provide other services.

The municipalities also tried to respond to citizens' and businesses' financial needs as economic activity slowed down. The initiation of fund-raising drives by the Ankara and Istanbul municipalities was another critical moment that revealed the partisan nature of inter-governmental relations. Given the polarised nature of politics in Turkey, CHP supporters with a higher than average income were expected to be eager to contribute to the municipalities' campaigns. In response, both President Erdoğan and Devlet Bahçeli, leader of MHP (*Milliyetçi Hareket Partisi*, Nationalist Movement Party), accused the CHP-led municipalities of creating 'parallel administrations' and 'states within states' and the funding drives were quickly blocked by the Ministry of Interior. The municipalities then initiated other projects such as *Askıda Fatura* (Bill on the Hook) that coordinated the payment of unpaid electricity, water and gas bills voluntarily by other citizens. Given shrinking municipal resources, borrowing emerged as another option for which the municipal council's approval was needed. In May, the mayor of Ankara asked for such approval and was blocked by the AKP-MHP majority in the municipal council. Similarly, when Istanbul's mayor needed the municipal council's approval to speed up the application process for municipal aid by eliminating in-house visits, it was rejected by the AKP-MHP majority. Social assistance forms an important element of electoral politics in Turkey. As such, it is not surprising that there was severe partisan competition over who was providing social and economic aid in response to the pandemic – and taking credit for this assistance.

Whether mayors from the incumbent AKP and its electoral alliance partner, MHP, left the pandemic response mostly to the central government, or their efforts were not covered in the media, they were not as visible as the opposition mayors. On the contrary, since the opposition parties have been out of power at the national level for almost 20 years, the control of local governments was seen by opposition politicians as an opportunity to showcase their capacity to govern efficiently and their efforts to improve inequality. This was especially true for CHP which, shortly before the pandemic, had been successful in the 2019 local elections. The party leadership tried to coordinate the CHP mayors' response to the Covid-19 crisis, and eleven metropolitan municipality mayors wrote a joint declaration, emphasising their efforts in social assistance and the need for cooperation with the central government.

Politics in times of crisis

AKP has been governing Turkey since the 2002 elections. In the 2018 presidential and legislative elections, the AKP and MHP ran together under the so-called People's Alliance (*Cumhur İttifakı*). Although MHP did not directly participate in the national government, it supported Erdoğan's minority government in the legislature. While the incumbent electoral alliance had received an overall majority (51.6 per cent) in the 2019 local elections (Esen & Gumuscu 2019), it had also suffered major setbacks. There was a drop in the two parties' total vote share compared to the 53.7 per cent in the 2018 legislative elections. They lost the metropolitan municipality in the capital, Ankara, and then through the June repeat elections the largest city, Istanbul. CHP and İyi Party (Good Party – a splinter from the MHP) formed the backbone of the opposition alliance (*Millet Ittifaki* – Nation Alliance). Although small parties left the formal opposition alliance in 2019, HDP (*Halkların Demokratik Partisi* – People's Democratic Party), the third largest block, tacitly supported the opposition in the Western part of the country by not nominating its own candidates. These local elections were important, not only in showing the strength of the opposition's electoral challenge, but also in making the incumbent-opposition cleavage apparent, especially in the repeat elections in Istanbul. When the pandemic hit Turkey, this fault line – with AKP and MHP on one side versus the opposition on the other – and the polarisation between these two groups, formed the general political context (Erdoğan & Uyan Semerci 2020).

Government and opposition faultline

During the onset of the crisis, some appearances of unity existed between the opposition and the government. CHP's deputy chairman met in person with Health Minister Koca on 21 March and presented the party's policy recommendations. The party's vice presidents visited the Minister of Interior and the Minister of Environment and Urbanisation with the purpose of improving the channels of communication between the local governments and the central government and increasing the municipal financial resources. CHP's policy recommendations included measures such as incorporating the Turkish Medical Association into the decision-making process, preventing violence against healthcare workers by passing legislation, making test kits widely available, and imposing restrictions on the export of critical medical supplies. At first, the opposition parties' criticisms mostly focused on the economic response package announced by the government. CHP suggested restructuring tax and insurance debts, easing the conditions for state support during furlough, providing extra payments for healthcare workers, and implementing a family insurance scheme. İyi Parti, in turn, accused the government of protecting business and not the citizens and suggested reductions in sales tax, delays in debt repayments for the farmers, and the restructuring of small businesses' payments to the government.

With time, however, tensions between the government and the opposition started to grow. CHP accused the government of not being transparent with the data and of risking citizens' lives by delaying a complete lockdown. The central government's intrusions into the opposition-controlled municipalities' initiatives discussed above contributed to this conflict. Another major area of disagreement emerged around an amnesty bill. Around late March, discussions started about the conditions in prisons during the pandemic. Early drafts of the bill excluded political prisoners and journalists, but included sex offenders and those convicted of violence against women, causing a major uproar not only within opposition circles but also more widely within society. Overall, HDP criticised the government the harshest. On 13 May, the party presented a report evaluating the governments' response over the previous two months and called for the resignation of three cabinet ministers for their delay in making preparations in the face of the crisis.

These tensions culminated when President Erdoğan accused the CHP of acting like a terrorist group. Precipitating this controversy, a dispute in Adana took place between a CHP member and Vefa Sosyal Destek group (aid groups organised by the governors and district-governors) when the latter was distributing social assistance. Given the populist rhetoric widely used by Erdoğan (Elçi 2019), this was not unexpected. In some other speeches, too, Erdoğan presented the political opposition as 'the enemy' that tried to prevent the government from dealing effectively with the Covid-19 crisis. This aligned with the general populist style of communication in times of crisis (Moffitt 2015). Indeed, AKP, is studied as a right-wing populist (Öniş & Kutlay 2020) or neoliberal populist party (Özdemir 2020). The stand of the party and its leader during Covid-19 showed elements consistent with this diagnosis. Especially in the initial stages, AKP constantly praised Turkey's performance in comparison to the 'West' (Europe and the US). Over time, the opposition parties were also targeted and blamed for the country's problems.

Populist elements in AKP can also be associated with the government policies. In general, the economic policies of the right-wing populist incumbents pose a problem. It is not always clear how the government can 'serve the people' and improve their economic conditions while also maintaining a close relationship with business. It was even harder to reconcile these two seemingly contradictory goals when the economic contraction caused by the pandemic took place. AKP, as a party that appeals to the low-income strata and especially to more vulnerable sectors in the informal sector (Özdemir 2020), was faced with the triple challenge of preventing the spread of the virus, maintaining the economic livelihood of the vulnerable sectors and keeping businesses economically active. Policies such as the partial lockdown that covered only the weekends, restrictions on age groups whose economic contribution is more limited and expansion of credit availability (and hence postponement of the financing of the crisis) all seem to be efforts to respond to these challenges. Exit strategies also seem to be reflecting this dilemma, such as in the apparent indecisiveness about extending the weekend lockdown on 6–7 June discussed earlier.

When making these difficult decisions, AKP mostly maintained the external support of MHP. There were moments of divergence such as when Soylu, formally a member of AKP, but also known to be close to MHP, received explicit support from Bahçeli against his resignation. Another instance occurred when the party vice chair, Semih Yalçın, hinted at his disapproval of MHP's alliance with the AKP. While there may have been negotiations behind closed doors, in the end MHP stood together with AKP in the critical moments. Bahçeli made efforts to publicly reaffirm his allegiance to the People's Alliance. He even joined Erdoğan and AKP in attacking CHP and accusing the party of hindering the government and Turkey's success. MHP together with AKP also proposed and voted for the controversial amnesty bill (Law no 7242).

In addition to the amnesty bill, only four other legislative bills between March and June 2020 included responses to the pandemic, confirming the recent executive dominance of the policy-making process in Turkey. They involved economic measures discussed earlier, such as the ban on layoffs, a short term work allowance, cash wages for workers on unpaid leave, authorisation of the President to approve delays in electricity and gas payments, delays in payments by the tourism sector, suspension of legal deadlines, authorisation of the Ministry of Education to shorten teachers' summer vacation, increases in penalties for violence against health workers, and an increase in the debt ceiling for 2020. MHP worked together with AKP to pass these proposals. For the opposition, parliament mainly served as a public arena to voice criticism through plenary debates and other institutional means such as parliamentary inquiries.

Polarised media and social response

The press and the media in Turkey are known to be partisan and polarised (Erdoğan & Uyan Semerci 2020). Taking four newspapers – two pro-government (Yeni Safak and Sabah) and two pro-opposition (Cumhuriyet and Sözcü) as identified by Erdoğan and Uyan Semerci (2020) – we analysed how they differed when reporting two controversial events: the first weekend lockdown and the government's intervention in the CHP municipalities' funding drives.

On 12 April, Cumhuriyet's front page headline was 'Chaos at the hand of the incumbent', referring to the panic rush to the stores prior to the start of the lockdown. Sözcü's headline was in the same vein: 'All efforts are gone in vain in two hours'. Yeni Şafak, on the other hand, ran the headline 'Most critical 48 hours' and continued by stating that the decision 'will play a critical role in breaking the pandemic chain in Turkey'. Finally, Sabah's headline was 'We stayed at home, we found security', referring to the drop in crimes during the social isolation period. Our second topic concerns the blocking of municipal bank accounts on 31 March. On 1 April, Cumhuriyet's headline read 'Decision worse than the virus', while Sözcü's main headline criticised the central government's initiative to collect voluntary contributions and reported the government's intervention regarding the municipalities lower on the front page as 'Blocks on CHP municipalities' donations'. In contrast, neither of the pro-government newspapers carried the story about the government's intervention in the municipalities on the front page. Both focused instead on the central government's donation campaign, which Sabah's headline referred to as 'Legendary Solidarity'. Although a more systemic analysis needs to be conducted, these examples suggest that the polarised pattern in the press continued during the pandemic.

Turkish society was not initially as polarised in its evaluation of the government's response. Among a representative sample of the Turkish adult population, 39.9 per cent of the respondents in early-to-mid April found the government successful, 30.6 per cent unsuccessful, and 29.5 per cent of the population stated a neutral position though supporters of the incumbent and the opposition differed in their evaluation (Aydın 2020). Probably due to the 'rally around the flag' effect, Erdoğan's approval rating jumped to 55.8 per cent

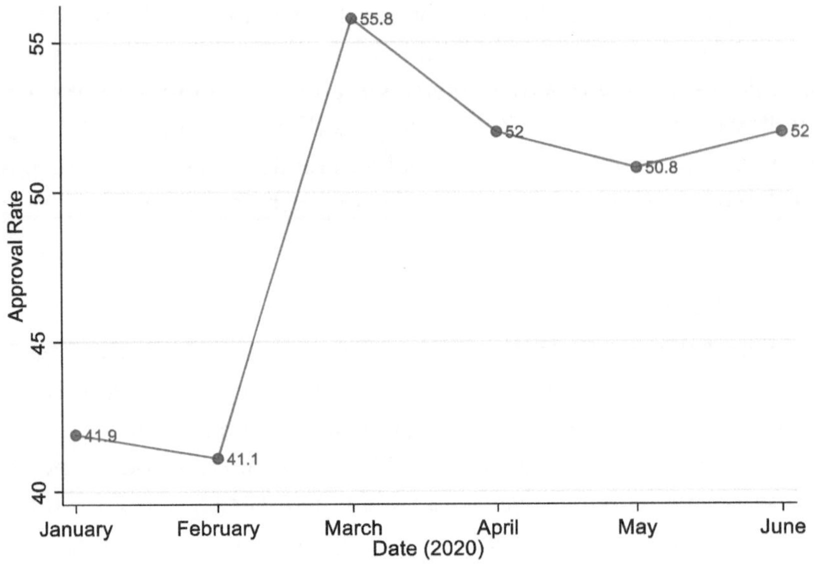

Figure 4. Approval ratings for President Erdoğan.

Source: Monthly public opinion surveys (*Türkiye'nin Nabzı*) conducted by Metropoll, gathered by the authors from press releases. Please see the following webpage for detailed information on their methodology: http://www.metropoll.com.tr/arastirmalar/turkiyenin-nabzi-17

in March from 41.1 per cent a month earlier, though it decreased to 52 per cent in June (Figure 4, Metropoll 2021). A study with a representative population of Istanbul found that the economic situation of a large section of the society was affected negatively by the pandemic (Çarkoğlu 2020). When a question was asked about the respondent's own household, 66 per cent stated a negative effect. In response to a question about the economic situation of Turkey, the negative effect increased to 76 per cent. According to Ipsos' report, 84 per cent had stated coronavirus pandemic as the most important problem on March 26–30, but this dropped to 39 per cent on 29 May-5 June. With time, the economy took over in importance, with those stating this was the most important problem increasing from 10 to 43 per cent over the same period (Ipsos 2020).

With respect to the organised sections of the public and civil society, unsurprisingly the Turkish Medical Association (TTB) was the organisation with most visibility and voice. The Ministry of Health has the legal basis to monitor the TTB but de facto, it is an independent professional association. It already had a conflictual relationship with the AKP, emanating mostly from the politics around the earlier health care reform (Yılmaz 2017). Initially, the association criticised the government for excluding it from policymaking in response to the pandemic. The association and the provincial chambers (*Tabip Odaları*), especially the Istanbul chamber, were also critical of specific policies, such as allowing *umre* (pilgrimage to Mecca), not freezing economic activities except for basic and immediate needs (İstanbul Medical Chamber 2020) and easing the restrictions too early. Within the broader context of a long ongoing struggle between AKP and the professional chambers (including those of lawyers, architects and engineers), in May the government started working on a legislative proposal to restructure the organisation of these professional associations.

Apart from business associations that lobbied for favourable policies, such as in insurance and construction, only a few other organised social groups were involved in the public discussions regarding the pandemic. Civil society organisations responded to the controversial amnesty bill discussed earlier and the Association of Rights for the Elderly over 65 (65+ Yaşlı Hakları Derneği) criticised the continuation of the lockdown for this age group as a whole.

Conclusion

Turkey seemed to have weathered the first wave of the Covid-19 crisis relatively successfully. Death rates were relatively low and the healthcare system was not overwhelmed with the growing number of cases. Different factors seemed to have contributed to this outcome. Compared to the European average, Turkey has a much younger population. The healthcare system had gone through a major restructuring and almost all the population had access to healthcare. Policy-wise there was an early intervention with school closures and the stockpiling of medicine. Though a full lockdown was never implemented and the timing of partial lockdowns was criticised, the elderly, who were at the highest risk, were isolated through restrictions on their mobility. Without analysing more systematically the relative impact of the demographics and policies with comparative data across countries, it is hard to evaluate the effectiveness of these policy measures. Here, we mostly derive conclusions about how these policies were made and how the pandemic's first phase affected Turkey.

Healthcare and economic policies in the first phase of the pandemic followed the right-wing/neoliberal populist path that the incumbent party has been taking in the last decade, including the earlier healthcare reform. The reform both created opportunities for the private sector and extended coverage for the lower income population, providing an ideal ground for the AKP to bridge the two seemingly contradictory interests of business and the low-income population. In a similar vein, the healthcare sector was able to deal with the pandemic by covering a large number of patients through the incorporation of privately owned facilities. Though improved after reforms, the healthcare sector still had limitations, especially in primary care services and personnel. Coupled with the growing pressures on the government budget, the healthcare policies' sustainability was challenged. Economic policies were, in turn, mainly based on the expansion of liquidity to help economic actors survive restrictions on economic activity. However, the risk of deficit financing with the expectation of a shorter crisis that made relative success possible in the first wave paved the way for the crisis of sustainability in the later stages of the pandemic.

Our analysis of the policymaking and implementation in the first phase highlights three characteristics of the populist rule in Turkey. First, both healthcare and economic policies were made and implemented under a highly centralised executive in the new presidential system. Possibly due to the personalistic nature of intra-government relations around the figure of President Erdoğan, however, there were some problems with coordination and consistency. Because Turkey relied on existing legislation and ministry circulars to issue restrictions, the restrictions sometimes appeared arbitrary and their legality was questioned, further challenging the weak rule of law in the country. Second, policymaking was exclusionary. While experts were consulted, critical non-state organisations, local governments, and opposition parties were not incorporated into the process. Since municipalities were rarely directly involved with treatment, this did not create a major problem in the more urgent healthcare dimension, but the governments' response to the growing financial needs ended up being more conflictual and ineffective. Finally, populist elements in the government's style which framed the opposition as the enemy exasperated the existing partisan polarisation.

Overall, the review of the political, economic, and social dynamics of the first phase of the pandemic in Turkey suggests that the sustainability of policies in the face of a prolonged crisis is challenged by the limitations of the earlier healthcare reform, the state of the economy, and the short-term focus of the measures. Growing suspicions regarding the reliability of the data shared by the government raised questions about its claim of success. In addition, the personalised, exclusionary, and polarising nature of the populist government's policy-making process led to inconsistencies and arbitrariness in implementation, hampering the effectiveness of the response.

Later phases of the pandemic

The growing economic pressures as the crisis entered its second year added to the characteristics of the populist policy-making process that we identified in the first phase and made these problems even more acute in the later phases of the pandemic (July 2020-May 2021). Yet, Erdoğan continued to praise Turkey's response, making comparisons with Europe and the US. In March 2021, AKP published a book on its 'success' with a prologue by the president.

Following the reopenings in June 2020, the pandemic remained mostly under control throughout the summer. One important policy reversal in July ended SGK's full coverage of Covid-19 treatment in private hospitals, but the decision was overturned again in September. Official Covid-19 figures remained low. Especially around August, however, doubts were raised about their reliability, mainly by the medical associations and the opposition-led metropolitan municipality mayors. In response to a leaked document shared by CHP that alleged that the number of positive cases was almost 20 times the official figure, Koca stated on 30 September that a positive case does not have the same meaning as a patient. This announcement led to a major uproar in Turkey and abroad. Following much pressure to share the number of cases, this data was made public only on 25 November. Compared to the 6,713 patients announced on 24 November, the number of positive cases shared the next day was 28,351. From late November 2020 till March 2021, Turkey opted for nationwide weekday curfews and weekend lockdowns.

The government was successful in getting the first batch of Sinovac vaccine, for which efficacy trials were underway in Turkey, and covered health workers and those over the age of 65 by around mid-February 2021. Eligible citizens were notified via an online system. They were then able to get vaccinated at a public or private health institution. AKP top cadres also got vaccinated on the first day of rollout. However, then the process slowed down. The government frequently made different promises of future vaccination shipments, but they were slow to materialise. As of 1 June 2021, the number of doses administered was 29,139,341 (Ministry of Health 2021).

According to IMF estimates, between January 2020 and March 2021, Turkey spent 1.9 per cent of its GDP on the pandemic response (IMF 2021). The basic pandemic-related economic policies continued with the short-work allowance system, cash wage support for workers on unpaid leave and ban on lay-offs. However, there were major macroeconomic policy reversals accompanying the turnover in high policy circles. The Minister of Treasury and Finance resigned in early November, just two days after the replacement of the Central Bank governor. The new governor remained in office for five months, only to be replaced in March 2021. On 27 July 2020, the central bank governor had shared his expectations of growth following the reopening and his expectations of improvement in the tourism sector. He publicly stated that this would be followed by a gradual contraction of liquidity. Yet, these calculations had assumed that there would not be a second phase of the pandemic.

The government, limited in its capacity to provide material benefits, offered its supporters favourable treatment in other areas. In July, hundreds of thousands joined in the first prayer after the historic Hagia Sophia was converted from a museum to a mosque. In September 2020, for Istanbul all outdoor activities like concerts and weddings were banned but that decision was postponed for two days, reportedly because AKP was holding an indoor meeting to celebrate its new party members. Although attendance at weddings and funerals was limited to 30 people, government officials attended crowded funerals. In the meantime, the pandemic was used as an excuse to ban protests against government policies. Schools remained mostly closed, with televised lessons offered to students without internet connection providing an inadequate alternative. Limited face-to-face teaching resumed in September 2020, only to close again in November.

AKP postponed its local congresses twice because of the pandemic. On 11 January, the party reinitiated the process and ended it with a grand congress on 24 March 2021, packed with thousands of members. A circular that had banned association meetings remained in effect, yet the exemptions provided by provincial health councils allowed party meetings, leading to public criticism about double standards. Easing of restrictions followed and the government introduced a system of local restrictions dubbed as 'Decision on the Ground'. Although it was announced that face-to-face teaching was going to resume on 1 March, because of problems of coordination, at the last minute it was delayed for a day.

With Turkey reporting its highest confirmed cases and highest daily death toll, Erdoğan reimposed restrictions at the beginning of April. Although vaccinated, the mobility of citizens above 65 was once again limited. Face-to-face teaching stopped. Full lockdowns were announced for the second half of Ramadan and the Eid festival. Although Koca tried to deflect blame by saying that the whole population is responsible for the surge, the exceptions allowed for the ruling party and its supporters made such statements sound hollow. To calm small shop keepers and farmers, the Ministry of Interior had to issue additional circulars to allow district bazaars. More than 7 million employees received work exemption permits. Mosques remained open, and the lockdown excluded tourists.

The pressure to make the country attractive to tourism became clear in anticipation of the second summer under the pandemic. The Minister of Foreign Affairs' declaration that they 'will vaccinate everyone that tourists can see' led to major criticism in social media. A ban on the sale of alcohol during the lockdown drew ire, because it lacked any semblance of legality. Although the President and the Minister of Interior gave oral instructions, the nationwide prohibition was not prescribed even in a ministerial circular. With some delay, several provincial public health councils took decisions to institute the ban, which was then extended to all non-essential goods. There was no police intervention in the case of anti-Israel protests or soccer fan celebrations. An aid package to small shopkeepers was introduced only after the end of the lockdown in response to public criticism, and a steep fall in Erdogan's approval rating (to 44.5 per cent in April) (Metropoll 2021). Economic limitations and the populist nature of policymaking clearly dictated the lockdown's features, as in the earlier stages of the pandemic. A gradual normalisation began on 17 May 2021, with the relevant circular laying out the restrictions issued only one day before.

Notes

1. For the information on the pandemic experience we mostly relied on news sources. Please see the Online Appendix for a list of these news sources.
2. The National Pandemic Plan was published in 2006 and the relevant directive on infectious disease surveillance and alert system was issued by the MoH in 2007. It was updated to include Covid-19 on 22 April 2020.
3. The share of doctors aged 55 and older is much lower than the OECD average (34 per cent) at 18 per cent (OECD Health at a Glance 2019, p. 175).
4. At the end of December 2019, Turkey's net external debt to GDP ratio stood at 32.5 per cent (Ministry of Treasury and Finance). As of January 2020 the unemployment was at 12.7 per cent and youth unemployment at 23.1 per cent. In January 2020 inflation rate was at 14.52 per cent (TÜIK). Turkey's foreign currency reserves had declined to $77.1 billion in December 2019 (IMF).
5. Turkey has only reported cases confirmed by PCR tests and did not report clinical or epidemiological diagnosis of Covid-19.
6. On 30 June 2020 MoH published its first report outlining the epidemiological situation (Ministry of Health 2020c). Daily and weekly reports are published, available in English at https://covid19.saglik.gov.tr/TR-68443/covid-19-durum-raporu.html
7. Besides health monitoring, the app's functions were developed to request masks, to get a code to travel by bus, ferry or plane after June 2020.
8. Art. 17 of Law No. 2911 on Demonstrations and Gatherings and Art. 32/Ç of Law No. 5442 on Provincial Administration.
9. In order to implement some of these measures, parliament had to make legislative amendments in two omnibous bills: Law no. 7226 (26 March 2020) and Law no. 7244 (17 April 2020).
10. The campaign is called *We are Enough for Ourselves, My Turkey* [Biz Bize Yeteriz, Türkiyem].
11. According to data compiled by the Turkish Medical Association (TTB), as of mid-July, 44 health workers including 23 medical doctors had passed away from Covid-19 (TTB 2020, p. 154).

12. These organisations under the leadership of governors and district-governors operated with public employees and voluntary activists from civil society organisations.

Disclosure statement

No potential conflict of interest was reported by the author(s).

ORCID

Özge Kemahlıoğlu http://orcid.org/0000-0001-7070-0844
Oya Yeğen http://orcid.org/0000-0003-4896-3538

References

Agartan, T. I. (2012) 'Marketisation and universalism: crafting the right balance in the Turkish healthcare system', *Current Sociology*, vol. 60, no. 4, pp. 456–471.

Agartan, T. I. & Kuhlmann, E. (2019) 'New public management, physicians and populism: Turkey's experience with health reforms', *Sociology of Health & Illness*, vol. 41, no. 7, pp. 1410–1425.

Akkan, B. & Canbazer, C. (2020) 'The long-term care response to COVID-19 in Turkey', *LTCcovid International Long-Term Care Policy Network*, CPEC-LSE, 10 June, available online at: http://ltccovid.org/2020/06/19/new-report-the-covid-19-long-term-care-situation-in-turkey

Akman, M., Sakarya, S., Sargın, M., Ünlüoğlu, İ., Eğici, M. T., Boerma, W. G. W., Schäfer, W. L. A. (2017) 'Changes in primary care provision in Turkey: a comparison of 1993 and 2012', *Health Policy*, vol. 121, no. 2, pp. 197–206.

Aydın, M. (2020) 'Covid-19 public perception survey (Turkey)', 6 May, available online at: http://www.mustafaaydin.gen.tr/source/Covid19PublicPerceptions_06052020_Eng.pdf

Bakir, C. (2020) 'The Turkish state's responses to existential COVID-19 crisis', *Policy and Society*, vol. 39, no. 3, pp. 424–441.

Bilim Akademisi (2020) 'It is problematic to subject scientific research on COVID-19 to permission', 26 June, available online at: https://en.bilimakademisi.org/it-is-problematic-to-subject-scientific-research-on-covid-19-to-permission/

Cakir, B. (2020) 'COVID-19 in Turkey: lessons learned', *Journal of Epidemiology and Global Health*, vol. 10, no. 2, pp. 115–117.

Çarkoğlu, A. (2020) 'Salgın günlerinde İstanbul'da yaşam-bir araştırma [Life in Istanbul during the pandemic days - a research]', *Sarkaç*, 13 May, available online at: http://sarkac.org/2020/05/salgin-gunlerinde-istanbulda-yasam-bir-arastirma

CHP Bilim Platformu Politika Notları (2019) 'AKP Sağlıkta Şiddete Göz Yumarak Halk Sağlığını Tehlikeye Atıyor [AKP by turning a blind eye to violence in health, is risking public health]', available online at: https://chp.azureedge.net/b544f676ca16400db785a36939b952ff.pdf

Corbacioglu, S., Celik, S. & Saran, U. (2016) 'Self-adaptation in dynamic disaster environments: response to the 2006 avian influenza crisis in Turkey', *Journal of Asian and African Studies*, vol. 51, no. 6, pp. 742–759.

Dorlach, T. (2015) 'The prospects of egalitarian capitalism in the global South: Turkish social neoliberalism in comparative perspective', *Economy and Society*, vol. 44, no. 4, pp. 519–544.

Ekmekci, P. E. (2016) 'An assessment of coherence between early warning and response systems and serious cross-border health threats in the European Union and Turkey', *Disaster Medicine and Public Health Preparedness*, vol. 10, no. 6, pp. 883–892.

Elçi, E. (2019) 'The rise of populism in Turkey: a content analysis', *Southeast European and Black Sea Studies*, vol. 19, no. 3, pp. 387–408.

Erdoğan, E. & Uyan Semerci, P. (2020) *Fanusta Diyaloglar: Türkiye'de Kutuplaşmanın Boyutları, [Dialogue in a Vacuum: The Dimensions of Polarisation in Turkey]*, İstanbul Bilgi University Press, Istanbul.

Esen, B. & Gumuscu, S. (2019) 'Killing competitive authoritarianism softly: the 2019 local elections in Turkey', *Southern European Society and Politics*, vol. 24, no. 3, pp. 317–342.

Esen, B. & Gumuscu, S. (2020) 'Why did Turkish democracy collapse? A political economy account of AKP's authoritarianism', *Party Politics*, pp. 135406882092372.

Güngör, B. (2021) 'Foreign aid during the COVID-19 pandemic: evidence from Turkey', *Southeast European and Black Sea Studies*, vol. 21, no. 3, pp. 337–352.

Hale, T., Angrist, N., Goldszmidt, R., Kira, B., Petherick, A., Phillips, T., Webster, S., Cameron-Blake, E., Hallas, L., Majumdar, S. & Tatlow, H. (2021) 'A global panel database of pandemic policies (Oxford COVID-19 Government Response Tracker)', *Nature Human Behaviour*, vol. 5, pp. 529–538.

HASUDER (2020a) 'Yeni koronavirüs hastalığı (Covid-19) pandemisine Türkiye'de hazırlılık ve yanıt: 28. gün değerlendirmesi [Preparedness and response to new coronavirus disease (Covid-19) pandemic in Turkey: evaluation on day 28]', 12 April, available online at: http://korona.hasuder.org.tr/pandeminin-28-gun-degerlendirmesi/

HASUDER (2020b) 'Yeni koronavirüs hastalığı (Covid-19) pandemisine Türkiye'de hazırlılık ve yanıt: 56. gün değerlendirmesi [Preparedness and response to new coronavirus disease (Covid-19) pandemic in Turkey: evaluation on day 56]', 10 May, available online at: http://korona.hasuder.org.tr/turkiyede-hazirliklilik-ve-yanit-56-gun-degerlendirmesi/

HASUDER (2020c) 'Halk Sağlığı Uzmanları Derneği'nin COVID-19 Süreci ile İlgili Görüşleri – 5 [Association of Public Health Specialists' Views on Covid-19 Process]', 14 June, available online at: https://hasuder.org.tr/halk-sagligi-uzmanlari-derneginin-covid-19-sureci-ile-ilgili-gorusleri-5/

Hoxha, J. (2020) *Network Policy Making within the Turkish Health Sector: Becoming Collaborative*, Emerald Group Publishing, Bingley.

Human Rights Watch (2020) 'Turkey: probes over doctors' Covid-19 comments', 10 June, available online at: http://www.hrw.org/news/2020/06/10/turkey-probes-over-doctors-covid-19-comments

IMF (2020) 'Policy responses to COVID-19', 25 June, available online at: https://www.imf.org/en/Topics/imf-and-covid19/Policy-Responses-to-COVID-19

IMF (2021) 'IMF fiscal monitor: database of country fiscal measures in response to the COVID-19 pandemic', April, available online at https://www.imf.org/en/Topics/imf-and-covid19/Fiscal-Policies-Database-in-Response-to-COVID-19

Ipsos (2020) 'Kontrollü sosyalleşme sürecinde ülkemizin en önemli sorunu nedir? [What is the most important problem of our country in the controlled socialisation process?]' 15 June, available online at: https://www.ipsos.com/tr-tr/kontrollu-sosyallesme-surecinde-ulkemizin-en-onemli-sorunu-nedir

İstanbul Medical Chamber (2020) 'İhtiyacımız olan "algı yönetimi" değil "salgın yönetimi [What we need is not "perception management" but "pandemic management". Is there a real programme to fight the pandemic in Turkey?]' 13 April, available online at: https://www.istabip.org.tr/5701-ihtiyacimiz-olan-algi-yonetimi-degil-salgin-yonetimi-turkiye-nin-gercek-bir-pandemi-mucadele-programi-var-mi.html

Karakaş, B. (2020) 'Migrants and refugees in a time of pandemic: access to healthcare services in Turkey', *Heinrich Böll Stiftung*, 18 May, available online at: http://eu.boell.org/en/2020/05/18/migrants-and-refugees-time-pandemic-access-healthcare-services-turkey

Kemahlıoğlu, Ö. & Özdemir, E. (2018) 'Municipal control as incumbency advantage: an analysis of the AKP era', in *Party Politics in Turkey: A Comparative Perspective*, eds S. Sayarı, P. A. Musil & Ö. Demirkol, Routledge, London, pp. 116–135.

Metropoll (2021) 'Türkiye'nin Nabzı Nisan 2021 [Turkey's Pulse April]', available online at: http://metropoll.com.tr/arastirmalar/turkiyenin-nabzi-17/1898

Ministry of Health (2018) 'Health Statistics Yearbook 2018', available online at: https://dosyasb.saglik.gov.tr/Eklenti/36164,siy2018en2pdf.pdf?0

Ministry of Health (2019) 'Pandemik influenza Ulusal Hazırlık Planı [Pandemic influenza national preparation plan]', available online at: https://grip.gov.tr/depo/saglik-calisanlari/ulusal_pandemi_plani.pdf

Ministry of Health (2020a) 'Minister Koca delivers presentation on Coronavirus efforts at Parliament', 23 March, press release available online at: https://www.saglik.gov.tr/EN,64638/minister-koca-delivers-presentation-on-coronavirus-efforts-at-parliament.html

Ministry of Health (2020b) 'Minister assesses the latest situation on coronavirus', 11 April, available online at: http://www.saglik.gov.tr/EN,65035/minister-assesses-the-latest-situation-on-coronavirus.html

Ministry of Health (2020c) 'COVID-19 situation report Turkey', June 30, available online at: https://dosyamerkez.saglik.gov.tr/Eklenti/37743,covid-19-situation-report-v4pdf.pdf?0

Ministry of Health (2021) 'Vaccination table of Turkey', 1 June, available online at: https://covid19asi.saglik.gov.tr/?_Dil=2

Moffitt, B. (2015) 'How to perform crisis: a model for understanding the key role of crisis in contemporary populism', *Government and Opposition*, vol. 50, no. 2, pp. 189–217.

OECD. (2019) *Health at a Glance 2019: OECD Indicators*, OECD Publishing, Paris.

Öniş, Z. (2009) 'Beyond the 2001 financial crisis: the political economy of the new phase of neo-liberal restructuring in Turkey', *Review of International Political Economy*, vol. 16, no. 3, pp. 409–432.

Öniş, Z. & Kutlay, M. (2020) 'The global political economy of right-wing populism: deconstructing the paradox', *The International Spectator*, vol. 55, no. 2, pp. 108–126.

Özdemir, Y. (2020) 'AKP's neoliberal populism and contradictions of new social policies in Turkey', *Contemporary Politics*, vol. 26, no. 3, pp. 245–267. doi:10.1080/13569775.2020.1720891.

Pala, K. (ed) (2018) *Türkiye'de Sağlıkta Kamu-özel Ortaklığı: Şehir Hastaneleri [Public-private Partnership in Health in Turkey: City Hospitals]*, İletişim, İstanbul.

Sakarya, S. & Uzunköprü, G. (2020) 'COVID-19 infodemisi ve yönetimi: türkiye ve dünya örneklerine karşılaştırmalı bir bakış [COVID-19 infodemic and management: a comparative perspective on the world and Turkey examples]', *Istanpol*, 15 May, available online at: https://www.istanpol.org/post/covid-19-infodemisi-ve-yönetimi-türkiye-ve-dünya-örneklerine-karşılaştırmalı-bir-bakış

Selçuk, O., Hekimci, D. & Erpul, O. (2019) 'The Erdoğanisation of Turkish politics and the role of the opposition', *Southeast European and Black Sea Studies*, vol. 19, no. 4, pp. 541–564. doi:10.1080/14683857.2019.1689902.

Tan, E. (2020) 'Quo vadis? The local government in Turkey after public management reforms', *International Review of Administrative Sciences*, vol. 86, no. 1, pp. 115–133.

Transparency International Turkey (2020) 'Şehir Hastaneleri [City Hospitals]', available online at: http://www.seffaflik.org/wp-content/uploads/2020/05/percentC5percent9Eehir-Hastaneleri.pdf

TTB (Turkish Medical Association) (2020) 'Covid-19 Pandemisi 4. Ay Değerlendirme Raporu [Covd-19 pandemic 4th month evaluation report]', available online at: https://www.ttb.org.tr/kutuphane/covid19-rapor_4.pdf

TÜİK (Turkish Statistical Institute) (2020) 'İstatistiklerle yaşlılar, 2019 [Elderly in statistics]', 18 March, available online at: http://www.tuik.gov.tr/PreHaberBultenleri.do?id=33712

Yilmaz, G. (2017) 'It is voluntary transfer! Exploring healthcare reforms in Turkey', *Turkish Studies*, vol. 18, no. 4, pp. 665–687.

Yılmaz, V. (2017) *The Politics of Healthcare Reform in Turkey*, Palgrave Macmillan, London.

Yılmaz, V. (2019) 'The emerging welfare mix for Syrian refugees in Turkey: the interplay between humanitarian assistance programmes and the Turkish welfare system', *Journal of Social Policy*, vol. 48, no. 4, pp. 721–739.

Index

Note: **Bold** page numbers refer to tables; *italic* page numbers refer to figures and page numbers followed by "n" denote endnotes.